Medieval Royal Mistresses

Medieval Royal Mistresses

Mischievous Women who Slept with Kings and Princes

Julia A. Hickey

PEN & SWORD HISTORY

First published in Great Britain in 2022 by
Pen & Sword History
An imprint of
Pen & Sword Books Ltd
Yorkshire – Philadelphia

ISBN 978 1 39908 194 8

Typeset by Mac Style
Printed and bound in the UK by CPI Group (UK) Ltd,
Croydon, CR0 4YY.

Pen & Sword Books Limited incorporates the imprints of Atlas,
Archaeology, Aviation, Discovery, Family History, Fiction, History,
Maritime, Military, Military Classics, Politics, Select, Transport,
True Crime, Air World, Frontline Publishing, Leo Cooper, Remember
When, Seaforth Publishing, The Praetorian Press, Wharncliffe
Local History, Wharncliffe Transport, Wharncliffe True Crime
and White Owl.

For a complete list of Pen & Sword titles please contact

PEN & SWORD BOOKS LIMITED
47 Church Street, Barnsley, South Yorkshire, S70 2AS, England
E-mail: enquiries@pen-and-sword.co.uk
Website: www.pen-and-sword.co.uk

Or

PEN AND SWORD BOOKS
1950 Lawrence Rd, Havertown, PA 19083, USA
E-mail: Uspen-and-sword@casematepublishers.com
Website: www.penandswordbooks.com

Contents

Illustrations		vii
Author's Note		viii
Introduction		ix

Chapter 1   Queen Emma and Ælfgifu of Northampton   1

Chapter 2   Edith Swanneck and her Daughter Gunnhild   10

Chapter 3   Herleva of Falaise   18

Chapter 4   Maud Peverel   25

Chapter 5   Robert of Gloucester's Mother and Ansfride of Seacourt   30

Chapter 6   Nest of Wales   40

Chapter 7   Sybilla Corbet   50

Chapter 8   Edith Forne Sigulfson and the Unknown Mothers of King Henry I's Illegitimate Children   55

Chapter 9   Elizabeth de Vermondois and her Daughter Isabel de Beaumont   61

Chapter 10   Eleanor of Aquitaine, Ykenai, Annabel de Baliol and the Count of Brittany's Daughter   69

Chapter 11   Rosamund Clifford, Ida de Tosny, Alys of France, Nesta and BelleBelle   78

Chapter 12   Ela de Warenne, Constance, Clemencia and Agatha de Ferrers and Isabella of Angoulême   87

Chapter 13   Magna Carta Mistresses   96

Chapter 14   Piers Gaveston, the Tour de Nesle Affair and the
Consequences of Adultery   103

Chapter 15   Hugh Despenser, Roger Mortimer, Unhappy
Marriages and the Further Consequences of
Adultery   115

Chapter 16   Katherine Mortimer and Margaret Drummond   131

Chapter 17   Alice Perrers   137

Chapter 18   Katherine Swynford   150

Chapter 19   Elizabeth Wayte   163

Chapter 20   Lady Eleanor Talbot Butler and Elizabeth
Woodville   168

Chapter 21   Jane Shore   175

Glossary   183
Appendices: English Kings, their Mistresses and Children Listed in
Chronological Order   187
Notes   195
Bibliography   202
Acknowledgements   210
Index   211

Illustrations

Table of Consanguinity (illumination)

Is this Edith Swanneck? Bayeux Tapestry – a house is burned by the Normans (wool embroidery on linen)

Falaise Castle (photograph)

Peverel Castle (photograph)

Robert, Earl of Gloucester, one of King Henry I's illegitimate sons (carved fireplace relief, Cardiff Castle)

Oseney Abbey founded by Robert D'Oyly the younger on the prompting of Edith Forne Sigulfson (print, 1643)

Eleanor of Aquitaine, alabaster effigy at Fontrevault

Fair Rosamund, J.W. Waterhouse (oil on canvas, 1917)

Full-page miniature of lovers walking in a garden, in April, fol 5v. (illumination, circa 1500)

Matilda FitzWalter, alabaster effigy in the Priory Church at Little Dunmow

Isabella of Angoulême by W. H. Mote (engraving, nineteenth century) after an illustration by J.W. Wright

Philip IV and his children (from l. to r. Philip V, Charles IV, Isabella, Louis X and Charles of Valois)

Illustration pour la Tour de Nesle: une orgie, Octave Nicholas Francois Tassert, (drawing, nineteenth century)

King Edward II (alabaster effigy in Gloucester Cathedral)

Alice Perrers at the deathbed of King Edward III (illustration, nineteenth century)

Elizabeth Woodville (print, circa 1800)

The meeting of Elizabeth Woodville and King Edward IV, (engraved and printed in colours by E. Evans. F.P, 1864)

Jane Shore 'Give gentle Mistress Shore one gentle kiss the more' (print, 1790)

Author's Note

A print depicting the ill-fated lovers Hellelil and Hildebrand by Frederic William Burton hangs in my study. It depicts the romance of a princess and her body guard. The ballad is the product of a darker side of medieval love and chivalry that also includes Malory's *Morte D'Arthur*. Chivalric values produced a medieval culture of courtly behaviour. The literature of medieval romance with love at its heart flourished. But the love was unattainable or lost and the focus was usually upon the chivalric knight rather than his idealised lady. Knights did not expect to win their ladies but romantic love had been given an identity. I grew up reading Jean Plaidy, Dorothy Dunnett and Anya Seton. *Katherine*, first published in 1954 has never been out of print since. It tells the story of Katherine Swynford, the mistress and third wife of John of Gaunt and unlike the story of Hellelil, it provides a satisfying story of romance, passion and a happy-ever-after. I re-read it during the first lockdown of 2020. Seton researched her book with attention to detail and remained within the constraints of documentary evidence. The facts became part of an absorbing story. However, the relationships and characters depicted in the novel are fiction based on supposition and conjecture. History cannot know the emotions of medieval princes or the women they took to their beds. It cannot know for sure when Lancaster first became attracted to his children's governess, the way in which the relationship evolved or Katherine's feelings. We do not even know for certain what she might have looked like. We might want to know about the depth of the relationships that developed behind the bed curtains and to empathise with the men and women whose lives are uncovered in the primary sources but the historical record is silent on the topic of what royal mistresses thought and felt. People's emotions have not changed across the centuries but personal happiness was not always a priority. A writer of historical fiction can fill the gaps between facts, human motives and passion in a way that a writer of non-fiction cannot. However, within these constraints, the history of the medieval royal mistress is significant and one to which popular culture keeps returning.

Introduction

This book is about some of the temptresses, Jezebels, harlots and repentant Mary Magdalens who slept with medieval kings and princes. The chronicles recount dramas and scandals surrounding beautiful women, and in the case of Edward II, handsome men. Whether mistresses were involved in a lengthy love affair; were innocents seduced and then discarded or were calculating courtesans willing to break the social rules, fiction imagines beautiful women dressed in silks and satins, the distant sound of ballads being played on the lute and soft throaty laughter as well as the occasional ripped bodice. However, history was written by monastic chroniclers of the medieval era, with their own agenda of Hell, repentance and salvation, depicted temptation, sin and debauchery drawing on the models of Eve, Jezebel and the Whore of Babylon. Also, later writers added to the stories which usually reflected the concerns of the day. And the reality? Rather than a spotlight played on desirable women it's more a case of 'find the lady' amidst charters, pipe rolls and legal documents in the hope that the echoes of the women who gave birth to countless royal bastards might be amplified. Most of the women, deemed unimportant at the time, have been erased from the written record – and effectively silenced.

The choice of dates is pragmatic from 1000 to 1485 and the ascent of Henry Tudor to the throne, a Beaufort descendant of Katherine Swynford. The Norman Conquest of 1066 is a key date in English history, it's certainly the best remembered. However, whilst the Saxon elite may have suffered a discontinuity in the political upheaval that followed, it is equally important to consider some of the cultural patterns that evolved more slowly. Marriage was an essential part of the dynamics of royalty before 1066 just as it was afterwards but the Church had not yet completely transformed itself into the arbiter of what constituted legal marriage. William of Jumièges writing the *Deeds of the Dukes of Normandy* in the mid-eleventh century described two forms of marriage; *more danico* and *more Christiano*. Both the Danish and the Christian forms of marriage were legal, a reminder that England was multi-cultural and there was co-existence rather than a single homogeneous nation. Kings and earls, eager for alliances and political gain, were able to take advantage of making more than one kind of marriage whilst the definition of a legal union remained unfocused. A century later, Church marriage was the only recognised form of union in England, and even then, a textbook of canon law known as the *Decretum* described concubinage combined with marital affection as a form of sanctioned union. The stories of women like Ælfgifu of Northampton and Edith Swanneck, eleventh-century women who married outside the Church, were written or even rewritten by monastic chroniclers with an interest in emphasising the sinfulness of women who indulged in sex outside the confines of a Church-sanctioned union. They were transformed into concubines or mistresses who were morally weaker than the men around them but who tempted kings like Cnut the Great and Harold Godwinson. William the Conqueror's contemporaries were more careful about the way they depicted his mother, Herleva, as they had no wish to rouse his anger. Her story became interwoven with her destiny as the mother of powerful kings but even Duke Robert I repented of his youthful indiscretions and set William the Conqueror's mother to one side.

If religion is an integral part of understanding medieval mistresses so is the evolution of the medieval state. The Norman Conquest imposed a new language, social system and culture. At the start of the period, a kingdom was the personal property of the king but there was dramatic social and political change. The diverse peoples who inhabited the realm became more cohesive. The Norman elite took more of an interest in the Anglo-Saxon past and re-imagined it so that rather than usurping it they became a part of it. Maud Peverel, the alleged mistress of William the Conqueror, was part of that reimagining. The tradition also enhanced the king's virility at a time when no one could believe that a monarch would not take the most beautiful women for himself – Maud's reputation mattered not at all.

Medieval monarchs were a powerful and privileged elite at the top of a patriarchal society. Whilst kings might have been guilty of sins of the flesh, the women that they associated with were, according to the religious beliefs of the time, the source of temptation thanks to the idea of Original Sin – Eve gave the apple to Adam. Christian ideals might have required monarchs to exercise self-restraint but medieval medical science throughout the period, and beyond, stipulated that physical health required the balance of bodily fluids. Medieval medicine was based on a system of four humours; blood, phlegm, black bile and yellow bile. If the humours were balanced good health was maintained. Galen, the Greek physician who influenced the development of western medicine, argued that 'sexual desire was the expression of the need to be rid of the seed whose retention was a potential health hazard'.[1] It followed that in order to be healthy a king needed an active sex life. As well as lengthy marital separations resulting from the business of overseeing empire, justice and military conflict, there were also times when the Church forbade the king his wife's company in the royal bedchamber including during pregnancy. But balance was the key. Physicians viewed too much sex as bad, if not worse, than too little as frequent ejaculation left the body depleted with potentially fatal consequences. And a king who became too obsessed with the women he slept with was likely to experience political disaster if monastic chroniclers are to be believed.

King Henry I fathered more than twenty illegitimate children but his contemporary biographers were sympathetic to his private lusts. He justified the number of mistresses he kept not because of his health or even his personal enjoyment but because of the need to have children to extend the security of his rule by marriage alliances forged through his illegitimate children and discarded mistresses. Throughout the period, medieval monarchs used their illegitimate children and, on occasion, their mistresses as diplomatic pawns to secure treaties and alliances through marriage. Marriage was a visible sign of the union of one house with another. Royal blood was a tradable commodity whatever its provenance. He married off his illegitimate offspring to legitimate heirs and heiresses to secure land and titles for them by right of marriage rather than birth. This had the effect of strengthening the Crown's ties to the nobility as well as controlling the distribution of wealth within his kingdom. It also helped to create a buffer zone of extended kinship around the margins of the king's territory as can be evidenced in his relationship with women such as Nest of Wales, Sybilla Corbet and Edith Forne Sigulfson. King Henry II pursued a similar policy with the offspring of his own mistresses although his extramarital relationships lacked the longevity of many of his grandfather's and he had an unsavoury reputation for casual whoring. Despite the censure of the Church and the possibility of public scandal many families were prepared to allow their daughters and sisters to become royal mistresses because the king's favour could yield rich rewards for the entire family. The women who took kings and princes into their beds during the late Norman and the Angevin periods were part of the medieval court scene and accepted as such as long as they remained in the shadows, submissive, silent and suitably ashamed of sleeping with the monarch for the preferment, protection or political salvation of their families.

When women refused to be silenced, they were often punished. Eleanor of Aquitaine defied the social mores of the time and both her husbands in a bid for her voice to be heard. As a consequence, monastic chroniclers blackened her reputation. Unlike Queen Emma, Eleanor did not leave her own version of her story. When Henry II's marriage to Eleanor of Aquitaine stalled, he turned to many women for comfort and imprisoned his wife for the rest of his life. The most famous of Henry II's mistresses, Rosamund Clifford, became the focus of romantic legend which conformed with the narrative of the submissive woman. Rather than Eleanor being depicted as the wronged wife, she was portrayed as a vengeful murderess by legend. Posterity found a new way of silencing wayward women in a narrative, written or painted by and dominated by men.

If adultery was acceptable for kings, it was entirely insupportable for queens to indulge in love affairs. It was essential that the heirs to the throne were the king's own issue. Royal marriages, it can be argued, were largely loveless alliances despite some notable exceptions. Freedom of action for medieval queens and princesses was not compatible with social or ecclesiastical perspectives. Aside from being described as beautiful, queens were expected to be good wives and mothers and to be peace weavers. The thirteenth-century *Speculum Dominarum* or 'Mirror for Ladies' was written as a guidebook for Joan of Navarre when she married Philip IV of France. It acknowledged that a queen had a role to play but it emphasised the importance of virtue. The French Tour de Nestle affair of 1314 illustrates the consequences of royal adultery for royal women, their children and their lovers. Failure to provide healthy sons weakened royal wives, as did ill-considered political alliances. Isabella of Angoulême, a child when King John took her as his second wife, suffered because the union was associated with the loss of his continental territories. The only medieval English queen known to have a lover was Isabella of France, the wife of Edward II. There was no suggestion of an affair whilst she lived with her husband who has become infamous for his favourites – men like Piers Gaveston and Hugh Despenser the Younger. The exact nature of Edward II's relationships with his favourites is uncertain given the lack of surviving evidence. An anonymous chronicler of the 1320s wrote of Edward and Piers that Edward 'bound himself with him before all other mortals with a bond of indissoluble love'.[2] By the 1390s *The Meaux Chronicle* stated that the King indulged 'too much in the vice of sodomy'.[3] Queens were expected to be chaste and virginal. Failure to comply with social and political expectations whatever the provocation, led to accusations of sexual voraciousness. There were no degrees of sinfulness. Women were either virtuous or whores.

There were some conventions imposed upon kings. They were not supposed to take foreign princesses or the women of their most powerful nobles for their own pleasure as it was likely to sow the seeds of resentment or rebellion. Henry II broke this taboo when he bedded Alys of France who was destined to be the bride of his own son Richard. As the feudal pyramid tottered, King John's licentiousness was used as a justification for rebellion. The chroniclers changed their narrative and wrote about wives and daughters debauched by the king. Harassment, rape and sexual abuse demeaned John's barons. The voices of the women themselves are largely absent, muffled by the very chroniclers who denounced the king and the stories that grew from the rumours. Their experiences, as exemplified by Matilda FitzWalter, are invalidated by lack of written evidence.

As well as political evolution stretching across centuries, there were also social changes most usually associated with the Black Death of 1348 which saw England's population plummet to below three million. The second half of the Middle Ages was a time when people were more free and able to exercise more control over their lives. They were better off as their wages increased and towns flourished. In a court setting the majority of women were unlikely to be from the lower social orders, even Alice Perrers who was castigated by chroniclers for being low born was one of Queen Philippa's damsels at the start of her relationship with King Edward III. She was vilified not because the king took her to his bed or even because she was seen to profit by it but because she stepped into the public arena. Not only did she have access to the king's ear but she controlled who else might influence him as well. History judged her for her greed and avarice predicated on the uncorroborated story of her prizing rings from the fingers of the dead king. Traditionally 'evil counsellors' were blamed for royal errors but Alice, like Isabella of Angoulême was also vilified and condemned as the Whore of Babylon. The politics of the period required the barony and, as it evolved, parliament, to trust the institution of the monarchy and when it failed as happened at the end of Edward III's reign when the early successes of the Hundred Years Wars stalled and there were insufficient funds to pay England's army.

Women who became royal mistresses were branded as whores and harlots by monastic chroniclers. Alice Perrers, who fell afoul of the so-called Good Parliament which weeded out King Edward's evil advisers, was imprisoned and her goods confiscated but she still fared better than Katherine Mortimer who displaced King David II of Scotland's wife, Joan of the Tower. Katherine was murdered by a cabal of Scottish nobles as a consequence of her perceived influence over the monarch. John of Gaunt's mistress Katherine Swynford, a contemporary of Alice's, was vilified only because her lover was unpopular with the Commons.

By the fifteenth century the private lives of kings were better recorded thanks to ambassadorial accounts but the Yorkist monarch King Edward IV shocked the country when he revealed his secret marriage to Elizabeth Woodville, an impoverished Lancastrian widow with two children. She became the first English-born queen to sit on the throne since the eleventh century. Irrelevant of the well-worn controversies surrounding the Princes in the Tower and the accession of King Richard III, it was Edward whose penchant for secret marriages set in motion the chain of events that caused the House of York to tumble. Following Edward's death and his brother, Richard of Gloucester's, rise to power, Jane Shore, the most sexually charged mistress of the period, was accused of conspiracy and forced to do penance for her promiscuous behaviour. Richard wanted the world to consider the extent of his brother's secret intimacies whilst they watched the so-called Rose of London parade through the street's dressed only in her shift showing the populace the fleshly delights enjoyed by the king, his friend Hastings and even his step-son, Thomas Grey. Jane Shore, penitential taper in hand, stepped out of history and into legend.

Kings, princes and earls made arranged Church-sanctioned marriages for dynastic and political reasons. Most of them took mistresses although one or two were fortunate enough to fall in love with their wives. King Edward I raised twelve crosses in memory of Eleanor of Castile following her death in 1290. The crosses mark the resting places of her coffin when her body was transported from Harby near Lincoln to Westminster Abbey. The pair had been married since he was fifteen years old and she was just ten years of age. The marriage was part of the negotiations to ensure English control of Gascony but the couple quickly became inseparable. After her death the warrior king retired for a time from public life to grieve, 'I loved her,' he said, 'in life; I cannot cease to love her in death'.[4] It was unthinkable for most of the medieval period that a member of the royal family would marry his mistress. Both Edward, the Black Prince and his brother John of Gaunt, married women they loved. Gaunt's scandalous duchess, Katherine Swynford, had been installed as his mistress before she became his bride.

The relationship between kings and the women they slept with had changed across five hundred years. It is remarkable that we know about any of them. Ultimately, mistresses and paramours had no choice, not much of a voice and were cast by the Church in the role of sinners. With the exception of Katherine Mortimer, and possibly Maud FitzWalter, they were survivors. It took a renaissance monarch proud of his chivalric values and learning to judicially murder the women he claimed he loved – not even King John did that. Imagine if you must, the sex life of King Edward IV, whose personal badge was the sun in splendour, reputed to pass his mistresses on to his friends when he tired of them. Having seized the throne in 1461 he mutated from chivalric knight to overweight debaucher of women. It is suggestive of the changes which society had undergone since the Norman Conquest, that the last Plantagenet king, was forced to promise marriage to women before they slept with him. Gone, it seems for two women at least, were the days of feminine compliance no matter how charming the man who propositioned them. But then, of course, there was his grandson, King Henry VIII, although that is another story entirely.

Chapter 1

Queen Emma and Ælfgifu of Northampton

I n 1000, a Danish army overwintered in Normandy. Sweyn Forkbeard was entertained by Duke Richard II and his family before launching an attack on England in the spring of 1001. King Æthelred sought a marriage with Normandy in an attempt to close Norman ports to the marauding Danes. Emma of Normandy, the daughter of Duke Richard I of Normandy and his wife Gunnor, married King Æthelred in 1002 in a Church-sanctioned marriage arranged by her brother Richard II in an attempt to broker peace between England and Normandy. Æthelred's first wife, Ælfgifu of York, who gave the king eleven children, appears not to have been crowned, possibly on the orders of Ætheldred's domineering mother Ælfthryth. She died in 1001, so there was nothing to prevent Emma's coronation either at the time of her marriage or shortly after. It was unlikely, however, that Emma's sons would rule as Æthelred had five sons from his first marriage who survived infancy. Unfortunately for Æthelred, the treaty with Normandy did nothing to prevent raiding longboats appearing on English shores from other ports. Their numbers continued to escalate, especially after the St Brice's Day massacre of Danes living in England in 1002. In 1003, Sweyn Forkbeard of Denmark, whose sister Gunnhild and her family may have been murdered in Oxford during the massacre, signalled his intent for vengeance when he burned Exeter and Wilton. By 1006 his army had 'left its mark on every shire in Wessex'.[1] Æthelred would spend the last ten years of his life trying to fend off Danish raiders. Three of his heirs died before 1015 including his eldest son Æthelstan. It was a time of murder, war and conquest when alliances forged through marriage could make or break kingdoms.

The situation continued to deteriorate as the annual raids drove deeper into the kingdom and men who should have been tending their crops found themselves called to defend their country. Famine, as well as Danish swords, began to bite. In 1013, Sweyn landed near modern-day Sandwich in Kent with the intention of conquering England. The earls of

Northumbria, Mercia and East Anglia quickly submitted to Sweyn who made his capital at Gainsborough. In London, Æthelred realised that the Danes were stronger than him and that pragmatic landowners preferred to accept Sweyn's rule rather than continue to resist. The king fled to Normandy along with his young wife and family. On 3 February 1014, after a reign of less than two months, Sweyn died suddenly. Too soon to be elected by the witan, the council of leading nobles, as England's king. He was succeeded by his son Cnut who was not so experienced in warfare. The Anglo-Saxons took the opportunity to summon Æthelred back from Normandy. The force that now marched against the Danes was sufficiently strong to drive Cnut out of England but not before he mutilated the hostages who had been taken by his father to ensure English compliance.

The kingdom continued to be troubled. Æthelred, some twenty or so years older than Emma, was unable to control his nobility. Two factions formed; one loyal to Æthelred's son Edmund Ironside and the other faction loyal to his son-in-law Eadric Streona, a Mercian who came to dominate Æthelred's council. In 1015, Streona had two leading Mercian noblemen, Sigeferth and his brother Morcar, murdered. Æthelred seized all of the brothers' land and bundled Sigeferth's widow off to the nunnery at Malmesbury. His son Edmund took the opportunity to seize the woman and make her his own wife before claiming all Sigeferth's confiscated estates for himself. As Edmund and Streona vied for power, Cnut returned to England with a fleet of ships and began raiding the south coast. Initially, the two factions put aside their differences to take on the Danish threat but Streona concluded that it would be more advantageous to pledge allegiance to Cnut. Æthelred, who was increasingly unwell at Cosham near Portsmouth died on 23 April 1016, leaving Emma widowed with three small children. Her position was precarious. She could either remain in England to retain control of the dower properties given to her at the time of her marriage or return to Normandy. Her own sons were too young to inherit their father's kingdom. Their elder half-brother, Edmund Ironside, was in the best position to take the throne.

The Battle of Ashingdon between the English and Cnut's army took place on 18 October 1016. It had the effect of dividing England into two regions with Edmund Ironside ruling the south of England and Cnut ruling Mercia and Northumbria. However, divided rule was brief as Edmund died on 30 November 1016. Henry of Huntingdon, writing in the twelfth century, claimed that Edmund was murdered whilst in the privy. Geoffrey Gaimar placed the blame on Eadric Streona's shoulders, stating that he murdered the king with a cross-bow. Other chroniclers believed that the young king either died from wounds or disease. Emma sent her children to Normandy for safety but remained in London herself, although as London was surrounded by Cnut's army, she may have had no choice. Æthelred's only remaining adult son, Edwy, was murdered on Cnut's orders. Edmund's infant children were sent into exile. By the summer of 1017, Cnut was king of the whole of England and Emma became a captive queen.

The *Anglo-Saxon Chronicle* recorded, 'before 1 August the king ordered the widow of the former king Æthelred, Richard's daughter, to be fetched to him as queen'.[2] The marriage was a political manoeuvre. Cnut, who was about ten years younger than Emma, ruled by right of conquest but his new wife was a recognised Queen of England whose coronation at the time of her wedding to Æthelred conferred political authority upon her. She represented continuity and the reconciliation of the opposing nationalities in the same way that Henry Tudor would one day transition rule from the Plantagenet House of York to the Tudor dynasty by the expedient of marriage to Edward IV's daughter Elizabeth. Cnut's marriage to Emma would also make Duke Richard of Normandy less likely to put the interests of his nephews fathered by Æthelred before those of his sister and any more sons that she might have with Cnut. In all likelihood, Emma enjoyed a higher status as Cnut's bride than she had as Æthelred's second wife. Although she had little choice other than to marry Cnut, Emma later described the negotiations around the wedding and her eventual agreement that she would be the 'partner of his rule'.[3]

The only difficulty was that Cnut already had a living wife at the time he married Emma. Ælfgifu of Northampton had two children, Sweyn and Harold named after Cnut's father and grandfather, suggesting a degree of permanence rather than a fleeting encounter of the kind enjoyed by many Scandinavian rulers at the time.[4] History has made Ælfgifu Cnut's mistress or handfasted wife despite the fact that there's no evidence whether they married *more danico* or *more Christiano*. History describes the two sons of Cnut's union with Ælfgifu as illegitimate but at the time there was no distinction made between Cnut's children by Ælfgifu or Emma.

Few English sources mention the shadowy Ælfgifu but it is clear that she had significant political leverage. She was the daughter of Ælfhelm, an influential *aldorman* from southern Northumbria. He and his brother, Wulfric Spot, founded Burton Abbey and attested to royal charters. Their political influence extended across the Midlands and North of England.[5] Although Ælfgifu's family were important they were not invulnerable. It seems that her father was murdered in 1006 and the family further weakened when both his sons were blinded on the orders of Eadric Streona who was eager to acquire power in Mercia and on the king's council for himself. It is also extremely likely that he was confident that he would not be punished for his crimes because he acted on the orders of King Æthelred. If the king was behind the murder and mutilation of Ælfgifu's father and brothers it explains why the family supported Sweyn Forkbeard during his invasion of the country in 1014.

Sweyn must have found it desirable to ally his son to Ælfgifu's family with a marriage of some description in order to strengthen relationships with leading families to further his plans for a conquest of England. If families to the north of Sweyn's army could be held in an alliance formed by marriage, he would run less risk of an attack from behind whilst he concentrated his campaign on Wessex and the south. The *Anglo-Saxon Chronicle* has nothing to say on the subject of Cnut's wedding to Ælfgifu either at the time or later. After Sweyn's death, Æthelred was able to repulse the invaders so the wedding between Ælfgifu and Cnut, if there was one, is unlikely to have taken place later.[6] Nor can we be certain what happened to Ælfgifu when Cnut returned to Denmark. It has been suggested that she could be the woman who took Sweyn Forkbeard's body back to Denmark before Æthelred was able to carry out a threat to disinter the corpse from its grave in Gainsborough.[7] Denmark would certainly have been safer for her but there is a lack of conclusive evidence that her husband arranged for her to cross the North Sea. She might also have remained hidden in an out-of-the-way location in the North of England with people loyal either to her own family or the Danes.

It is also possible that a canonical marriage was entered into between Ælfgifu and Cnut but that it became expedient for Cnut to repudiate Ælfgifu after he conquered all of England. By then the alliances his father wished to secure were redundant. Ælfgifu became a 'temporary wife'.[8] Divorces were not uncommon at the time but there is no evidence of a formal repudiation. It was not unusual for unwanted wives to find themselves behind a convent wall. Adam of Bremen writing in the second half of the eleventh century assumed that Ælfgifu was a 'concubine' but his main source was Cnut's nephew, Sweyn Estrithsson, who kept several wives, mistresses and sex slaves. Adam believed that it was common Danish practice and expressed his disgust with Estrithsson whilst besmirching Ælfgifu's reputation.[9] Cnut's own actions show that both Ælfgifu and Emma were important to him. Ælfgifu was the mother of two of his children. The Danes did not use primogeniture as a method of selecting their kings and marriage was not a necessity for an heir to be throneworthy. It was for this reason that Scandinavian kings were welcome to have sexual relationships with women of noble birth outside marriage because if a woman became pregnant with a future leader, the status of the whole family would be elevated.[10]

Cnut succeeded to the Danish throne in 1018 after his brother Harold II of Denmark's death and took the throne of Norway in 1028. Ælfgifu assumed a role as Cnut's representative in his Scandinavian kingdoms. She was sent first to Denmark and then to Norway with her eldest son, Sweyn. Ælfgifu was a political power in Norway where the period is remembered as 'Ælfgifu's time'. Scandinavian tradition tells the tale of Ælfgifu being St Olaf's lover before becoming Cnut's woman. It provides a neat, though unlikely, explanation for the enmity between Norway and Denmark at this time. She was no less significant to Cnut than his wife Emma, who held the royal treasury in Winchester and acted on occasion as his regent in England. The story promoted by the *Encomium Emmae Reginae* (Praise of Queen Emma) written around 1041 attempted to belittle Ælfgifu's status by describing her as 'some other woman'[11] but Cnut sought to control his empire through both the women who shared his bed.

The historical ambiguity of Ælfgifu's position was not helped by the fact that Emma was careful to make alliances with leading churchmen during her marriage to Æthelred as well as during her marriage to Cnut. In 1029, she and Cnut presented Wulfstan, the Archbishop of York, with a precious book known as the York Gospels and more famously she is depicted in the Winchester *Liber Vitae* with her husband. It is perhaps not surprising Ælfgifu of Northampton is regarded as the 'other woman' given that the record keepers of the time were all monastic chroniclers.

In addition, Cnut issued a legal code drawn up by Archbishop Wulfstan including a law that stated that a man who kept more than one wife was to be excommunicated.[12] Cnut may have accepted the wording of the archbishop's rigorous standards but who was going to object to his own relationship with Ælfgifu?

By 1034 Ælfgifu and her son were back in Denmark because the Norwegians led by Magnus the Good rebelled against Cnut's overlordship. Traditionally, punitive taxation and a harsh rule are cited as the reasons that Danish overlordship collapsed in Norway. By the following year Cnut's son Sweyn was dead and so was the king. By that time Emma's son Harthacnut was in Denmark where he was acting as regent and learning the business of kingship. The witan, or king's council, held a meeting in Oxford to decide which of Cnut's sons would be their next king. Northern earls favoured Harold Harefoot, the son of Ælfgifu, whilst the southern earls, notably Earl Godwin of Wessex, favoured Harthacnut the son of Emma. Both women used their familial networks and political leverage to promote their own sons recognising that their own position was dependent on which of Cnut's sons was victorious. The *Anglo-Saxon Chronicle* recorded the mudslinging that accompanied the campaigning. It was claimed that Ælfgifu tricked Cnut into believing that Harold Harefoot was his. A rumour spread that one of her children was the child of a servant smuggled into Ælfgifu's bed. If Cnut's union with Ælfgifu was an illicit one, there would have been no need for a smear campaign. Later John of Worcester stated that Harold Harefoot was the son of a cobbler and that Sweyn was the son of a priest's concubine.[13]

The Council of Oxford composed of the country's leading *ældormen* arrived at a compromise, Harold would rule as king north of the Thames whilst Harthacnut would rule Wessex. England's rule fractured along the line of the Thames with Godwin of Wessex and Leofric of Mercia urging their supporters to elect the king that they themselves favoured. However, Harthacnut remained in Denmark. There was a growing threat from Norway so he had no option other than to remain where he was. Harold Harefoot who was in England at the time, used the opportunity to seize the royal treasury from Emma in Winchester and take control of the whole country. By 1036, Emma decided that if Harthacnut was tarrying in Denmark that her sons by Æthelred might be more interested in wresting the kingdom from Ælfgifu and Harefoot. A letter arrived in Normandy inferring that the current instability in England was a chance for them to reclaim their birth right. The author of the *Encomium* maintained that the letter purporting to be from Emma was in fact a forgery sent by Harefoot to lure the Saxon princes into danger. Edward, who was the elder of Emma's sons, arrived with vessels supplied by his uncle but met with a hostile reception so returned to Normandy. John of Worcester recorded that Edward's younger brother, Alfred, arrived separately with six hundred men. He was met by Earl Godwin of Wessex at Guildford. Alfred had no reason to distrust him; Godwin was a friend of his mother's. But the earl recognised that in supporting Harthacnut he had made a blunder which he needed to redress if he was to maintain his place in Harold Harefoot's regime. Godwin captured Alfred and murdered his men or sold them into slavery. He handed Alfred over to Harold Harefoot and Ælfgifu in Ely where they blinded their prisoner.

Resistance to Harefoot's claim to the throne collapsed. The *Anglo-Saxon Chronicle* recorded that Harold's mother settled in Winchester to 'hold all Wessex in hand for him'.[14] Emma was forced into exile in Bruges. With King Harold I on the throne, Ælfgifu held the upper hand. Cnut's second marriage did not invalidate his first one even if some of the writers of the *Anglo-Saxon Chronicle* thought Harold's claim was dubious. The succession seemed secure. During this time no question arose about Ælfgifu's status. Unfortunately for her, victory over Emma was not a lasting one. Harold Harefoot died in Oxford on 17 March 1040 without any legitimate heirs.

Harthacnut was summoned back to England. He was an unpopular king, remembered for his high levels of taxation and for disinterring his brother's body from its grave in Westminster, having the corpse beheaded and then ditched in the Thames. At about the same time that Harthacnut was wreaking his vengeance on his brother, Emma commissioned the *Encomium Emmae Reginae* ensuring that her version of history was the one to survive for future generations. It developed her political position by emphasising her partnership with Cnut. It also sought to strengthen the claim of her children to the throne. The book described Ælfgifu as a concubine and placed the blame for Alfred's death squarely on Harefoot's shoulders. Emma stated that she made Cnut swear that her sons would take precedence over any other woman's – if Ælfgifu's children were deemed illegitimate in the eyes of contemporary society there would have been no need to do this. Later chroniclers embroidered Emma's account so that by the time Florence of Worcester wrote his version of events just over eighty years later, Ælfgifu was little better than a harlot.

There is no further mention of Ælfgifu in the *Anglo-Saxon Chronicle*. She may have retired to a convent in the Midlands but England was no longer safe for her. Denmark remained in Harthacnut's hands so it becomes reasonable to assume that she could not return there if she fled into exile. A story contained in a twelfth-century cartulary from the Monastery of Sainte-Foi at Conques in Aquitaine suggests that Ælfgifu may have lived out her days in the south of France. An Englishman called Alboynus or Elfwine, who was said to be the illegitimate son of King Harold, came to the area on pilgrimage with a woman called Alveva, the latinised form of Ælfgifu. The record describes the woman as Elfwine's mother but equally might have been his grandmother. The man persuaded the authorities to rebuild the church and make him its prior.[15]

Harthacnut died in 1042 and was succeeded by his half-brother, Edward the Confessor. He stripped his mother of her power and she retired from court. She died ten years later and was buried in Winchester. Her legacy, *In Praise of Queen Emma*, written between 1041 and 1043, is the earliest surviving account of a female political figure. It justified Emma's own actions and reduces Ælfgifu to the status of mistress. The account tarnished Ælfgifu's reputation to ensure the queen's own legacy. However, the marital status of Emma's own ancestors was not without doubt. Her Norse great-grandfather Rollo became the first duke of Normandy having arrived at an accommodation with Charles the Simple of the West Franks. The treaty between the two men was sealed with an alliance. Rollo married Charles' daughter Gisla despite the fact that he was already married *more danico* to a woman called Poppa. Rollo's newfound Christianity and marriage to Gisla, who died soon after, did not invalidate Rollo's relationship with Poppa or make his children with her illegitimate. Rollo's son William Longsword continued the semi-bigamous marriage habits of his father as did Emma's own father Duke Richard I who married Emma of Paris, the daughter of Hugh the Great, as part of an alliance between Normandy and Paris against King Louis IV of West Francia. The duke had no children with Hugh's daughter but he did have a number of other more fertile relationships including with Emma's mother Gunnor. Later chroniclers created a distinction between

Gunnor and the other women in Richard's life by suggesting that she was married *more danico* to the duke before Emma of Paris's death and then married according to Christian rites to legitimise her children. William of Jumieges, writing during William the Conqueror's lifetime, tactfully made no reference to illegitimacy and talks only about marriage after the Danish custom. This kind of marriage has been described as an 'alliance-building relationship',[16] that was entirely respectable. It was arranged without detriment to the woman's reputation. If the union was dissolved neither the alliance nor the status of the woman was harmed. The term has been described as meaning a 'common law wife' but realistically there is no modern equivalent. Even concubinage, which could be best described as a long-term relationship without the benefit of any kind of legal agreement, was seen as an imperfect form of marriage. It was not until the second half of the twelfth century that the Church was acknowledged as the sole authority for contracting lawful marriage. The cultural change impacted the way in which women like Ælfgifu of Northampton and Gunnor were written about. At a stroke of the pen, monastic chroniclers shifted their status from respectable women to wanton wenches.

Chapter 2

Edith Swanneck and her Daughter Gunnhild

There were other women in the eleventh century who married after the Danish custom but by far the most famous is Eadgifu Swanneshals or Edith Swanneck, who loved King Harold and entered the pages of history when she found his body in the bloody aftermath of the Battle of Hastings. King Harold II was one of Earl Godwin of Wessex's nine children. Godwin gained his earldom in 1018 and then married King Cnut's sister-in-law Gytha in 1022. Harold was born circa 1022 and created Earl of East Anglia at about the same time his sister Edith married King Edward in 1045. The family relationship with the king was a difficult one as he held Earl Godwin responsible for the capture, mutilation and death of his younger brother Alfred in 1036. He also resented the political dominance of the family preferring his own Norman advisers.

Harold may have been handfasted to Edith Swanneck at the same time that he took control of East Anglia. It is also conceivable that a union was arranged to provide Harold with political power backed by Edith's landholdings which totalled more than 270 hides, making her one of the wealthiest landholders in pre-Conquest England.[1] They may have been related as they married *more danico* rather than in a church. The papacy forbade marriage within seven degrees of consanguinity as incestuous. The papacy set about regulating and influencing marriage by determining whether a couple were free to marry one another; by setting standards for consanguinity, or the degree at which relationships became incestuous, and by providing safeguards against deception, bigamy and the taint of illegitimacy. After 1215 couples were required to count back up their family tree for four generations. If they shared a common ancestor the marriage would be deemed incestuous. Affinity and spiritual ties complicated matters. But equally, marriages between Danish families were often handfasted weddings. Edith probably already knew Harold as some of her manors adjoined his estates at Brightlingsea and East Bergholt. She was not a mistress or concubine and her children were viewed as legitimate. Harold's non-Church marriage to Edith left him free to make a politically advantageous second marriage in exactly the same way that Cnut and the dukes of Normandy married both by the Danish and Christian customs.

The couple's eldest surviving son, Godwin, was born in 1049. Within two years Harold was forced to flee to Ireland when Edward the Confessor took an opportunity to seize political power from the Godwin clan. The confrontation between Edward and the Godwins was sparked after the death of men in the household of Eustace, Count of Boulogne, at Dover. Eustace and his men having visited King Edward sought overnight accommodation prior to returning to their homes. When they were refused board and lodgings, the resulting skirmish led to the death of twenty of Eustace's men. He was quick to lay the blame on the townsfolk of Dover. Edward ordered Earl Godwin to harry the town but Godwin refused as it lay within his own domains. The opposing factions gathered their armies but the country avoided civil war when Godwin agreed to stand trial in London. There was little chance of reconciliation. The king wanted vengeance for the death of his brother and was implacable in his demands. Godwin and his five sons were banished. Harold and his brother Leofwine went to Ireland. There is no mention of where Edith Swanneck might have been at this time. Godwin's wife, Gytha, is chronicled in John of Worcester's account of the episode as is Judith, the wife of Harold's brother Tostig as accompanying their husbands into exile in Flanders at the court of Judith's father. Harold's younger brothers may already have been hostages in Normandy and Queen Edith was banished to a nunnery. Edith Swanneck, who retained administration of her own lands, appears to have been left unmolested. She may have retired to her estates and lived quietly.

Harold's exile was brief. His father was re-established at court by 1053 and Harold inherited his father's earldom of Wessex the same year when Godwin died unexpectedly. He relinquished the earldom of East Anglia where Edith's landholdings were situated making the political element of their union redundant but their family continued to grow, although we cannot be certain of how many children there were in total or what their names might have been. The couple's youngest daughter, Gunnhild, was born in 1055. Harold, now Earl of Wessex, not only had his own estates to run but also led military campaigns against the Welsh and served Edward the Confessor as a diplomat in Europe. Edith was welcome at a court ruled by a king known for his piety. So far as the society she lived in was concerned she was married to Harold but the couple was used to leading separate lives and meeting when circumstances permitted. At some point in 1064, Harold found himself in Normandy. The events of his visit are recorded on the Bayeux Tapestry from the Norman perspective and included an oath promising support for Duke William in his pursuit of the English throne.

By 1065 Harold and Edith had been living together as man and wife for about twenty years. They had between five and seven children depending on the source. Edward the Confessor died on 5 January 1066 and was buried the next day. Harold was crowned King of England on 6 January. For a very short time, Edith was effectively Queen of England although she was not crowned as her husband's consort. But it was expedient for Harold to make a new marriage to secure essential alliances if he wanted to be secure on his throne. He needed the support of the witan, the council who advised and chose England's kings, and more importantly the affirmation of the two northern earls Morcar and Edwin. To achieve that end he married the earls' widowed sister Ealdgyth of Mercia, in a Church-sanctioned ceremony during the spring of 1066. She was the widow of Gruffudd ap Llewelyn, killed during a campaign led against the Welsh by Harold and his brother Tostig in 1063. The marriage also had the effect of weakening Edwin and Morcar's links with the new rulers of north Wales. Ealdgyth, the widow of a prince of Wales, was more throne-worthy than Edith not least because she had a more powerful family. The *Anglo-Saxon Chronicle* makes no comment about the wedding or when it happened although it does describe Harold making a journey to York before Easter. It is likely that Ealdgyth returned with him. Shortly after Easter, Halley's Comet appeared in the skies warning of dangers ahead. There was no time for a coronation for Ealdgyth thanks to a summer spent awaiting invasion from the Normans and from Harold's own brother Tostig who was allied to the Norwegian king Harold Hardrada, a descendent of Cnut. Ealdgyth was in London on 14 October 1066 but was moved to Chester soon after by her brothers Edwin and Morcar when they learned of Harold's death. By that time, according to a later chronicler, she was heavily pregnant. From Chester she could escape with her son, Harold Haroldson, into Wales or cross the Irish Sea. For the time being, Chester was safe from the Normans so she may have remained. But in 1069, Eadric the Wild rose against the Norman hegemony and besieged Shrewsbury. As well as Welsh allies he was supported by a contingent from Chester. Soon after William the Conqueror squashed the rebellion, he turned his attention to Chester. If Ealdgyth had not fled before, she did so now. She disappeared from the written record although it is said that her son grew up in exile and died in 1098.

History does not record Edith Swanneck's views on Harold's marriage to another woman. What is noticeable is that she remained close to the man she loved in the days before Hastings. She waited throughout the summer for William of Normandy to invade England. As the season drew to a close, news of an invasion arrived but it was not on the south coast. The threat came from the north. Harold Hardrada, King of Norway and Tostig landed in the north of the country and defeated an army led by the brothers Morcar and Edwin. Harold marched north with his army, arriving in York just four days after hearing news of the English defeat at Fulford. At the battle of Stamford Bridge on 25 September 1066, Harold was victorious. Three days later William of Normandy landed at Pevensey on the south coast.

Emma may have been at one of Harold's manors in Sussex at the time of the Norman invasion. It is possible that the woman and child fleeing the burning building depicted on the Bayeaux Tapestry are Edith and one of Harold's younger children.[2] William of Poitiers states that the destruction of property on the south coast was one of the reasons that Harold increased the pace of his return south.[3] Whether or not the figure is Edith, she is representative of the Saxons who were now powerless in the face of Norman aggression. As the king turned to face the new threat, his family held a conference. His mother, Gytha, tried to persuade him not to fight William. Harold's brother Gyrth offered to lead the army because he had made no oath to the duke. The arguments raged back and forth but of Edith, nothing more is heard other than when the army led by Harold arrived at Senlac Hill on 14 October 1066 that Edith was behind the lines in the English camp along with Harold's mother. Together the women waited to hear the outcome of the battle. It must have been a terrifying day with the sounds of battle drifting on the wind and fragments of information reaching their ears taking them from early optimism to the crushing news that Harold, his brothers and most of the king's house carls were dead and that the Normans were victorious.

As darkness fell, the women who had waited with the baggage train throughout the battle took to the field to reclaim the bodies of their loved ones. Edith knelt amongst the mutilated remains of the two armies searching for the body of Harold undoing chain mail to peer more closely at the shattered corpses of men who had refused to surrender. Harold was recognisable, according to the *Anglo-Saxon Chronicle*, by secret marks known only to Edith. Some sources suggest that William the Conqueror ordered the body to be buried secretly and without ceremony despite Gytha's pleas for him to give her Harold's body. She is even said to have offered William its weight in gold. The Conqueror retorted that it was unfair for Harold's body to be buried when so many remained unburied on the field on his account. William of Jumièges recorded that Harold was buried on the shoreline beneath a cairn. Bosham Church in Sussex also lays claim to Harold's remains following the discovery of the body of a wealthy man in a grave next to King Cnut's young daughter who was said to have drowned nearby whilst she was playing. Following the Conquest, the manor and the church fell into the hands of William FitzOsbern who was the Conqueror's trusted kinsman. It is possible that the new king dispatched the remains of the old king to a secret resting place but it is largely supposition. William of Poitiers makes the point that William was a God-fearing man and that he would not have refused his opponent a Christian burial.[4]

The monks of Waltham Abbey told their own tale, that Edith Swanneck, her heart broken by the death of the man she loved, accompanied by two priests, Osgod Cnoppe and Elthelric Childemaister, found Harold's body and took it to Waltham where he was cured as a child of paralysis. The Waltham Chronicler writing about the same event in 1180 demoted Edith from wife to concubine because the monks did not recognise marriage *more danico* as legal. In 1205, the *Life of Harold* written by the same monastic community changed the story yet again to leave Harold alive after the battle and ending his days in Chester.

William the Conqueror was crowned king on Christmas Day 1066. Harold's estates were confiscated as were the properties of his brothers Gyth and Leofwine. Their sister, Queen Edith, the widow of Edward the Confessor, was permitted to keep her dower rights to estates in Winchester and other landholdings in Wiltshire. She found it politically expedient to confirm that Edward the Confessor nominated William to be his heir. Edward's widow lived quietly until her death in 1075 when she was buried alongside her husband in Westminster Abbey. It has been suggested that Harold's mother Gytha was also allowed to keep her extensive lands immediately after the conquest because she was not regarded as a threat.

Edith Swanneck's sons Godwin, Magnus and Edmund fled to Dublin where they recruited mercenaries and planned to regain the kingdom their father lost. In the summer of 1068, they returned and attacked Bristol before making their way along the coast to Somerset. A battle was fought at Bleadon with heavy casualties. The fleet of mercenaries returned to Ireland but, undeterred, Edith's sons made a second attempt the following year in Devon and were beaten back again. A Norman army advanced towards Exeter where Gytha plotted on behalf of her grandsons. An eighteen-day siege followed until Gytha was forced to escape to the island of Flat Holm in the Bristol Channel. She went from there to Europe taking Edith's thirteen-year-old daughter, Gytha, with her, her youngest grandsons and her daughter Gunnhild. Gytha's nephew Sweyn Estrithson who was king of Denmark arranged that Edith's daughter should marry Vladimir, Prince of Smolensk and Kiev. It was an advantageous marriage. Although young Gytha's father lost both his life and his kingdom, so far as Sweyn and Vladimir were concerned, she was a kinswoman of Sweyn's who could be used to seal an alliance. One of her descendants was Isabella of France who married King Edward II, another was Catherine of Valois who married King Henry V and after his death married Owain Tudor.

As a female magnate with a large landholding in her own right, it is likely that had Edith Swanneck remained in England, William would have arranged a new marriage for her but there is no evidence of this or of her whereabouts. The hand-fasted wife of King Harold disappeared from the pages of history and into the realms of legend.

Initially, much of Edith's estates were given to Ralph de Gael before being passed to Alan Rufus 'the Red' of Brittany following de Gael's rebellion in 1075.[5] Edith Swanneck's younger daughter, named after her aunt, Gunnhild was educated in Wilton Abbey as her aunt Queen Edith had been. It is likely that she was there in 1066 and that like many other women at the time it was decided that it was safest for her to remain within the confines of the convent in the immediate aftermath of the conquest. During her stay at the abbey, she was said to be cured of an eye tumour by Bishop Wulfstan of Worcester. It is not clear whether she took vows as a nun or whether she stayed there for her own safety in the care of her aunt, Queen Edith. Also in the abbey was Edith of Scotland, the daughter of King Malcolm and Queen Margaret who was the daughter of Edward the Exile (the son of Edmund Ironside sent into exile by King Cnut in 1016). Edith was descended from the royal house of Wessex making her a valuable marital prize. Perhaps for that reason, her Aunt Christina made her wear a nun's veil at Romsey and the practice continued at Wilton. In 1093, Malcolm and Alan Rufus negotiated an arrangement by which Alan, by now the wealthy lord of Richmond, would marry Edith.

In August that year, Malcolm attended the dedication of Durham Cathedral and from there he travelled to Gloucester for a meeting with King William II better known as William Rufus. The meeting was a disaster. Malcolm felt that he had been disrespected. William Rufus forbade the union between Alan and Edith as it would have made Alan too powerful in the north of England as well as extending Scottish influence south. Malcolm's anger was so great that he led a raid into England immediately afterwards and was killed at the Battle of Alnwick along with his heir Edward. Edith seems to have left Wilton at around the same time and disappeared from the known historical record until 1100 when Rufus's younger brother Henry married her upon becoming king.

Meanwhile, Alan Rufus met Gunnhild, who was in her thirties by then, perhaps whilst he was visiting Edith at the abbey and carried her off – it is open to debate whether she went willingly or not. By forming a union with Gunnhild either as a handfasted wife or concubine, Alan was aware that his tenants were more likely to be loyal. Gunnhild, and women like her, were a route by which earlier landowning bloodlines could be followed, legitimising the change from Saxon to Norman ownership. Archbishop Anselm of Canterbury wrote to Gunnhild demanding that she should return to her convent. He believed that she had taken the veil. Gunnhild repudiated the claim but Anselm did not accept her reasoning. Alan died at the end of 1093, perhaps before the couple could marry according to the rites of the Church. Gunnhild, who received a second letter from Anslem exhorting her to return to Wilton, had no intention of returning to the cloister. She became mistress, or possibly the handfast wife, of Alan's brother, Alan Niger 'the Black' who died in 1098. History does not know what became of Gunnhild after his demise. She may have returned to the anonymity of a cloistered life as her mother and stepmother may also have chosen to do.

Chapter 3

Herleva of Falaise

Duke Richard II of Normandy, brother of Queen Emma, left the duchy to his eldest son Richard. His second son, Robert, would inherit the County of Hiémois in southern Normandy. When he became its count upon his father's death, Robert would be required to give fealty to his brother which would help to secure the succession.[1] Instead, when Richard II died in August 1026, the new duke's younger brother rebelled. Richard besieged Falaise, the administrative capital of Hiémois, and Robert was forced to swear fealty to his brother. Duke Richard III died unexpectedly the following year, poisoned by his brother if the rumours at the time are to be believed, and Robert became duke in his turn. He ruled from 1027 until his death in 1035.

The story of Duke Robert and Herleva, told by William of Malmesbury, was one of love at first sight. Robert happened to look down from the ramparts of Falaise Castle perched on the edge of a cliff to the treetops and tanneries below. He saw a beautiful girl washing clothes in the River Ante or even bathing herself. A knight was sent from the castle to find the girl with orders to bring her back to Robert. William of Malmesbury, who told a slightly different tale, wrote, 'her beauty had once caught his eye as she was dancing, and he had become so smitten with it, as to form a connexion with her'.[2] Setting aside young Robert's supernaturally good eyesight, he might reasonably have expected the girl to make a shame faced entrance by a side gate and to spend an afternoon between his bedsheets. Instead, Herleva arrived at the main castle gates on a white horse and having met and publicly acknowledged her, Robert fell in love. Or at least that was what the legend recorded. The monk continued with his account that 'for some time (he) kept her in the position of a lawful wife'.[3] There was no evidence that Robert married his lover *in danico* but the retrospective tale gave a degree of formality to the union.

The truth is that details of Herleva's life are scant and more complicated than the love match depicted, at a later date, by both William of

Malmesbury and Orderic Vitalis. Robert's relationship with Herleva began before he became duke when he was about eighteen years old. He was a second son but his father gave him responsibility for Hiémois in southern Normandy prior to his death. In due course, Falaise would become Robert's base for his rebellion against his elder brother Duke Richard III. The relationship between Robert and Herleva began against a stormy political backdrop and ended only when Robert left Normandy to go on pilgrimage to Jerusalem in repentance of his sins. There was nothing noteworthy about a wellborn young man taking a local girl into his bed. Writers became interested in Herleva because her son became a duke and then a king.

It was said that Hervela's father, Fulbert, was a tanner. The main source for this is Orderic Vitalis, of Anglo-Norman descent writing from about 1123 until his death circa 1143. The area around Falaise was known for its tanneries and leather works. More recently, the term *polinctores* from which the idea arose has been re-translated from 'animal skins' to a more classical form of Latin meaning 'one who prepares bodies for burial', so perhaps Fulbert was a tanner, a furrier, an undertaker or even an embalmer.[4] Rather than being on the lowest rung of the social ladder, Herleva's father was likely to have been a wealthy burgher or even an administrator whose ancestors had once been tanners.[5] Certainly it seems unlikely that Robert would have found the stench associated with the tannery trade, which required urine and faeces, attractive no matter how beautiful Herleva might have been. Later, her brothers appeared as attestors on a number of their nephew's, Duke William's, papers. It is unlikely that the children of a lowly tanner would have been deemed appropriate for such an important role no matter how fond the duke was of his maternal family. What is certain is that William was sensitive about his grandfather's social status. When he besieged the town of Alençon in 1051, its defenders hung pelts and furs from the wall as an insult. It was a mistake. When he took the town, William ordered his soldiers to cut off the hands and feet of thirty-two of the defenders. Three generations later Bishop Hugh of Lincoln watched King Henry II stitch a 'bandage wound round an injured finger on his left hand'. He quipped 'How you resemble your cousins at Falaise'. Fortunately, Henry II who was famous for his rages also had a sense of humour and 'dissolved in helpless laughter'.[6] He even explained the jest for the benefit of those around him.

Herleva's son, William, was born circa 1028 in Falaise, the year after his father became Duke Robert I of Normandy. Herleva, or Arlette as some sources call her, was somewhere between eighteen and twenty-five years old at the time. William of Malmesbury, writing in 1125, told the story that during her pregnancy Herleva dreamed that 'her intestines were stretched out, and extended over the whole Normandy and England'.[7] Duke William may have been a child destined by Fate for greatness but his birth was a difficult one. Malmesbury continued that the baby was laid on the floor by the midwives struggling to save Herleva's life. He claimed that the child grabbed the floor rushes demonstrating that he would grow into a warrior with a strong hand. Wace and Benoît de Saint-Maure also recount the dream. Herleva became a device by which later writers were able to justify William's place as Duke of Normandy and King of England – God willed it. In reality, the infant was the bastard offspring of a duke who might reasonably have been expected to marry and have legitimate sons.

Soon after her son was born Herleva left Falaise to live in Rouen, Normandy's capital, with her lover. William's birth was followed, in the account of Robert of Torigny, by a sister named Adelaide or Adeliza. There is little or no record of William's early years or Herleva's life. Duke Robert II raised his children in his household and either made Herleva's father his chamberlain or promoted him from his position at Falaise. Instead of marrying to form an alliance and secure the duchy's future, he kept Heleva by his side. He could not marry her because of their difference in social status. There were negotiations for him to marry a sister of King Cnut called Estrith but it came to nothing. Early dukes of Normandy bedded a succession of women but Herleva emerged from the period as the love of Duke Robert's life and the mother of his successor. Herleva inspired Robert's devotion and their son revered them both throughout his life.

In 1035, Herleva's life at her lover's court came to an end. Duke Robert, sometimes known as 'the Devil' because of his supposed involvement with the death of his brother, repented of his youthful sins. In addition to the presence of Herleva in his life, he had confiscated the property of the Bishops of Rouen and Bayeux forcing them both into exile. Now, he founded a monastery at Cerisy and a convent at Montivilliers and recalled the exiled bishops. He also decided to go on pilgrimage to Jerusalem to demonstrate how fully he atoned for his sins. Herleva, well endowed by the duke, was married to Herluin, Vicomte de Conteville, a middle-ranking lord who owned land south of the Seine. The marriage provided protection for Herleva. William's mother bore at least three more children. Odo, who would become Bishop of Bayeux, could have been born as early as 1030. He is best known for his role at Hastings and the commissioning of the Bayeux Tapestry. A second son Robert was born a year after Odo. William gave both his half-brothers large landholdings in England. A third child, a daughter, would eventually marry William, Lord of the La Ferté-Macé. In time Herleva's family would become the nucleus of William's administration. Herluin acquired land that stretched across Normandy. In the aftermath of the Conquest, William's half-siblings and extended family would benefit from large landholdings in England. Orderic's account of the Conqueror's life draws attention to the Conqueror's devotion to his mother and her family whilst William of Malmesbury noted that William treated Herleva with generosity.

Duke Robert, having no wife or legitimate heirs, made William his heir during the Christmas and New Year festivities that heralded 1035. The duke required all his nobles to swear an oath in support of his decision. His relationship with Herleva was long-standing, stable and she had an acknowledged place in the duke's life but it was a risk to identify an illegitimate child as his heir. Archbishop Robert of Rouen, Count Alan of Brittany, Osbern the steward and Turold, who was one of the boy's tutors, were appointed as the boy's guardians. Their job was no sinecure. There were men with a better claim to rule even if, in 1035, they did swear that they would support Robert's son. According to Jumièges, everyone 'unanimously acclaimed', Robert's son and 'pledged him fealty with inviolable oaths'.[8] Duke Robert was only twenty-five years old and was on the verge of becoming one of Normandy's most important dukes. It seemed unlikely that he would not return, marry and provide legitimate heirs. Before he left for Asia Minor, the duke took the precaution of ensuring that the French, who saw the Normans as their vassals, recognised William's status as his heir. Having settled the succession, Robert emptied the treasury and set off on foot to Jerusalem travelling via Constantinople. He fell ill and died, some reports said by poison, on his return journey at Nicaea on 2 July 1035.

William was either seven or eight years old when he became Duke of Normandy. A French writer, Ralph Glaber, wrote that the lack of a legitimate heir was 'a cause of great distress',[9] but added that the Normans accepted children who were the issue of concubines. The Church was still struggling to achieve supremacy in the matter of what constituted marriage. Herleva, an openly acknowledged mistress with a long-term familial relationship with the duke, was of a similar ilk to women including Emma of Normandy's mother Gunnor. Young William's birth was not so different from that of earlier dukes but Christianity had a tighter grip on Normandy than in previous centuries. His accession resulted in a time of political instability that escalated into civil war before William was old enough to bring his nobility to heel.

The next five years of William's life were brutal and dangerous. A number of Norman barons rejected their new duke's right to rule them. The Normans vied against one another for power and settled old grudges. One of William's guardians, the archbishop, an old man, died in 1037. Three years later Alan of Brittany was killed during a siege. Gilbert, Count of Brionne took over William's guardianship. He was William's kin although one tale suggested that he had enjoyed Herleva's favours before she met Robert. According to the story, his illegitimate son Richard FitzGilbert was Duke William's half-brother. There is no evidence for the relationship in the historical record other than the esteem in which William held Richard. Gilbert was soon murdered by his own cousin Ralph de Gacé. Normandy descended even deeper into chaos. Malmesbury wrote, 'fire and slaughter raged on all sides'.[10] In 1041, Turold was murdered and then Osbern's throat was cut one night whilst the duke was staying at Vaudreuil. William was asleep in the same room as the murdered man. Orderic Vitalis' version of the tale dramatised the dangers that the duke faced and demonstrated, using a classical model, that he was chosen by God to rule. He also recounted episodes from William's life that showed that the boy was loved by his mother, even though the pair were separated. Herleva's brother, Walter, cared for William during this time, moving him from castle to castle, often fleeing at a moment's notice to evade his enemies. William later recalled that his uncle even smuggled him out of his bed chamber and hid him in the home of some nearby peasants when the need arose.

There were a series of attempts on the duke's life, his subjects rebelled and, in 1047, Guy of Brionne who had his own claim to the duchy gathered an army that predominantly came from the west of Normandy to take Normandy by force. William turned to King Henri I of France for help. The Battle of Val-ès-Dunes fought by a combined force of Norman and French against William's cousin Guy resulted in a victory for twenty-year-old William but it took more than a decade for him to establish his rule throughout his duchy. Soon after William's victory in 1047, his full sister Adelaide married Enguerrand of Ponthieu to procure an ally for the duke.

Two years later Adelaide's marriage was deemed to be incestuous based on the rules of consanguinity. William's proposed marriage to Matilda of Flanders was also questioned by Pope Leo IX. William had no intention of losing an alliance with Baldwin V of Flanders but Enguerrand was excommunicated and Adelaide's marriage annulled. She retained Aumale which was part of her dower and was styled Countess of Aumale in her own right. William had arranged his sister's first marriage to forge alliances to help secure his position. As his grip on his duchy became more certain he looked beyond his borders for her second husband in order to create a buffer zone around Normandy. Adelaide's second marriage may have been to the Count of Lens who was killed in 1054; a subsequent marriage was made to Odo, Count of Champagne. She was one of the few Norman women in the Domesday Book of 1086 to hold manors in her own right demonstrating the affection in which her brother held her.

Herleva was at Eu on the eastern border of Normandy with her husband when William married Matilda of Flanders in 1050. The alliance with Flanders was an indicator that her son was secure in his position as Duke of Normandy. Herleva would have watched Baldwin V of Flanders and his wife arrive at the head of a colourful retinue dressed in all their finery. She would have been part of an equally magnificent gathering. The marriage to Matilda of Flanders was a turning point. By 1060 William had emerged as a strong ruler intent on expanding his domain.

History does not record exactly when Herleva died. Herluin married a second time to Fredesendis and it is her name listed amongst the benefactors of the monastery of Grestain where Herleva was buried. Herluin was the father to at least two more children from his second marriage, Ralph and John. Robert of Torigny believed that when Herluin died before, or very shortly after 1066, he was buried next to Herleva.[11] William remained close to his extended family. Richard FitzGilbert who was certainly his cousin, if not his half-sibling, accompanied William to England in 1066. He became England's chief justice and helped to suppress a number of the rebellions that arose against the Conqueror. By the time of the Domesday Book, he was recognised as Richard de Tonbridge from his possessions in Kent. He also held a large number of lordships across East Anglia and the South. Odo, Bishop of Bayeux, William's half-brother and trusted adviser, was created Earl of Kent in the aftermath of the Conquest. Robert is recorded in the Domesday Book as holding tracts of land in the southwest of England. William appointed Robert as Count of Mortain prior to his invasion of Maine in 1063 demonstrating a continued strategic use of family ties to secure his borders. Even Herluin's son Ralph, who was no relation to the Conqueror, acquired estates in Somerset and Devon.

By 1570 the story grew that the word harlot, meaning a wanton woman, came from the name Herleva, or Arlette, as some sources identified her. In fact, the word derives from the Old French word *herlot* that first appeared in English during the thirteenth century. It meant rascal and was initially a description applied to men. By the fourteenth century, a harlot was a jester, clown or entertainer. It was only in the fifteenth century that the word was used to describe women. In 1560 it was used in place of strumpet and whore in the Geneva Bible resulting in its current derogatory meaning.[12] Herleva remains largely in the shadows but the monastic chroniclers suggest that she was a woman who inspired the love and devotion of two dukes of Normandy, her husband and her family.

Chapter 4

Maud Peverel

Wwilliam the Conqueror, perhaps understanding better than most the stigma of illegitimacy, had no known children out of wedlock. He appears to have been faithful to his wife Matilda of Flanders although that did not stop rumour providing him with a mistress and an illegitimate son. Dugdale's *The Baronage of England* written in 1605 claimed that Ingelric's daughter, Athelida, was William's concubine and that the duke's children by her carried her husband's name. There was also a claim that Maud, to give her the name that the Normans knew her by, was the duke's cousin which might go some way to explain his later generosity to the family.

The story was retold throughout the eighteenth and nineteenth centuries. J. R. Planché, a nineteenth-century Somerset Herald defended the idea and expressed the view that 'every ancestor of the Conqueror had left illegitimate issue, and therefore in the summary of his crimes and vices no contemporary would have dreamed of including incontinence'.[1]

Maud was also provided with a link to the royal house of Wessex to ensure that she was a suitable mistress for the man who conquered England. Æthelred the Unready was the father of fourteen legitimate children. Later stories, with no substantiating evidence, provided him with several illegitimate offspring by various women. According to legend, one of those children was called Ingelric who became the Earl of Essex and founded the Collegiate Church of St Martin-le-Grand in the City of London. It was even said that he was descended from Joseph of Arimathea, the man who provided Christ's tomb after his crucifixion. If that were not enough, Maud's father was also reputed to be one of the wealthiest men in England. The suggestion that Ingelric was the Earl of Essex only grew after his death and nothing is known about his family background other than the fact that Ingelric or Engelric were names more commonly found amongst Continental-German families. It is more likely, despite the evidence of substantial wealth, that he was a clerk in holy orders who came to England during the period before the conquest than part of Edward the Confessor's extended family.[2]

It is true that Ingelric and his brother, Eirard, founded the church of St Martin-le-Grand in the City of London in 1056. The foundation was confirmed by William the Conqueror in 1068. Ingelric had sufficient resources to establish the collegiate church because of his landholdings, identified through the Domesday Book of 1086, in Essex, Suffolk and Kent. Edward the Confessor granted him land for the specific purpose of building St Martin-le-Grand including, in 1056, the living of the church at Maldon as well as two hides of land. This grant was confirmed at a later date by King William. Ingelric's extensive land acquisitions can also be explained by the fact that he was a royal commissioner who had influence both in the courts of King Edward and King William. He added to his landholdings through royal reward, by purchase and annexation. After the Conquest, William allowed the English, whose fealty he accepted, to buy back their lands. The majority of English landowners found themselves in reduced circumstances but Ingelric's were much improved.

Maud 'being a woman of celebrated beauty'[3] was believed to have become the mistress of William Duke of Normandy and given birth to a son named after his father prior to William's marriage to Matilda of Flanders in 1051. Later, Maud married Ranulph Peverel whose father Payne was said to be Duke Robert II's standard-bearer although there is no known evidence of the Peverel family in Normandy before the Conquest. Planché argued that Peverel or Piperell, and in the Domesday Book *Piperellus*, was a mistranslation caused by a mis-spelling of the Latin *puerulus* -meaning a boy, to distinguish William the boy from William the father.[4]

Maud's son, William Peverel, listed on the Roll of Battle, was at Hastings. The roll is not completely trustworthy as it is a copy of an earlier document. The author explains William's wealth by adding that 'he was by all accounts, his son (the Conqueror's) by a noble and beautiful Saxon lady'.[5] A note provides the counter-argument that the story is 'altogether uncertified'.[6] The Peverels were undoubtedly an important family in post-Conquest England. The year after Hastings, William Peverel held Nottingham Castle on behalf of the king and became the first Lord of Nottingham. The Conqueror also made Peverel bailiff of the Royal Manors to the north and west of Derbyshire and gave him the land to build a castle named the Castle of the Peak and the town below the castle which appears to have been planned at the same time. Castleton still retains some evidence of a grid pattern. Peveril Castle, as the Castle of the Peak is better known today, in Castleton, Derbyshire, was a small castle including a curtain wall built from stone rather than wood as was more usual at the time. The keep was added in around 1176 by Henry II who confiscated the Peverel estates.

The Domesday Book of 1086 reveals that Ranulf Peverel held thirty-seven manors in Essex and a further eighteen manors in Suffolk as well as knights' fees in Norfolk, Oxfordshire and Shropshire. William Peverel held 162 lordships and berewicks called the Honour of Peverel in Nottinghamshire and Derbyshire as well as being granted property in Nottingham itself. In addition, he held a large amount of land in Northamptonshire. Between them, Ranulf and William held more than three hundred manors. It appears that because there was a mystery surrounding Peverel's parentage and that the Conqueror showed him marked favour, that before long the conclusion was drawn that Peverel was the king's son. It was not a bad thing to have a royal connection, albeit an illegitimate one. The story makes a printed appearance in 1610 in Robert Glover's *Catalogue of Honor, or Treasury of True Nobility, peculaier and proper to the Isle of Great Britaine*. Glover, the Somerset Herald of Arms, catalogued the genealogies of some of England's families whilst on official business. Before the seventeenth century, the story would have been kept alive through repetition. Other noble houses had their own stories of royal illegitimacy. In a hierarchical society, it made families seem more influential within their own social and geographical settings.

If Maud did have an affair with William, she and her father may have gone to Normandy with Edward the Confessor whilst he was in exile between 1016 and 1035. It might even have been possible that William met Maud when he visited his cousin, Edward the Confessor, in 1051. William's marriage to Matilda of Flanders was essential for the security of both the duke and his duchy. However, if the Confessor promised William, who was his kinsman, that he would succeed to the throne during the visit of 1051, it is not unreasonable to think that a Saxon royal connection would have helped William's claim to the throne. It is also true that the Normans used marriage alliances following the Conquest as a way of establishing themselves in England. The Conqueror betrothed one of his daughters to Earl Edwin of Mercia but he died before the marriage could go ahead. The Earl Waltheof of Huntingdon married the king's niece Judith of Lens. Intermarriage led to assimilation and later writers perhaps provided William with a beautiful mistress descended from the Royal House of Wessex to exemplify the merging of two cultures as well as explain the favour shown to the Peverel family. The romance of William's meeting with Ingelric's daughter had echoes of Duke Robert's meeting with Herleva. Both were young men who were not yet married. And like his father, William was besotted with the beautiful girl who captured his heart. He 'desired nothing more than to be her prisoner in arms'.[7] Maud, being virtuous, had to be wooed and William set about this by 'enriching the college of St. Martin's-le-Grand'[8] and offering other 'unavoidable allurements'.[9] She was at length made his mistress. The story was unencumbered by supporting evidence but made William the conqueror of a people, the captive of one beautiful Saxon girl.

There is no proof that Maud had an affair with William the Conqueror or that William Peverel was his illegitimate child. The ambiguity of many charters and rolls makes it difficult to confirm that everyone with the Peverel name dwelling in England in the aftermath of the Conquest was a direct relation of Ranulph and Maud. There is even some doubt that Ranulph was William's stepfather. Freeman, writing in the 1860s, dismissed Glover's claims as 'uncorroborated assertions,' and concluded that the affair and possibility of an illegitimate child were an 'almost impossible scandal'.[10] Ranulph and William were more likely to have been brothers than stepfather and son. Planché, writing ten years after Freeman, counter-argued that William Peverel made no mention in the foundation charter for Lenton Priory of his parentage which would have been more usual, preferring instead to found and endow the priory for 'the health of the soul of King William' and his family. The wording of Peverel's charter implores assistance for the souls of King William I and his two sons as well as Peverel's wife and children. Planché suggests that this tenuous indication demonstrated that the Conqueror was Peverel's father.

Maud is thought to have married Ranulph Peverel in about 1058. She had several children between 1060 and 1068. She founded Hatfield Peverel Priory, a college of secular canons in Essex during the reign of William Rufus and remained there until her death. Her son William confirmed the charter and all the possessions that Maud granted to the priory but converted the foundation to a Benedictine one with monks from St Albans Abbey. Dugdale's *Monasticon Aglicanum* provided a reason for the foundation of the college which was initially dedicated to St Mary Magdalen. Maud wished to atone for her sins and expiate her guilt before her death. Hearne's 1715 edition of Leland's *Collectanea* embellished the tale still further. As Maud approached the end of her life the Devil vowed that her soul would be his if she was buried outside the church. Her family avoided the problem by burying her in the wall of the collegiate church at Hatfield Peverel renamed St Andrew's by her son. The effigy, purported to be Maud's, can be seen to this day although it dates to the thirteenth century rather than the earlier period in which Maud lived and is the effigy of a man rather than a woman.[11]

Maud's son, William Peverel founded or re-founded the priory between 1108 and 1116 during the rule of King Henry I. Dugdale's *History of Hatfield Peverel* begins with William's act.[12] Peverel offered his own home to the monks and confirmed the gifts made by his predecessors. He did not name his father in the deed although he did state that the gift was for the souls of his parents as well as King William and King Henry. By then Norman England had seen the rule of two Williams. History cannot even be sure that William Peverel, in this instance, was the man alleged to be the Conqueror's son – William Peverel of Nottingham and William Peverel of Dover were both alive during this time. Forester writing in 1853 believed them to be half-brothers, one the son of the Conqueror, the other the son of Maud's husband.

The Honour of Peverel was taken back by the Crown in 1155 when William Peverel the Younger, Maud's grandson, was accused of killing Ranulf, Earl of Chester by poison when the earl was Peverel's guest. Evidence shows that the earl survived the assassination attempt as King Henry II granted him much of Peverel's lands. More likely, the forfeiture of the Peverel estates was caused by the fact that William backed King Stephen rather than the Empress Matilda during the Anarchy that followed the death of King Henry I. It was said that Peverel retired to an abbey, like his grandmother, to repent of his sins.[13] He may simply have been guilty of supporting the losing side during England's first civil war. It can be stated however that Maud Peverel was the mistress who never was. She became a convenient means by which commentators explained William's favour towards the Peverel family.

Chapter 5

Robert of Gloucester's Mother and Ansfride of Seacourt

William the Conqueror died on 9 September 1087. William Rufus succeeded his father as King of England whilst his elder brother Robert Curthose became the Duke of Normandy. Henry, the third of William's sons received £5000 but no land other than estates in England which had once belonged to his mother. For the next thirteen years, Henry moved around his brothers' domains as William and Robert vied against one another for supremacy until William Rufus was killed by a stray arrow in the New Forest on 2 August 1100. Henry was with his brother, according to the chronicler Orderic Vitalis, but rather than tending to William's body he seized a horse and galloped to Winchester where he appropriated the royal treasury. Under the terms of a treaty made in 1091, it was Robert who should have inherited England after William's death. However, the duke was absent from Normandy at the time of Rufus's death having gone on the First Crusade in 1096. He was on his way home from the Holy Land but had paused in his journey to marry Sybilla of Conversano in order to secure the funds he needed to pay back 10,000 marks he borrowed from William to fund his part in the crusade. Henry was crowned in Westminster Abbey on 5 August 1100. He ruled until his death on 1 December 1135 having won Normandy from his elder brother Robert Curthose in 1106.

Henry took the opportunity not only to hold his coronation before Robert returned to claim the Crown but also to reissue his brother William's coronation charter. In November 1100, 'not wishing to wallow in lasciviousness like any horse or mule'[1] Henry allied himself with the royal house of Wessex when he married Edith of Scotland declaring that he would give up his mistresses. Henry's bride was the great-niece of Edward the Confessor whom the Normans esteemed and the *Anglo-Saxon Chronicle* noted was 'of the true royal family of England'.[2] Her lineage lent Henry's rule the legitimacy that the youngest son of the Conqueror lacked having usurped a throne that belonged to his elder brother.

Before the wedding could take place, Edith was required to demonstrate to Anselm, Archbishop of Canterbury that she had not taken the veil during her education at the nunneries at Romsey and Wilton. The marriage canon found in the *Decretum* of Gratian specifically forbade widows and virgins who passed many years in a monastic foundation to marry. Both Romsey and Wilton had long traditions of educating royal women but difficulties arose because Edith had been seen to be veiled from childhood onwards. Anselm believed that she could have been dedicated to God by her parents or that she took Holy Orders during her time inside the cloister. Edith was adamant that she took no vows and was prepared to testify to Anselm himself that her Aunt Christina, the abbess at Romsey had forced her to wear a veil for her own protection. The matter was taken before a council at Lambeth. It decided in Edith's favour. No record exists to explain what happened to Edith between 1083 when Alan Rufus's suit for her hand was turned down and her marriage to Henry. It is possible that she spent some time at William Rufus's court because Malmesbury and Orderic Vitalis both stated that Henry knew her and that he had been attracted to her because of her many virtues. A key factor in the decision reached by the council was that after the conquest, Archbishop Lanfranc ruled that women who took refuge in nunneries were not held to be sworn nuns. The alternative was that Edith would have been required to return to a convent or have faced excommunication.

Edith became Queen Matilda upon her marriage, adopting her godmother, Matilda of Flanders, name and signalling the unity of William the Conqueror's family with the remnants of the House of Wessex. The wedding was followed by a miscarriage the following year but in February 1102 the queen gave birth to a healthy daughter named Adelaide (who incidentally changed her name to Matilda following her marriage as a child to the Holy Roman Emperor, Henry V). In 1103, a boy named William was born. Charters and chronicles demonstrate the queen's involvement with ruling the country and the fact that Henry relied upon her running of governmental affairs whilst he travelled more widely to establish his control of Normandy and expand his territories. It has been suggested that although Matilda played a role in public life, once she had provided the king with two children the couple no longer shared a bed. There were certainly no more children after 1103. William of Malmesbury wrote, 'the bearing of two children, one of either sex left her content'.[3]

Henry may have loved his wife but once his son was born, he returned to the beds of the women who kept him company before his marriage. The king, it seems, was never short of willing partners. There is little known about many of Henry's mistresses, some of whom were casual encounters whilst others could be described as having familial intimacy with Henry given the number of children that they each gave him. Henry of Huntingdon talked about the 'king's secrets' after his death, 'And debauchery, since he was at all times subject to the power of women, after the manner of King Solomon'.[4] Even Orderic Vitalis who was an admirer of the king's policies described him as 'possessing an abundance of wealth and luxuries, he gave way too easily to the sin of lust; from boyhood until old age, he was sinfully enslaved by this vice'.[5] William of Malmesbury, writing after the event saw things differently. He stated that King Henry I was 'wholly free from impure desires'.[6] Given that he fathered more than twenty illegitimate children and had numerous mistresses in both England and Normandy this seems to be a bit of a stretch of the imagination. Malmesbury rationalised his view of Henry's libido:

He partook of female blandishments not for gratification of his lust, but for the sake of issue; nor did he condescend to casual intercourse, unless where it might produce that effect: in this respect (he was) the master of his inclinations, not the passive slave of desire.[7]

It is difficult to imagine that Henry planned to use his children as pawns on the diplomatic chessboard whilst he was a landless younger son with two apparently healthy elder brothers but he was swift to utilise their political potential after he became king. Henry would marry eight of his illegitimate daughters to neighbouring nobility. In some cases, although the names of Henry's children are known, their mothers are not. There were rumours and inferences about some of the women for whom no written record remains and Henry may have had other children for whom there are no records, only tantalising clues. The wife of Fergus of Galloway, for example, seems to have been the king's illegitimate daughter Elizabeth FitzRoy since her own son, Uhtred, was identified as a cousin of Henry II when he was sent as a hostage to the court of Malcolm IV of Scotland.[8]

Robert of Caen, who supported his half-sister Matilda's right to the English throne is probably the best known of Henry's illegitimate children but we know nothing about the affair that produced the earl apart from the fact that the woman who gave birth to him shared Henry's bed in 1090. Robert's education, abilities and seniority of birth made him one of the most influential figures of the period. In 1120, following the death of Henry I's only legitimate son, William Ætheling, the king raised Robert to an earldom having already arranged his son's marriage to a wealthy heiress. But who was Robert's mother? Nest of Wales and Sybilla Corbet, both known mistresses of Henry, have been suggested. Robert became lord of Glamorgan with a power base in South Wales that fits geographically to either Nest or Sybilla. However, Robert did not grow up with the sobriquet 'of Wales'. Robert's mother could have been an unknown woman of Caen as the name 'de Caen' would suggest. Equally, it might be a later addition deriving from Robert's role as governor of Caen which he held by right of his wife Mabel FitzHamon. William of Malmesbury wrote about the earl's Flemish and French ancestry. The name Robert is also suggestive of location as the boy was born at a time when Henry was on good terms with his elder brother and seeking to cement his position within Normandy.

In 1087, Henry was known to be in Caen arranging his father's funeral. In 1088 he came to an agreement with Curthose who wanted support from Henry to launch an invasion of England. He purchased lands in the Cotentin from his elder brother for £3,000 at this time but his brother William confiscated estates in England that the Conqueror had said should be given to Henry. Neither of his brothers trusted him and both came to believe that he was siding with the other. Henry returned to England in the autumn of 1088 to try and persuade his brother William to regrant him their mother's estate. By the time he returned to Normandy, Curthose was convinced that Henry was conspiring against him so gave orders for his brother to be imprisoned in Neuilly-la-Forêt. He remained in custody for the next six months during which time Robert stripped him of the Cotentin. Upon his release, Henry continued to control the west of Normandy although he was no longer its count. He demonstrated his loyalty to Robert during a riot in Rouen at the end of 1090. Subsequently both his brothers unified against Henry. He found himself banished from Normandy and living as an exile in France. It is not known exactly where Henry stayed during this time but Orderic Vitalis suggested the French Vexin which marched along the border with Normandy. By 1092, Henry had regained a foothold in Normandy when the citizens of Domront invited him to take control from Robert de Bellême. Henry's later reputation for a series of mistresses located across different geographic regions implies the existence of many unknown women during this period of Henry's life of whom Robert's mother was one.

There is another theory that Robert of Caen's mother was from Oxfordshire. Henry made himself at home in Woodstock from the 1080s onwards whenever he stayed in England. At the time there was a hunting lodge at Woodstock. When he became king, Henry established a park there and it became a 'favourite seat of his retirement and privacy'.[9] Three of his mistresses are known to have lived near Oxford. It has been argued that Robert's mother was a daughter of Rainauld Gay or Gayt of Hampton Gay and Northbrook Gay in Oxfordshire. Evidence for this comes from the chronicle of John of Worcester who described the siege of Bristol in 1138 during the so-called Anarchy when Henry's daughter Matilda and his nephew Stephen of Blois vied for the throne. Worcester describes one of Bristol's defenders, Philip Gay or Gayt, as Robert's *cognatum* meaning cousin. The family held lands at Hampton and Northbrook near Henry I's residence at Woodstock.[10] A charter of gifts made to St Mary's Church, Kirtlington identifies Philip as the son of Stephen Gay.[11] In 1086, according to the Domesday Book, Rainauld Gay, the father of Stephen, held two hides of land as tenant to Roger d'Ivry. The Gay family were much lower down the social scale than might be expected for the mistress of a prince but Henry was a third son and unlikely to become king. Henry, like his father and grandson, was an enthusiastic hunter. He roamed the countryside looking for game to chase and if he met a beautiful woman along the way he might have been diverted by another kind of entertainment. The only problems with the theory are that there is no documented evidence that Rainauld had a daughter and *cognatus*, which is taken to mean first cousin but can also mean any kinsman in any degree.

Henry acknowledged Robert as his son and arranged for him to be educated. For a time, the boy's tutor was Otuel who would become guardian to the king's only legitimate son William Ætheling. In 1107, Henry married Robert to Mabel FitzHamon providing him with a wealthy inheritance. It set the pattern for the way that the king would treat his natural children. He oversaw their welfare and education but did not provide for his illegitimate sons from Crown land when they reached maturity. Instead, he arranged for them to marry wealthy heiresses ensuring that no overmighty magnates grew to contest the monarchy. A network of landowners evolved who were part of Henry's extended family but who owed everything they had to the monarchy ensuring their continued loyalty.

Ansfride, the widow of a knight called Anskil, appears in the records as the mother of at least three of Henry's children and was one of the women associated with Henry who came from the Oxford area. Ansfride's husband Anskil of Seacourt held land in Oxfordshire and Berkshire as the tenant of Abingdon Abbey. The luckless knight fell out with William Rufus who threw Anskil into prison, where he died, and seized all of his lands leaving Ansfride without a home or a husband. She appealed to Henry for help. He was very happy to 'support her in her troubles'[12] first by taking the woman into his own household and then by negotiating the return of her dowry lands. Meanwhile the Abbot of Abingdon who was the overlord of Seacourt, the manor being granted out since before the conquest as a knight's fee to a military tenant, retrieved the manor from William Rufus on payment of a substantial fine. It seemed unlikely that Ansfride's legitimate son William would be able to reclaim his inheritance but Henry intervened. He arranged a marriage for the boy to the niece of the Abbot of Abingdon and Seacourt was returned to the family. Later Ansfride's youngest son, Fulk, would become a monk at the abbey and Ansfride, would be laid to rest in its hallowed precinct despite the number of children she gave Henry outside marriage. It is likely that her final resting place was granted as a favour to the king. It provides circumstantial evidence of Ansfride's importance to Henry.[13] Although the Church taught the importance of chastity for women there was much more freedom for Henry who was part of the elite and could lay with whoever he wished.

Ansfride may already have been Henry's mistress or he was attracted to her, helped her and expected sexual favours in return. There was even a medical theory influenced by Ovid, relating to balancing the humours of the body that a woman's body was hot and that, as a consequence, they were more lustful than men. This was complicated by the fact that men were considered active partners in lovemaking whilst women were passive recipients. Whilst chivalric love was for upper-class women, the lower classes did not need to be wooed in the same way. Kings and sons of kings were at the top of the social pyramid, widows like Ansfride without land or a family to protect them were without rights. At least she was in a better position than many comely peasants or servants. Capellanus' text entitled *On Love* written at the end of the twelfth century, proclaimed that women from the lower classes were not capable of true love. Their natures were more earthy and they coupled like animals. The writer's advice for his aristocratic readers was to 'puff them (peasant women) up with praise and then, when you find a convenient place, do not hesitate to take what you seek'.[14] There is no evidence that Henry ever needed to force himself on the women in his life and Ansfride was not a quick tumble to be quickly forgotten. Henry helped her to regain her husband's land and provided for their children. Juliana was born before Henry became king. Her brother Richard was either born around 1100 or as late as 1110 depending on the source. Her youngest son, Fulk, was born several years later.[15] The pattern of the births reflects the longevity of many of Henry's extramarital relationships. Ansfride nurtured her children until they had survived the dangers of infancy and then Henry arranged for their education as part of the extended royal family. History does not record where Juliana was educated but Richard was raised in the household of Robert Bloet, Bishop of Lincoln as was his half-brother Robert of Caen for a time. Both boys were acknowledged as *filius regis* – sons of the king.

King Henry eventually arranged for Ansfride's daughter, Juliana, to marry Eustace of Bréteuil. Eustace's lands lay on the Norman border so were strategically important. Henry hoped to ensure Eustace's loyalty through the ties of kinship. Eustace was himself illegitimate and had seized his father's lands after he died. He was probably successful because the legitimate heirs came from outside the duchy and Henry was looking to his own interests rather than what the Church might have thought on the issue of inheritance. Problems arose when Henry installed his own garrison at Ivry Castle in 1119 securing his position despite the newfound familial alliances. Eustace withdrew his support for his father-in-law. Peace was eventually restored when Eustace recovered the castle along with the son of Ralph Harenec, the castellan, who was to be a hostage to guarantee a cessation of hostilities. The boy was blinded either accidentally or on the command of Eustace. Orderic Vitalis records that Henry ordered that Julianna's two daughters, the king and Ansfride's own grandchildren, were to be handed over to Harenec that he might be revenged. The boy's disability meant that he would never be able to lead men or govern a castle. In a militaristic society, Harenec's heir had lost his value. Both girls were blinded and as a further compensation to Harenec, they were mutilated by having their noses split. It made it unlikely they would ever find husbands. Family affection seems to have had little to do with the king's response. Mistresses and their families might benefit from their links to the king but Crown interests came first. The result was a breakdown of the familial ties that Henry I cultivated. Eustace rebelled. The king arrived at Bréteul and besieged the castle. Juliana led a spirited defence which included an attempt to shoot her father with a crossbow from the battlements under the pretext of negotiating a surrender. Orderic Vitalis recorded that she made her escape by leaping from the castle walls, exposing her bare buttocks as she fell, into the moat before fleeing to Pacy sixty miles away. The couple were eventually reconciled with the king thanks to Juliana's brother Richard of Lincoln but much of Eustace's land was given to Ralph de Gael, a son of the Earl of Essex.

Malmesbury described Richard of Lincoln, the second of Ansfride's children with Henry, as 'dear to his father for his obedience'.[16] Richard grew up to be an able warrior and an accepted part of the royal circle being a favourite companion of William Ætheling, Henry's only legitimate son. In 1120, Henry betrothed Richard to Amice, the only child of Ralph de Gael, who held the lands originally belonging to Eustace of Bréteuil. If the marriage had gone ahead, it would have made Richard a wealthy landowner in Normandy and Brittany at the expense of his sister and brother-in-law. Orderic thought that the proposed marriage was unfitting, not because Richard was base-born but because Ralph, a Breton, held territory against the will of its Norman population.

On 25 November 1120, King Henry was about to return to England with his court having waged a successful military campaign against the French. The fleet was due to sail from Barfleur to Southampton. After twenty years Henry had established his rule in England and Normandy and had a seventeen-year-old heir to succeed him. Amongst the silk-clad throng of the Anglo-Norman elite who gathered for the voyage were Richard of Lincoln and another of the king's children, Matilda, who was married to the Count of Perche. She was a favourite with William Ætheling as well as her father. While the king waited for a favourable wind to carry his fleet to England, he was approached by Thomas FitzStephen, the son of the man who captained the Conqueror's flagship Mora in 1066. Thomas asked for the honour of carrying the king in his vessel the *Blanche-Nef* or the White Ship. He claimed that its crew of fifty oarsmen would arrive home faster than any other ship in Henry's fleet. The king declined to change his plans but put his treasure chests in the hold of the White Ship and suggested that there were other members of the royal family who would be glad to travel with FitzStephen. The king and his fleet left the harbour at Barfleur leaving the White Ship and a crowd of young men and women to follow including William Ætheling, Richard and Matilda of Perche.

William ordered a large quantity of wine to be fetched aboard the vessel. Having drunk the wine, the inebriated crew and their passengers attempted to overtake the king's fleet. The general drunkenness caused a number of the vessel's passengers to disembark before the White Ship cast off. They reported that there was a breakdown in order on the ship. As well as two monks, Stephen of Blois, who was the king's nephew, got off the boat. The drunken sailors did not take the care they should have when leaving harbour. The boat was one mile out of the harbour just before the moment when it reached open seas when it struck a rock in the darkness. Men and women were thrown into the water as the stricken vessel tipped over. The prince was hustled into the White Ship's only rowing boat and sent in the direction of safety. All around him the screams of drowning men and women filled the night. Richard of Lincoln, clutched in the embrace of his former tutor Otuel FitzEarl, was dragged beneath the water by their combined weight. Meanwhile, William ordered that the boat taking him to safety should be turned back when he heard the screams of his half-sister Matilda, Countess of Perche. Her mother was a woman called Edith about whom very little is known. If the account is a true one rather than the imagination of William of Malmesbury, it shows that Henry raised all his children as one family. The boat was soon swamped by men and women desperate to save their own lives.

Thomas FitzStephen was said to have initially survived the wreck, being one of the few people not to panic and who knew how to swim, but on discovering that the king's son was dead preferred to die rather than face Henry's wrath. Richard of Lincoln's body washed up on the shore. He was recognisable only by his fine clothes. William Ætheling's body was never recovered. The king's treasure chests were still in the hold of the White Ship which was broken on the Quillebœuf Rock. These were recovered as were many of the passengers' personal possessions. In England, it gradually became clear that the White Ship was unaccounted for. No one wanted to tell the king what had happened. Henry's beloved son was dead as were two more of his children, both cherished members of the royal family. It fell to Theobald of Blois-Chartres to tell his uncle the news. The boy was mourning his own sister and brother, not yet knowing that Stephen of Blois had not sailed with the ill-fated ship. The court was turned into a place of mourning.

Chroniclers were quick to see God's judgement in the death of as many as three hundred men and women including the crew. All of Henry's strategies and plans had been for nothing. Despite fathering a large number of children, he only had one legitimate son. In earlier times Robert de Caen, who was well-liked and held all the qualifications of command and education, might have succeeded to the throne rather than his half-sister or cousin. In 1035, the illegitimate son of Herleva became duke of Normandy but less than one hundred years later little thought was given to the potential of the Conqueror's illegitimate grandson. The idea of different kinds of marriage and the fluid interpretations of legitimacy had changed. The concept of a Christian marriage approved by the Church meant that only children, usually sons, born inside the sheltering confines of wedlock could expect to succeed their royal fathers. There was nothing King Henry I could do other than marry again. He chose Adeliza of Louvain to be his bride. They married on 24 January 1121 – two months after the White Ship's sinking. Despite his love of women and record for siring children out of wedlock, Henry died without a male heir.

Chapter 6

Nest of Wales

One of the women whose company King Henry I sought when he was no longer welcome in his wife's bed was the beautiful Princess Nest of Wales. She was the daughter of Rhys ap Tewdwr, King of Deheubarth. The territory which included modern Dyfed and Ceredigion was one of Wales' four main kingdoms. Rhys became king in 1079 after the death of his second cousin. The kingdoms to the north and east of Deheubarth waged war on an annual basis and although the wars were not so bitter after Rhys became king, old aggressions remained as did the unsettling presence of the Normans to the east. William the Conqueror pushed west so far as Offa's Dyke then stopped. He preferred to make alliances with the Welsh rather than continue with a policy of conquest.

One of the rulers who arrived at an accommodation with William was Rhys who, according to the evidence contained in the Domesday Book, made some kind of submission to the Conqueror recognising the king as his overlord. By 1081, despite some incursions by Norman settlers, Rhys felt secure on his throne. As well as arriving at an understanding with the Normans he also married Gwladus, the daughter of Rhiwallon of Powys. She was sent to Deheubarth as a peace weaver to put a stop to the intermittent warring between the two kingdoms. She was almost certainly the mother of Nest and her two brothers even though history cannot be certain about the date of Nest's birth. When she was a small child, Nest would have lived within her mother's household and been educated as the daughter of a king. An illustration in a medieval text by Matthew of Paris held by the British Library depicts her and Henry in bed wearing nothing but their crowns demonstrating her equality in rank to her lover.

Between 1081 and 1087, Deheubarth was at peace but then William the Conqueror died. The understanding that Rhys reached with the Conqueror did not extend to his son, William Rufus. It was an opportunity for land-hungry Norman barons on the marches of Wales to extend their territorial possessions while England and the Welsh marches seethed with rebellion against Rufus in 1088. The following year Rhys's kingdom was invaded by three princes of Powys; Madog, Rhirid and Cadwgan. They saw a chance to acquire land for themselves. Rhys was taken by surprise and forced to flee to Ireland but the following year he counter-attacked and regained his kingdom. For Nest, it must have been a frightening time. The threat of Norman invasion grew with each annexation of land along the Welsh borders. In April 1093, Rhys said farewell to his wife and children and marched with his army to Brycheiniog to check the territorial ambitions of Bernard of Neufmarché. Rhys was killed during the ensuing battle at Brecon. Within two months his kingdom was completely overrun by Norman invaders. Arnulf de Montgomery, a younger son of the Earl of Shrewsbury, set about establishing his dominance in the region from his base at Pembroke.

The first Nest would have known of the disaster was when ragtag bands of survivors from her father's army trickled home. Her brothers were too young to take their father's place. The eldest, Gruffydd, was sent to Ireland for safety whilst her youngest brother, Hywel, who was probably a very small child, stayed in Wales where he was eventually taken into the custody of Arnulf de Montgomery. Welsh chronicles relate that the young boy was not only imprisoned but also castrated before he eventually escaped Norman clutches. Two of Rhys' illegitimate sons were executed and Nest's mother disappeared from the historical record. Nest was taken prisoner at the same time. She was probably a child of seven or eight years. Under Welsh law, she could not inherit her father's throne and neither could her descendants but the inheritance system did allow daughters to inherit a share of parental estate. Nest became an heiress who would enable a new Anglo-Norman landholder to add a veneer of title to Rhys' former estates by right of marriage.

The Welsh regrouped and fought back against the invaders. Nest was sent into England to prevent her rescue. It is likely that she was sent first into territory belonging to the Earl of Shrewsbury. She may have even been sent to a convent for safety or else she could have been placed with a family patronised by the earl. One such family on the borders was the Corbet family. They had a daughter, Sybil, who was a similar age to Nest. Wherever she was sent, Nest would have learned to speak

Norman French. Another possibility is that William Rufus may have been concerned that Arnulf intended to marry Nest which would have made the Earl of Shrewsbury's family an almost royal power in the Welsh marches. The family, part of the Conqueror's extended kinship network, had rebelled against Rufus in 1088 and although they had been pardoned, Nest was too valuable an asset to leave in their custody. She may have been taken to live at the court of William Rufus in Windsor. Her position lay somewhere between hostage and royal ward.

Whilst at the English court, aged between ten and fifteen, she attracted the attention of Rufus's brother Henry. William Rufus's court was a place of feasting, drinking and gambling. Orderic Vitalis described it as a place of lewdness. Henry and Nest became lovers. As well as being handsome and charming, Nest may have seen Henry as a potential protector. He may have been genuinely attracted to her, or he was thinking of her father's lands in Wales. It is unlikely that the king would have welcomed a union between his land-hungry little brother and Nest any more than he contemplated a marriage for Nest with one of the Earl of Shrewsbury's relations.

When Henry became king and married Edith of Scotland in 1100, he set his mistresses, including Nest, to one side until his wife provided him with an heir. The *Myvyrian Archaiology of Wales* written during the eighteenth century told the tale that the Welsh princess was Robert of Gloucester's mother but it is highly unlikely. Henry arranged for Nest to marry Gerald de Windsor, the steward of Pembroke Castle, who was much older than her. It is also possible that Nest may have been married to Gerald much earlier on the orders of Arnulf de Montgomery. It has been suggested that Nest may have had her first child with Gerald in 1096.[1] If so, it was a momentous year for her husband. Gerald, the son of the constable of Windsor Castle, originally held Pembroke as steward to Arnulf and had retained it despite a prolonged siege in 1096.

Gerald's patrons, the Montgomery family supported Robert Curthose's claim to the English throne and rebelled against King Henry I's rule. The year after he was crowned Henry accused Arnulf and his brother of treason. Arnulf trusted Gerald sufficiently for the steward to travel to Ireland on his behalf to negotiate a marriage for Arnulf with the King of Munster, and for mercenaries and ships to carry them. At the end of the rebellion when Henry offered Arnulf the choice between exile or submission, Gerald remained in Pembroke where he avoided being attainted as a traitor. He was initially removed from his post and replaced by a knight called Saer, one of Henry's own men. By 1105, Henry came to trust Gerald sufficiently to re-establish him as castellan of Pembroke. Gerald had been an officer in the area for more than ten years. He may even have spoken Welsh. It was likely that he knew about Welsh laws and customs. Henry viewed him as an asset to help control the region. By offering Nest as a wife to Gerald, Henry was not only providing for her but also giving Norman rule in Wales an aura of legitimacy. The marriage demonstrated Henry's trust in Gerald and also tied the steward into an extended royal circle. In addition, Gerald would not be able to use Nest's status to further his own position in Wales as he was only a minor member of the nobility without extensive landholdings in the area or an extended kinship network. Within four years Nest was the mother of two sons, William and Maurice, and a daughter Angharad. Gerald began to build a new castle near Pembroke on land that was part of Nest's marriage settlement. Carew Castle became Nest's home. Territory disputes rumbled along the marches between England and Wales throughout the period. Gerald continued to build fortifications. In 1108, he started work on Cilgerran Castle. In time the couple had a third son called David.

William of Malmesbury believed that the union between King Henry and Edith/Matilda was a love match as did other chroniclers but the king proved unable to remain monogamous. At some point, probably after the birth of his own heir and when Henry visited Shropshire in 1102, the king resumed his relationship with Nest. She bore the king a son named Henry FitzHenry sometime after 1103 and possibly as late as 1114 depending on the source. He was raised alongside Nest's other children. Meanwhile, Queen Matilda endured 'with complacency, when the King was elsewhere employed'.[2]

In 1109, Cadwgan ap Bleddyn, the King of Powys and the dominant power in mid-Wales held a winter feast in Ceredigion. Nest and her husband were invited. Seasonal feasts were a way of maintaining social and political bonds. Nest was part of Bleddyn's extended family as well as being part of the region's Anglo-Norman elite. Her cousin, Cadwgan's son, Owain – sometimes called the Lion of Powys – paid her and her husband a visit at Cilgerran, or possibly Carew, at around the same time. He had heard much about Nest and wanted to see her for himself. According to the story told in the *Brut y Tywysogion* he was so overwhelmed by her beauty that he was 'instigated by the devil'[3] to have her for his own by any means available. Owain and a small band of his men returned during the night, having already found a weak spot in the castle's outer gate, where the original timber fortification met new stonework or where the mortar was still uncured. They dug beneath the gateway and fired the wooden buildings in the outer bailey of the castle before the castle guard was aware of what had befallen them. As the timber smouldered and began to burn more fiercely the little group of men scaled the inner castle wall and began battering the keep door. Gerald realised that he might be killed and panicked. Nest remained calm and quick-thinking despite the noise of Owain and his men trying to gain access to the keep and the acrid smoke from the burning buildings. She persuaded her husband to escape from Owain and his men by climbing down the midden chute in the garderobe adjoining their chamber. Nest waited until she knew Gerald was safe before shouting down to the castle's attackers;

> 'Why do you shout in vain? He whom you were seeking has escaped.' And then they came inside and searched for him everywhere. And when they did not find him, they seized Nest and her two sons and a third son, whom Gerald had by a concubine, and a daughter. And they utterly pillaged the castle and burned it. And he violated Nest and lay with her and then returned home.[4]

Cadwgan, who had spent thirty years resisting Norman advances into Wales, on hearing what his son had done demanded that Owain return Nest and her children to de Windsor. He was not only alarmed by what had befallen Nest but also by the grievance suffered by Gerald who was the king's officer. Owain refused. Nest was the victim, not only of Norman aggression, but of her own people's determination to punish the invaders by any means. Norman reprisals were directed at both the King of Powys and his son despite Cadwgan's horror at Nest's abduction. Richard of Beaumaris, Bishop of London, the king's justiciar, who was based at Shrewsbury took advantage of Nest's seizure and the resulting conflict to deprive Owain's father of his lands and to deal severe retribution to the men who were judged to be guilty of her kidnapping and rape. History cannot know whether Owain loved Nest, whether she went willingly or whether her abduction was a political statement that impugned her husband's honour. The laws of the time took no account of Nest's views on the matter regarding her abduction as a theft of property appropriated by force. Owain's destruction of Gerald's newly built castle, his escape through a passageway caked in excrement and the theft of his wife were humiliations for Gerald which were gleefully retold by the Welsh chroniclers. Even worse, Nest was beloved by King Henry I and Gerald had failed to protect her.

The Victorians concluded that Nest, Welsh and a cousin of her kidnapper, conspired with Owain. They decided that her loyalty to her Welsh family was greater than her loyalty to her husband. They named her the Helen of Wales because they saw her as a treacherous woman who betrayed her husband rather than a victim of Norman aggression or Welsh abduction. Owain's failure to return his cousin caused a bloody war. Nest was said to have given Owain two sons, Llewelyn and Einion, but if she did, they remained with Owain and dropped from the historical record. Her story became a romantic tale of seduction and deceit culminating in the arrival of a Norman army in Wales. It did not help Nest's long-term reputation that she was known to have had three lovers during her lifetime other than her husband as well as the encounter with Owain. Conflicting versions of the story cloud its interpretation. *The Red Book of Hergest* suggested that Owain became Nest's lover. Rather than blackening Owain's reputation by the inclusion of an act of violence against a Welsh princess it was Nest's standing that was damaged.

Depending upon the version of the story recounted, Nest could have endured almost five years as Owain's prisoner. The chronicles do not record where Nest was kept during her captivity. Owain spent some time near Aberdyfi so it is reasonable to assume that she was somewhere nearby. Tradition places her and her children at a hunting lodge by the Edlwyseg Rocks near Llangollen. Nest's quick thinking saved her husband's life and she was also able to persuade her captors to release her children which Owain did because, according to the medieval stories, he was infatuated with Nest. The chronicles depicted Nest as a *femme fatale* persuading Owain to release her children because if he failed to return them to their father the consequence would be her failure to remain faithful to her kidnapper. In reality, Nest's own release was probably negotiated within eighteen months of her abduction as a result of the combination of forces opposing Owain.

King Henry I offered the kingdom of Powys to anyone who could rescue her. Owain's cousins, Madog and Ithel ap Rhiryd, joined the campaign against Owain and his father because they coveted their uncle's lands. Owain's estates were burned and his people killed. Eventually, he fled to Ireland leaving Gerald to nurse a grudge against the man who abducted his wife and humiliated him. Cadwgan regained Ceredigion on payment of a fine and an oath to have nothing further to do with his son. Nest was returned to her husband. There is no indication of how the couple came to terms with Nest's kidnap or rape. Nor does history know whether any of her children by her husband remained in her care at this time. It is also unclear the extent to which King Henry renewed his own suit with Nest or where any assignations may have occurred.

Nest's abduction and its immediate consequences triggered a bloody period in Welsh history. Owain did not spend long in Ireland. He returned to Wales and resumed his campaign of burning Norman settlements and stealing their livestock as well as destroying settlements in Dyfed. He also made an alliance with his cousin Madog ap Rhiyd and a campaign of guerrilla warfare followed. Henry's response was to strip Cadwgan of his lands once more and make him live in England where he was murdered in 1111 by his nephew Madog who also killed Iorweth ap Bleddyn, the current king of Powys who replaced Cadwgan. Owain assumed the kingship of Powys and had his revenge for the murder of his father in 1113, when Madog was captured and mutilated.

In 1112 or 1113, Nest's brother Gruffydd ap Rhys who she had not seen since they were children also returned from Ireland. Once again Nest was placed in a difficult position. She was representative of a royal Welsh lineage but she was married into the Anglo-Norman elite. Gruffydd spent almost two years in Wales following his return from exile. As well as visiting Nest and staying at Pembroke with her family, he may have tried to persuade the king to return his father's kingdom to him. He travelled in Deheubarth and in Gwynedd, sought allies and a marriage alliance but his negotiations with King Henry were ultimately unsuccessful. Disaffected Welshmen joined his cause and he began his own campaign of destruction. Gerald of Windsor was ordered, by a furious Henry, to find his brother-in-law. Gruffyd fled Pembroke for the kingdom of Gwynedd. In Welsh texts, Gruffydd only turned to violence when it became clear that Henry intended to deny him his birthright whilst English texts describe a more established plot to seize the territories that had once belonged to Rhys ap Tewdwr. To further his intention, Gruffydd allied himself with Gruffydd ap Cynan, the King of Gwynedd. War always smouldering along the marches and in the troubled kingdoms of Wales burst into flames once more.

In 1114, King Henry invaded Wales. His intention was to subdue the kingdom of Gwynedd and to bring the rebels to heel. Many Welsh leaders, including Owain, elected to come to terms with Henry rather than to confront him. King Henry chose to recognise Owain as the Prince of Powys but took the precaution of taking Owain with him to Normandy the following year. Despite the fact that he kidnapped the king's former mistress and possibly abducted his son by Nest, Henry was a pragmatist. Owain was allowed to enjoy possession of his land once he submitted to the king. Some historians think that Henry I renewed his relationship with Nest during the campaigning season of 1114 and that Nest's son with the king was conceived during a summer of violence.

In 1115, Nest's brother Hywel escaped from his prison and joined his brother Gruffydd in Gwynedd. History does not record how Nest might have felt about the news. It is unlikely that she had seen Hywel since they were both children. It remained Gruffydd's intention to recover his father's kingdom but the king of Gwynedd came to terms with Henry who offered the king his lands free from fee. In one version of the story, Gruffydd ap Cynan promised to send Nest's elder brother to the king as a prisoner, or if that proved difficult, his head. According to the same version of the story, a relation of Nest's husband heard of the plot and related the information to Gerald. Nest, once again torn between her Anglo-Norman marriage and her credentials as a Welsh princess 'sent messengers in great haste to her brothers'.[5] Discovering they were betrayed, Nest's brothers fled to Ceredigion with the king of Gwynedd's daughter Gwenllian who married Gruffydd and became Nest's sister-in-law. The brothers set about regaining territory in the heartlands of Deheubarth by waging a successful guerrilla campaign.

The following year, King Henry ordered Owain to join his own Anglo-Norman forces to fight against Nest's elder brother. On his way to join the royal army, Owain met with Nest's husband and a party of Flemings. Despite the fact that he was a royal ally Gerald took the opportunity to avenge his wife's abduction and rape as well as his own shame by killing Owain. The *Brut y Twysogion* described Gerald as King Henry's 'particular friend'[6] which perhaps explains why there were no recorded repercussions against him. In time Gruffydd ap Rhys arrived at an accommodation with Henry and was restored to a reduced kingdom, the majority of which remained in the hands of the Normans.

Nest herself disappeared from the written record after Owain's death. She was widowed before 1130. Gerald was no longer the steward of Pembroke Castle by then and he would have been an old man given that he first appears in the records in 1093 as Arnulf de Montgomery's castellan. When rebellion broke out in 1136, it was Nest's sons who were listed amongst the Norman forces putting down the rebels. It is impossible to know how Nest felt about her Norman husband or the kind of relationship they might have enjoyed. For Nest, the alternatives to widowhood were remarriage or a convent. She chose to re-marry, or to live with, the castellan of Cardigan Castle, Stephen by whom she had another son, Robert FitzStephen, who succeeded his father as Constable of Cardigan. He was one of the Norman invaders of Ireland along with his half-brother Maurice FitzGerald. He also fought for King Henry II in North Wales. It is possible that Nest bore Cardigan's constable a second son called Hywel because he made a claim on Stephen's lands at Lampeter. Other records identify another son of Nest's called William who was the son of Gerald's successor at Pembroke, a man called Hait who was a Fleming. The circumstances of his birth are not known. Nest is thought to have died in 1136 but there is no record either of her death or where she was buried.

The Welsh princess had at least eight sons and two daughters by three or four different men. King Henry and Nest's son was the only one of the king's many illegitimate sons known to have been given his father's name, Henry FitzHenry. He was granted estates near Narbeth and fought on behalf of his cousin King Henry II. He was killed on campaign in Anglesey in 1157. William, the son of Hait, became Lord of St Clears. One of Nest's sons by Gerald, David, became the bishop of St David's. His brothers were William FitzGerald who inherited Carew Castle and Maurice FitzGerald who became Lord of Llanstephan as well as gaining land in Ireland. He married the daughter of Arnulf de Montgomery who changed the course of Nest's life when she was still a child from that of Welsh princess to Norman lady and one of King Henry I's concubines. She became the mother of a renowned and formidable family in Ireland. Maurice, an Anglo-Norman adventurer, founded the Geraldine dynasty at the same time that Richard 'Strongbow' de Clare, the son of another of King Henry's mistresses set about making Leinster his own. One of Nest's descendants was President John FitzGerald Kennedy.

Nest's daughter, Angharad, married William of Manorbier. They were the parents of Gerald of Wales. Nest's grandson wrote in his *Journey Through Wales* about his Norman grandfather but barely mentioned his grandmother 'the nobly born daughter of Rhys ap Tewdwr'[7] in his extensive writings other than to list his aunts and uncles including the fact that his uncle Henry was the son of the king and to mention that Robert FitzStephen was the son of a different father. It is unlikely that Gerald approved of his maternal grandmother. Nest, a celebrated mistress of King Henry I, was notorious for failing to meet the Church's rigorous moral standards. Yet, she had no choice in the matter – she was taken as a hostage from her home as a child and, having become Henry's mistress, was used as a pawn to lend legitimacy to the Anglo-Norman campaign to settle Wales. She was required to act as a 'peace-weaver' between the Normans and the Welsh. It was a difficult position to be placed in as the two groups grappled with one another. Even so, the accounts of her show her to be not only a strikingly beautiful woman but a shrewd and intelligent one. She was also a woman who endured difficult situations, survived as best she could and whose family flourished.

Chapter 7

Sybilla Corbet

Ansfride and Nest were mistresses of longstanding as was Sybilla Corbet of Alcester who gave King Henry five children; Sybil, Reginald, Rohese, William and Gundrada.[1] It has been suggested that Robert of Gloucester could have been Sybilla's son but there is little evidence to support the idea. It was even proposed that Henry married Sybilla and set her aside in order to marry Edith/Matilda of Scotland in 1100 when he became king.[2] The social difference in rank would have been an inappropriate match even for the third son of the Conqueror. Sybilla Corbet, sometimes known as Lucy or Adela, was the daughter of Robert Corbet, Lord of Alcester, a middle-ranking Marcher lord. The Corbet family were amongst the tenants-in-chief of the Earl of Shrewsbury who gave the family a large amount of land in 1071. Two generations of the Corbet family owed fealty to the earls of Shrewsbury; Hugo le Corbet who may have been at Hastings died before 1086 followed by his sons Roger and Robert who were listed as holding more than forty manors between them at the time of the Domesday Book. The latter held the barony of Longden and Alcester. Eventually, his estates would be divided between his two daughters, the elder of whom Sybilla was born between 1075 and 1077 and her younger sister Alice who may have had a different mother given that she married much later than Sybilla. Roger, the elder Corbet brother, can be found witnessing the Earl of Shrewsbury's charters and giving a donation to Shrewsbury Abbey for Earl Roger's soul in 1094. The association between the Corbet family and the earls of Shrewsbury continued with Earl Hugh and in 1098 when Hugh also died with his brother Robert de Bellême.

De Bellême revolted against King Henry I in 1102. He supported Robert Curthose's claim to the English throne. The king came to Shropshire with an army to put down the insurgency. Robert, Sybilla's father, retreated to Shrewsbury. His brother, Roger, held Bridgenorth Castle against the king for three months until its townspeople betrayed him. Having submitted, the king allowed him and his men to depart with honour. Henry went on to capture Pembroke Castle which was in the hands of Arnulf de Montgomery and his steward Gerald of Windsor. Whilst de Bellême and his brother forfeited the earldom of Shrewsbury and its associated territories both the Corbet brothers benefitted from additional landholdings in the region soon afterwards. They speedily returned to Henry's favour because he recognised the duty that men liked Corbet owed to their tenants-in-chief as well as the fact that in promoting men like the Corbets he created a tier in society who owed their place in it entirely to the Crown.

Sybilla's daughter, named after her mother, was born circa 1092 in Domfront, Normandy so it is difficult to know where Henry met Sybilla or exactly when their relationship began. The family retained landholdings in the Pais de Caux. It is also unclear where Sybilla resided at the time that her father joined in with the rebellion against the king. She may have been at the family home in Alcester in Warwickshire. The affair, paused during the king's post-wedding fidelity to his queen, resumed by 1104. Sybilla's son William was born the following year. Another son, Rainald, was born as late as 1110. Her parentage, relationship with King Henry, and her subsequent marriage were established from a charter in which Rainald confirmed ownership of Cornish lands originally given as a marriage portion to his Aunt Alice which must have occurred after 1140 as he only became earl in that year.

Shortly after the birth of her last child by the king, Sybilla was married to Herbert FitzHerbert, the Chamberlain of England whose father had been the king's chancellor and treasurer. His mother Emma, was alleged by fourteenth-century sources to have been the daughter of Stephen Comte de Champagne and Blois although more recent research suggests otherwise and that she was the daughter of a Dorset landowner.[3] After his marriage, Herbert acquired estates in Yorkshire and Gloucestershire as well as property in the marches of Wales. Amongst the papers of the Archbishops of York is a grant of property made to Herbert the Chamberlain and his son in the same year. It is possible that the king was providing 'for his mistress at no expense to himself'.[4]

It is possible that Henry returned to the arms of his mistress after her marriage as evidence about Gundrada's date of birth is lacking and about whom very little is known. In due course, Sybilla had legitimate children with her husband. Her son Henry was born circa 1112 suggesting that a marriage may have occurred in 1111. Another son, Robert, followed in about 1116. He succeeded his father and grandfather as King Henry II's chamberlain and was followed in his turn by his younger brother, Herbert, who inherited Robert's position at court in 1165. The king's ex-mistress, a wife with a large brood of children, was completely respectable once more and seems to have avoided being involved with anything that warranted a mention in the chronicles and accounts of the period. There is a final glimpse of her in the Pipe Roll of 1157. It records a payment made to Sybilla, identified as the Earl Reginald's mother from an estate at Mienes in Sussex. She also held land in the county which was granted to her the previous year by King Henry II. The gifts were perhaps a recognition of the loyalty which the earl had shown to Henry's mother during the civil war between King Stephen and the Empress Matilda.

King Henry I's strategy for stability included the marriage of a flock of illegitimate daughters, including Sybilla's children, to facilitate the establishment of closer familial ties both within his realm and beyond. He recognised the political capital to be gained from their blood relationship to the monarchy. Rohese married Henry de la Pomerai. He was a loyal supporter of the king as well as one of his household knights. He attained fame as a commander in 1124 at the Battle of Bourgtheroulde near Rouen. The marriage may have held an element of reward for his service to the Crown. Henry's elder daughter, Sybilla of Normandy, married King Alexander I of Scotland in 1107. Alexander was the son of King Malcolm III of Scotland and Margaret of Wessex. This meant that Alexander was both brother-in-law to the king and son-in-law. William of Malmesbury suggested that the marriage was not a happy one because the bride lacked both the decorum and refinement of a royal upbringing. She may have remained with her mother throughout her childhood or been educated at a nearby convent in much the same way that Rosamund Clifford was allegedly educated at Godstow Abbey. For the English and the Scots, it would have been sufficient that Sybilla was Henry's acknowledged daughter. She died on 12 July 1122 on the island of *Eilean nam Ban* between Mull and Iona. Despite what Malmesbury might have thought about Sybilla, the couple appear to have enjoyed an affectionate marriage. Alexander founded a priory on the island in her memory and never remarried even though Sybilla failed to provide him with an heir.[5]

Sybilla Corbet's son William went to Scotland with his sister at the time of her marriage and witnessed several charters made by Alexander I during the 1120s. The new queen consort of Scotland was not alone in a foreign country and it gave William an opportunity to create a future for himself as well as to extend King Henry I's sphere of influence in Scotland. William eventually returned to England and was provided with a wife and land in the West Country near at hand to his brother Rainald de Dunstanville who was created Earl of Cornwall in 1141 by his half-sister the Empress Matilda despite the fact she was never crowned. Rainald's position in Devon and Cornwall was established by Henry I when he arranged his son's marriage to Mabel FitzRichard. It was Orderic Vitalis who first linked him with the Dunstanville family but it is unclear how he or his mother were connected to them. Like the Earl of Gloucester, Rainald supported his half-sister's claim to the throne. Illegitimate children were entirely dependent upon the goodwill and continued success of their royal father and legitimate half-siblings. They would never be rivals for the throne but they might be bulwarks upon which their siblings could rely. In supporting Matilda, Rainald risked everything his father had given him. He was with Earl Robert of Gloucester in 1141 at the Siege of Winchester and the subsequent rout which saw the Angevins defeated. He led the advance guard that moved Empress Matilda to the safety of Gloucester whilst his half-brother Robert, protecting his half-sister's retreat, was captured by troops loyal to Stephen. Rainald's association with his father's family continued into the reign of King Henry II. He witnessed charters issued by Henry; he was part of the Council of Northampton in 1164 and sought to act as an intermediary between his nephew and Thomas Becket. By 1165 his barony in Cornwall was made up of 215 1/3 knights' fees.[6] The earl's children married into the wider Angevin hegemony and continued to work as part of the extended royal family to create affinities to the Crown through ties of marriage. After his death, and despite his loyalty to the Crown, King Henry II claimed Rainald's lands for his youngest son John ignoring the claims of his uncle's daughters although part of the estate was returned to the family during the reign of King Richard I. Rainald was buried in Reading Abbey which his father, King Henry I, founded and in which he was also buried.

Sybilla Corbet's death is unrecorded as is that of her younger sister, Alice. However, Asthall Church in Oxfordshire between Minster Lovell and Burford is the final resting place for one of them – probably Alice. The earls of Cornwall held the lordship of Asthall which marched with royal woodland. After 1154 the manor of Asthall became part of Wychwood Forest. A stone coffin can be found on the north side of the church 'it is said to contain the remains of Alice Corbett, concubine to King Henry I, the daughter of Sir Robert Corbett of Warwickshire'[7] which raises the questions about who, exactly, is buried in Asthall? Was Alice who married William Boterel also a mistress of the king? And how much of the later notice at Asthall reflects the way in which oral history can resemble nothing so much as a game of Chinese whispers with information becoming distorted across succeeding generations? The mystery of the occupant of the stone coffin demonstrates the difficulty of pinning the elusive mistresses of King Henry I into the historical record with any certainty.

The echoes of her story in the margins of history add to the voice of the women who Henry took to his bed but who are little known. Sybilla's significance in history, like Nest's, was that her children extended the influence of the Angevins and served their legitimate family with loyalty throughout the difficult period of the Anarchy. The marriages that Henry made for Sybilla and her children created alliances that linked the southwest with the marches of Wales. The relationship that Henry had with Sybilla might have been an enduring private one of which little is known but her family had an impact on the political geography of the region not only during Henry's reign but also in the Angevin fight to maintain control of the throne.

Chapter 8

Edith Forne Sigulfson and the Unknown Mothers of King Henry I's Illegitimate Children

Politics, patronage and family alliances went hand in hand. Henry I's mistresses and illegitimate children often provided the method of bringing those alliances close to the Crown, especially on the edges of Henry I's territories. William of Malmesbury described the north of England as a desolate and violent place. Norman settlement in Cumberland had been slower than in the Welsh marches which made the business of government and of forming alliances more complex. There were also the intricacies of the Anglo-Scottish relationships to be negotiated. William Rufus commenced work on Carlisle Castle in 1092. The lordship of Carlisle was granted first to Ivo Taillebois, a favourite of William Rufus, who married Lucy, who later chroniclers believed to be a relation to the earls of Mercia. Taillebois had demonstrated his capacity for dealing with the challenges facing Norman administrators and soldiers during the revolt against Norman rule in Lincolnshire led by Hereward the Wake.[1] Following the death of Taillebois and also Lucy's second husband, Carlisle was granted to her third husband Ranulf Meschin along with the Eden Valley and the Cumbrian lowlands north of the Derwent. He served King Henry I as a semi-independent governor of the northwest founding the baronies of Burgh by Sands and Liddel Strength on the border with Scotland. When Meschin's cousin Richard d'Avranches died in the White Ship disaster in November 1120, Ranulf became the 3rd Earl of Chester but was required to surrender the lordship of Carlisle as Henry had no intention of permitting overmighty subjects to flourish.

Henry extended the Norman landholding class throughout England's northern counties as a way of bringing administrative order to the region and rewarding his own supporters.[2] In addition, some lordships were held by families who were present before the Norman Conquest. Edith was the daughter of Forne, son of Sigulf. Forne, of Norse descent, was the Lord of Greystoke in Cumbria. He served Henry until his death in 1130. Forne was one of the men that Orderic Vitalis described as 'being raised from the dust'.[3] It is impossible to know whether Forne's father Sigulf was a figure of power before the Conquest and before the Normans came to Cumbria in 1092 but he held lands in Yorkshire listed in the Domesday Book. It is likely that Sigulf was a local leader, a thegn, whose landholding predated the Conquest. References to Forne as a king's thegn in Yorkshire and elsewhere may not necessarily be Edith's father, even if the name is an unusual one. It is impossible to know what other possessions either Sigulf or Forne held in 1086 as Cumberland was not recorded in the Domesday Book. The Conqueror had not quelled the region which Scotland also claimed. Forne was sufficiently important to have witnessed Ranulf Meschin's charter founding Wetheral Priory in 1090 and he was also known to be present at a gathering of northern magnates in Durham in April 1121.

King Henry visited York and Carlisle the following summer. His illegitimate daughter Sybilla, the queen consort of Scotland, had only recently died and it is possible that he was concerned about the Scottish succession. Henry sought to strengthen his position in the north by establishing new alliances. It was at about this time the king arranged the marriage of his illegitimate daughter Elizabeth by an unnamed mistress to Fergus of Galloway.[4] As an officeholder, Forne would have been present to welcome the king in either York or Carlisle. It is plausible that Henry's eye fell upon Forne's daughter at the same time. Edith's date of birth is unknown but she is unlikely to have been born before 1090. The king was fifty-four years old and had married his second wife Adeliza of Louvain on 2 February 1121 in an attempt to father a legitimate son, his only male heir having drowned in November 1120.

Although Henry fathered no more legitimate children, his relationship with Edith produced two offspring; Robert FitzEdith and Adeliza or Alice. Little is known about Adeliza other than her identification on a charter together with her brother and the possibility that she may have married Ernulf de Mandeville assuming that Alice d'Oilly is Henry's daughter rather than a later child from Edith's subsequent marriage.[5] Robert's history can be tracked through the Pipe Roll for 1130–1131 which identifies his lands in Devon being administered by guardians indicating that he was underage at that time. Henry ensured that his son by Edith became part of the enclave of illegitimate royal sons with land in the southwest. Together with Robert of Gloucester and Rainald of Cornwell, Robert FitzEdith remained loyal to his legitimate half-sister after the death of their father. He was at the Siege of Winchester and the rout which followed along with the earls of Gloucester and Cornwall in 1141.

In Cumberland during Henry's lifetime, Edith's family gained land and prestige as a consequence of her relationship with the king. Henry confirmed Forne's lands and granted him the right to hold them in fee in 1120. This meant that the land was his rather than the king's and that Forne's heirs could inherit the estates. Edith's brother, Ivo, inherited all of his father lands across four counties circa 1129. The writ-charter confirming his inheritance, including the barony of Greystoke, was witnessed by David, the King of the Scots, as well as Robert de Brus, Lord of Annandale.[6] King Henry II would confirm Ivo's son Walter in the same way. Direct succession was established. Ivo's great-grandson, Thomas, was the first of his family to be known as de Greystoke.

As with his other mistresses, Henry found a suitable husband for Edith. He married her to Robert D'Oilly, the nephew of Robert d'Oilly the Elder, a warrior who fought for Duke William at Hastings. The elder D'Oilly built castles at Wallingford and also Oxford which he held for the king as its hereditary constable. His only heir was a daughter named Maud but both her sons were lepers which meant that they could not inherit their grandfather's estates. When he died in about 1092 his property passed to his brother Nigel and then to his nephew also named Robert who was the third baron of Hook Norton as well as the constable of Oxford Castle. The king gave Edith the royal manor of Steeple Claydon in Buckinghamshire as a dower which also had the effect of bolstering the wealth of the D'Oilly family. As with his other alliances, Henry aimed to create a network that would be loyal to the Crown.

In 1129, Edith persuaded her husband to endow the Church of St Mary, in the Isle of Oseney near Oxford. As well as land, Robert granted the church several advowsons including Steeple Claydon, Water Stratford and Hook Norton. In 1149, the church was settled with further endowments from Edith's sons by Robert and her son by Henry. The church became an abbey by 1154. Eventually, the Augustinian house would become the wealthiest monastery in Oxfordshire ensuring that Edith gained a place in the history books. The story of its original foundation was written and retold by historians including John Leland, the antiquarian, during the sixteenth century. Leland wrote that Edith habitually walked by the river with her ladies but that she often heard magpies chattering in a tree. No one else heard them unless she was close at hand. It seemed to Edith that they were talking to her and she was afraid. She sought the counsel of her confessor who told her that the chattering magpies made the noise of souls in Purgatory. He instructed her to build a church or an abbey so that her own soul would be spared punishment for her youthful dalliance with the king. The story gained ground with each retelling until the birds were messengers who came to her in a dream, warning her to repent. The monastic chroniclers did not pause to consider that refusing a king was not something to be countenanced.

Along with the rest of Henry I's extended illegitimate family, Edith's husband remained largely loyal to the Empress Matilda after Henry's death. She arrived in Oxford in 1141. At the beginning of autumn her cousin, King Stephen, marched an army from Bristol intending to capture the city and his cousin. Oxford and the castle were besieged from the end of September until Christmas. During the three months of warfare, the city of Oxford was burned to the ground and inside the castle, the defenders were on the verge of starvation. The Empress only avoided capture by escaping through a postern gate and crossing the frozen River Isis before walking through the snow to Abingdon. She and her three companions were swiftly moved to the safety of Wallingford Castle. D'Oilly surrendered the castle the morning after Matilda's escape.

Edith's husband died soon after the siege ended and was buried in Eynsham Abbey. D'Oilly was a patron of the foundation as was his uncle. Edith lived until 1152 and after her death was buried in Oseney Abbey near the high altar in the most sacred part of the church rather than next to her husband. In 1163, Edith's son Henry d'Oilly was buried near his mother. Leland visited her tomb shortly before the monastery was dissolved. He wrote that Edith was a 'woman of great piety'.[7] He described her effigy dressed in the 'abbite of a vowess, holding a hart in her right hand, on the north side of the high altaire'.[8] The hart may have been symbolic of the fact that Edith was a pious Christian who sought to change her dwelling place from the world to heaven.[9] Nearby there was an image of magpies depicting the myth of the abbey's foundation.

King Henry I had other mistresses and several more children but it is impossible to determine whether they were the product of long-term relationships. Many of the women remain anonymous. They are hidden in the minutiae of charters or pipe rolls or they are still awaiting re-discovery. They did not establish monastic houses or start wars because of their beauty. Another of Henry's women was called Edith but nothing more is known other than she bore a daughter called Matilda who became the Countess of Perche and who drowned alongside her half-brothers when the White Ship sank off Barfleur on 25 November 1120. William de Tracy is also known to have been one of Henry's sons. Like so many of Henry's children, he was born before Henry became king. His mother may have been part of the de Tracy family or he was born at Tracy, near Vire, in Normandy. Like Sybilla Corbet's sons, he was granted land in Devon but is not to be confused with the William de Tracy who murdered Thomas Becket. Rainald of Cornwell cited their relationship in a charter witnessed by William Vernon which identifies 'William, my brother'[10] probably meaning Tracy. An illegitimate daughter, Constance or Matilda depending on the source, married Roscelin, Viscount of Beaumont-le-Maine. After the couple married Henry granted Roscelin the manor of South Tawton in Devon.[11] It is likely he acquired land in the county in connection with his bride's dowry.[12] Constance's great-granddaughter, Ermengarde de Beaumont, was married by King Henry II to William the Lion of Scotland, demonstrating that even a very diluted royal bloodline could be used to strategic advantage on occasion.

King Henry I arranged for many of his illegitimate daughters to be married to lords associated with the Norman marches in order to create a network of alliances with an affinity to the Crown. Another of his illegitimate daughters married Conan III of Brittany whilst 'others married the lords of Montmorency, Montmirail, Beaumont-sur-Sarthe and possibly Laval'.[13] When Henry I recognised his illegitimate children, he also recognised the need to educate and support them. They became part of his extended kinship network as did several of the women he bedded. It becomes plausible to suggest that the women who mothered his children were not peasants or serving wenches, even if some of them did have Saxon names, but from the knightly classes at the least. The various relationships must have been sufficiently longstanding, or monogamous on the part of the woman, for Henry to have recognised their children as his own.[14] Henry's mistresses and daughters, chattels in the royal collection, became the reward for his magnates who demonstrated their worth in terms of leadership and control of a region. Contrarily, Henry I and his Angevin descendants were largely successful in separating the intimacy of the bedchamber from public written record. Women bedded by feudal kings of England were often only identified in the documents of the period if there were children from the union, sometimes not even then. Confirmation of the existence of many mistresses has to be gleaned from accounts and charters which often recognise their children rather than the women themselves – they were expected to be submissive and silent.

Chapter 9

Elizabeth de Vermondois and her Daughter Isabel de Beaumont

In the mid-1050s William de Warenne, the second son of a minor Norman nobleman, achieved joint command of a Norman army and became one of Duke William's most trusted advisers. He was also part of the duke's extended kinship network as his mother was related to the duke's paternal grandmother, Gunnor. By 1086 he was the fourth richest man in England holding extensive lands in Sussex, East Anglia and Lincolnshire as well as the Honour of Conisbrough in South Yorkshire which had once been held by King Harold Godwinson. He continued to acquire lands throughout his life both by fair means and foul. It was said that he stole lands belonging to the Church including property in the hands of the Abbot of Ely. William Rufus created him Earl of Surrey weeks before his death in 1088 as a reward for loyal service. De Warenne's title and his estates in England passed to his son also called William whilst his lands in Flanders were handed to his second son Reginald. After Reginald's death in 1106, those lands passed into the keeping of his brother.

William de Warenne, 2nd Earl of Surrey wanted to acquire a bride with royal blood so he asked for the hand of Edith of Scotland, the daughter of Malcolm III and Margaret of Wessex. His request was refused just as Alan of Richmond's request for Edith's hand was turned down. This may have resulted in de Warenne joining Robert Curthose in 1101 when the duke attempted to take the kingdom of England for himself. As a consequence of his insurgence, William's title and estates were escheated by the Crown and he was exiled to Normandy. The matter was resolved two years later when Henry and Robert Curthose came to an agreement. William's title and lands were returned to him. It was during this period that Henry contemplated marrying the recalcitrant earl to one of his own illegitimate daughters as a means of ensuring future loyalty. However, before the king could arrange the wedding, Archbishop Anselm of Canterbury objected to the match on grounds of consanguinity because of the shared ancestry of the prospective bride and groom to Duke Richard I's wife Gunnor.

In 1118, de Warenne, now in his forties, finally married his royal bride. Elizabeth, or Isabel, de Vermandois was the widow of Robert de Beaumont, Count of Meulan. She was a granddaughter of King Henri I of France and descended from both the royal Capet and Carolingian lines. She had the blood of kings in her veins but she was a woman with a scandalous past, having openly rejected her husband and taken a lover. Fortunately, de Warenne had been Elizabeth's lover before her first husband's death.

Elizabeth had been married off to Beaumont in 1096 becoming his third wife. Beaumont's first wife died without children and his second marriage was annulled. Orderic Vitalis described Elizabeth as 'the beautiful Isabel, niece of the King of France'.[1] He failed to mention that the groom was thirty-five years older than his bride who was eleven at the time of the wedding. The legal age for marriage was twelve years but Elizabeth's father, Hugh, Count of Vermandois, was preparing to take part in the First Crusade alongside Robert Curthose so was able to persuade Pope Urban II to issue a dispensation permitting the ceremony to go ahead. The Pope was also required to grant a dispensation for consanguinity. Elizabeth's prospective husband shared a common great-grandfather with Hugh making the marriage incestuous in the eyes of the Church. Despite the age difference, it was regarded as an excellent match for the girl as Beaumont was both wealthy and influential. Her new husband had led the right-wing of the Conqueror's infantry at Hastings and was a respected adviser to both William Rufus, Robert Curthose and Philip I of France. Although they were married in name, the actual consummation of the marriage is unlikely to have taken place until Elizabeth was older. Her first child, Emma, was born in 1102 when she was somewhere between fifteen and seventeen-years old. Twin sons, Waleran and Robert, followed in 1104. They were sent to Abbot Faritius of Abingdon to be educated.[2] Another son and four more daughters followed including a daughter called Isabel or Isabella who was born before 1108. In 1107, Robert de Beaumont's service to the king was recognised by his elevation to the earldom of Leicester.

At some point between bearing children, managing her home and visiting the royal court, Elizabeth fell in love with William de Warrenne.

Details of the affair were recorded by Henry of Huntingdon who suggested that the affair took place across several years. De Warenne attempted to kidnap Isabel in 1115 but her husband refused to seek a divorce even though Elizabeth remained with her lover by whom she already had one child. Abduction and *raptus* (rape) were a form of property theft rather than a crime against a woman nor did it matter if the woman in question went willingly or not. Rumour hinted that at least one of de Beaumont's children were sired by de Warenne although there was no supporting evidence. De Beaumont died on 5 June 1118. Huntingdon wrote that the Earl of Leicester was a broken man because his wife had deserted him and destroyed his honour.

Elizabeth and de Warenne married very soon after de Beaumont's death with the king's approval. De Warenne, who was nearing fifty, needed a legitimate heir to inherit his title and estates. The couple's first legitimate child, a son, named William was born the following year. A least four more children followed in swift succession. Elizabeth spent much of her adult life in various stages of pregnancy and facing the all too real dangers of childbirth. Many medieval women had little or no say in their marriages. Romantic love was not for women of the countess's status. Her role, once married, was to be a dutiful wife and good mother to de Beaumont's children but she chose her own future both before and after her first husband's death. Society took a dim view of carnal unions made by mutual attraction rather than political consideration. The couple were blatant in their love for one another or, more prosaically, de Warenne wished the world to know his wife and heir were descended from kings. Upon his marriage, de Warrenne assumed the Vermondois coat of arms. Elizabeth may have had a hand in the blue and yellow check pattern that became known as 'Warenne chequer'.

When Elizabeth remarried it is likely that her four daughters and her younger son, Hugh, remained with her but her eldest sons were the heirs to de Beaumont's vast estates in England and Normandy. Waleran and Robert were thirteen years old when their father died so they became the wards of the Crown. Robert became the Earl of Leicester whilst his brother became the Count of Meulan. The king kept them with him at court rather than selling their wardships along with the right to arrange their marriages when they reached adulthood because it meant he could control their estates in Normandy. Waleran inherited the county of

Meulan in the French Vexin on the border between France and Normandy as well as four strategically important castles. Robert Curthose's son, William Clito, had come to terms with Louis VI of France in 1116 and King Henry faced insurrection in Normandy as well as invasion by the French so he could ill afford to permit Waleran's estates to drop into the hands of someone who might rebel. He arranged for four men to govern the Beaumont lands but retained oversight of their administration. One of the men appointed was William de Warenne who was now the boys' stepfather as well as being a trusted advisor of the king.

Once Waleran attained his majority he was drawn into a plot on behalf of William Clito. Orderic Vitalis explained this treachery as Waleran's youthful desire to prove himself on the battlefield. It was no spur of the moment action. He arranged the marriages of three of his sisters to ensure the support of their husbands for Clito's cause.[3] In October 1123, the king took action against the conspirators and by March the following year, the royal army had besieged Waleran's castle at Vatteville. Elizabeth's son was captured on 26 March 1124, his horse having been shot full of arrows. Waleran was initially imprisoned in Rouen but he was transferred from there to Bridgnorth and then Wallingford. He remained imprisoned until 1129.

Isabel de Beaumont was the only daughter of Elizabeth's by her first husband who remained unmarried. She either visited Henry's court with her mother and stepfather or the king took the precaution of bringing her to court to prevent any more unwanted marital alliances. In due course, she caught Henry's eye and he began an affair with the girl. Many of Henry's mistresses, though 'genteel'[4] were the daughters of knights or middling lords but Isabel was the daughter of a politically important house and the sister of an earl. Her virginity was an all-important part of her worth as a bride. Her affair with the ageing king began before her brother Waleran was released from captivity in 1134. Isabel, the youngest of Henry's mistresses, was the sacrificial virgin exchanged for her brother's freedom. It might also have been 'regarded as the sign and seal of the (re) establishment of good relations between the king and the Meulans'.[5] Before long Waleran and his twin brother Robert were back at the heart of the court.

In 1129 or 1130, Isabel gave birth to the king's daughter. The child was named Isabel or Elizabeth.[6] Henry settled the manor of Barrow in

Suffolk upon Isabel as her dower and married her to Gilbert de Clare who was something of a favourite with the king. Gilbert's grandfather was Richard of Tonbridge who was at Hastings in 1066 and part of William the Conqueror's extended family. The de Clare family profited from their connections to the Crown throughout the period. It has been hypothesised that one reason for Gilbert's prominence was that Isabel was one of Henry's favourite mistresses although another reason might lay in the theory that the de Clare family was involved in a conspiracy to murder William Rufus in 1100. However, it was only during the reign of King Stephen that Gilbert received the lordships of Pembroke and Netherwent. He was known as the Earl of Striguil because of his lordship of Netherwent which had previously belonged to one of his uncles.

Isabel was permitted to take her infant daughter with her from court when she married but it is unclear whether the little girl survived into adulthood. Her first child with Gilbert, Richard, was born at the end of 1130 in Tonbridge Castle, joining his elder half-sister in the de Clare nursery. In time another daughter, Basilia, joined them. Richard would be more commonly known as 'Strongbow' and like his father supported King Stephen during the civil war between King Stephen and the Empress Matilda.

William de Warenne, 2nd Earl of Surrey, husband of the scandalous Elizabeth de Vermandois died in 1138. He was buried at Lewes Priory. When Elizabeth died, in about 1147, she was buried with her beloved second husband. During the so-called Anarchy which followed Henry I's death, King Stephen raised Elizabeth's son Waleran to the Earldom of Worcestershire. His brother Robert also supported Stephen as did their half brother the 3rd Earl of Surrey and Gilbert de Clare, Isabel's husband. Elizabeth and Isabel's extended family formed a powerful faction that appeared to get on well amongst themselves suggesting that Elizabeth created a cohesive family unit despite the circumstances in which she left her first husband.

Waleran came to terms with Henry FitzEmpress in 1153 and was a trusted member of the king's court but Richard de Clare was one of the few men who remained steadfast in his loyalty to King Stephen. As a consequence, when he became king in 1154, Henry II deprived Isabel's son of the earldom of Pembroke and granted most of his estates in Wales to another member of the de Clare family. The relationship with King

Henry II remained strained. Strongbow was forced to borrow heavily during the next decade in order to maintain his home at Chepstow. Matters were worsened by the fact that the king refused to allow him to marry in case he made an alliance that restored his position in the marches. In 1167, Strongbow saw an opportunity to advance his fortunes, perhaps even to gain a crown of his own, when he agreed to help Dairmait Mac Murchada, the deposed King of Leinster, recover his kingdom in return for marriage to the king's daughter. De Clare made sure that he asked King Henry's permission before setting off on his venture but Henry's consent was imprecise. It was only as Strongbow was about to leave Milford Haven that a messenger arrived from King Henry II forbidding him to attempt the enterprise but de Clare ignored the order and went to Ireland anyway. By 1172 Strongbow was married to Dairmait's daughter, Eva or Aoife, and was Leinster's de facto ruler. The unauthorised marriage and annexation of a part of Ireland which the Crown regarded as within its province led to Henry II threatening to confiscate Strongbow's remaining estates in England, Wales and Normandy. The king was afraid that Strongbow, battle-hardened and once again wealthy, would defy him and turn Ireland into an independent monarchy which would draw to it men disgruntled with the Plantagenet regime.

Isabel's husband, Gilbert de Clare had died at the beginning of 1148 and was buried in Tintern Abbey which had been founded by his younger brother Walter. After Gilbert's death, an arrangement was made for Isabel to be married to Hervey de Montmorency who was Gilbert's half-brother and her son's representative in Ireland. The exact nature of the relationship was established in a charter giving property to Thorney Abbey in Cambridgeshire. It is not known whether Isabel was finally permitted to follow her mother's example and marry for love or whether it was a strategic familial marriage made to protect either Isabel from an unwanted second marriage arranged by the Crown or as a strategy for keeping the de Clare estates together. Gerald of Wales was vitriolic in his condemnation of the man when he wrote his account of the conquest of Ireland. The writer's hatred stemmed from the twists and turns of Montmorency's rivalry with Nest of Wales' grandson Raymond, known as le-Gros, FitzWilliam who was Gerald's own cousin. Isabel's husband Hervey de Montmorency was sent to see the king on Strongbow's behalf. A compromise was reached when de Clare announced that his campaign had been undertaken to win land for the king and renewed his oath of fealty as well as handing over key towns on the Irish coast including Dublin. He also agreed to join in the king's forthcoming campaign against the French. Both men wished to avoid conflict as they each had much to lose. Strongbow demonstrated his loyalty to the king in 1173 during the military campaign at Verneuil and at the siege of Breteuil. By the end of the summer's battles in France, Strongbow was appointed the justiciar for all Ireland but almost immediately faced a rebellion from his own barons who objected to the king's policy of non-aggression towards the Irish.

After Isabel's death circa 1172, Montmorency married again to Nesta, Maurice FitzGerald's daughter, named after her beautiful grandmother Nest of Wales. Strongbow's own daughter, Aline, was given in marriage to Maurice's eldest son William. The marriages were part of Strongbow's attempt to restore harmony with the FitzGerald family which had become strained after a quarrel with Raymond-le-Gros who wanted to be made the constable of Leinster and to marry Strongbow's sister, Basilia. Both demands had been refused so Raymond returned to Wales from Ireland in 1174. It was only after Strongbow was besieged in Waterford that the earl agreed to the marriage of his sister Basilia to Raymond and his appointment as constable. When Strongbow died in May 1176 his titles and estates passed to his young son who died in 1185. The inheritance passed to Strongbow's daughter Isabel, named after her grandmother, and her husband, the great knight, William Marshal. The earldom was granted to Marshal within a month of Richard the Lionheart becoming king in 1189.

Isabel's son was a powerful man and like many of Nest's family 'Strongbow' became a pivotal figure in Irish history. Isabel, another shadowy mistress is largely absent from the official record even her final resting place is unknown to history. The lack of documentary evidence, and public voice, makes it easy to ignore women like Isabel and the rest of King Henry I's elusive mistresses. But part of Isabel's story can be heard in the lives of the men she lived with. She affected the career and prestige of her husband and gave much more to her son than a bloodline. She almost certainly helped to form his attitudes to life and cared for him as most mothers seek to support their children whether they are infants or adults. Unfortunately, this means that most medieval women, mistress to royalty or not, can be heard only through the records of their male relations. The records have to be unpicked so that the women are less muted than before.[7] Why, for instance, did Isabel's brothers, husbands and sons choose to support King Stephen rather than King Henry I's designated successor? It might imply that whereas Henry's long-term mistresses and families felt a degree of love and affection for the king that Isabel was coerced into the royal bed and that her family resented the way in which she was treated. Accusations of abduction might have been better applied to the king than William de Warenne, 2nd Earl of Surrey who chose to wait until the woman he made his mistress was free to marry him. The difficulty with this idea is that there is no evidence to support the theory and without evidence, Isabel and women like her are almost erased from history.

Chapter 10

Eleanor of Aquitaine, Ykenai, Annabel de Baliol and the Count of Brittany's Daughter

Henry II became king of England in 1154. Aged twenty-one years, he was already the ruler of Anjou, Maine and Touraine by right of his father and Aquitaine by right of his marriage to Eleanor. England and Normandy were settled on him by King Stephen in 1153 but Henry saw the right of succession coming from his mother, the Empress Matilda. Her very public role gave her a voice in history not afforded to her father's many mistresses or those of her son. Like his grandfather, Henry II's illegitimate sons were placed at the highest level of society and served the Crown with loyalty. One was Geoffrey Plantagenet and the other William Longspée 'Longsword' who became the Earl of Salisbury but their mothers can only be found by sifting through legal documents and charters.

Henry's marriage to Eleanor of Aquitaine took place before he became king. Louis VII of France divorced her in 1152 and eight weeks later she was married to Henry. William of Newburgh believed that the pair had come to an arrangement before Eleanor's divorce from Louis while Matthew Paris described the bitterness that existed between Eleanor and her first husband. The pair married in 1137 but almost immediately ran into trouble although Louis loved his wife 'almost beyond reason'.[1] One of the problems was that Eleanor, an intelligent and capable woman, was marginalised by Louis' inner circle of advisers who had a clear view about the new queen's place at the French court. Over time Louis gained a reputation for piety and marital coldness. Eleanor failed to conceive an heir during the early years of her marriage. In 1145, she gave birth to a daughter Marie, but Louis needed a son. It was seen by the queen's detractors as a sign that God was displeased with the marriage.

A further difficulty was the love affair between Eleanor's younger sister Petronella and Count Raoul I of Vermandois, a grandson of Hugh of Vermandois who gave his daughter, Elizabeth, in marriage to Robert de Beaumont. It was a passionate affair that began in the summer of 1141 at Poitou even though Raoul was much older than Petronella and blind in one eye. He was also already married to Eleanor of Blois, a sister of King Stephen. Eleanor had no real influence at the French court but pushed for Raoul's divorce from Eleanor of Blois so that he and Petronella could marry. A marriage between the pair would have ensured that the queen was able to develop a court faction of her own and that her beloved younger sister would remain by her side. King Louis agreed to the match, no doubt wishing to please his queen. Raoul found several bishops, including his own brother, who were prepared to annul his marriage to Eleanor of Blois on grounds of consanguinity. The following year Petronella married Raoul. Count Theobald IV of Blois protested at the way his sister had been treated but more significantly Abbot Bernard of Clairvaux disapproved the annulment and subsequent union. He called Raoul 'an adulterous tyrant'.[2] The newlyweds, together with the bishops who married them were excommunicated in the summer of 1143 by the Pope although it did not stop them from living together as man and wife. The couple had two children regarded as illegitimate by the Church before Eleanor of Blois died and their marriage was eventually approved by the papacy in 1148. Petronella and Raoul would not have long to enjoy their newly sanctioned union as Raoul died in 1151 to the grim satisfaction of Abbot Bernard who predicted that their illicit love would be punished by a vengeful God. The affair and Eleanor of Aquitaine's involvement in it was a disaster for her status and her own relationship with her husband. France was placed under interdict as a consequence of Petronella's unsanctified union and war broke out between France and Blois. The burning of Virty-sur-Marne in 1143 haunted Louis for the rest of his life leading him to turn to Abbot Suger, his own father's principal adviser and friend, for guidance, further marginalising Eleanor.

John of Salisbury implies that Henry FitzEmpress made Eleanor his mistress whilst she was still married to the French king. Later chroniclers, including Gerald of Wales, would accuse Eleanor of sleeping with Henry's father, Geoffrey of Anjou, before taking Henry into her bed. If her marriage to Louis was incestuous, a second marriage to the son of a previous lover was even less likely to meet with papal approval. Helinand of Froidmont blamed Eleanor's desire to divorce Louis on her lust for

Henry. He accused her of behaving like a whore rather than a queen. Even worse, Eleanor's reputation was already damaged by rumours that circulated whilst she was with Louis on Crusade to the Holy Land in 1148. William of Newburgh regretted the fact that Louis did not leave his wife behind when he went to the Holy Land as it meant that many other nobles took their wives with them so that rather than concentrating on war against the infidel their minds were occupied by the opportunities for sin. John of Salisbury expanded the story. Eleanor's uncle Raymond of Antioch, who was only a few years older than her, paid too much attention to his niece. There were whispers of an affair that started because Eleanor did not think it strategically sensible for her husband to depart the Holy Land. Eventually, Louis' suspicions were aroused. The rumours grew to the proportions of a full-blown scandal that saw Eleanor as her own uncle's lover. The 'black legend'[3] of Eleanor – an incestuous, sex-mad whore was born. She might have been more offended by William of Tyre's claim that she 'was a foolish woman'.[4] All that can be said with certainty is that Eleanor did enjoy Raymond's company, that she disagreed with Louis about strategy and that it was the queen who told her husband that they were too closely related to be married without papal dispensation. By the time the couple arrived back in France the royal marriage was in tatters but Eleanor was pregnant. The birth of a second daughter, Alix, in 1150 convinced Louis that God would never give him a son while he remained married to Eleanor. The marriage was annulled in 1152 but Marie and Alix who both travelled to the households of their betrothed the following year were declared legitimate because their parents were unaware that their marriage was incestuous at the time of their births.

The arrival of Henry FitzEmpress (the future King Henry II of England) in Paris in the summer of 1151 gave Eleanor the opportunity to begin afresh. As Queen of France, she was denied power and influence but with Henry, she might be allowed to rule her own duchy even if Henry gained the territory by right of marriage making him one of the most powerful rulers in Europe. If Louis had discovered what was planned, he would never have let Eleanor depart. Aquitaine and Poitou were a third of the size of France. As it was, when Eleanor journeyed south to meet and marry Henry, she avoided kidnap not once but twice. The first man who sought to claim Eleanor and her territories for his own was the Count of Blois. The second would-be kidnapper was Henry's own younger brother

Geoffrey but Eleanor and her men gave her would-be suitors the slip and arrived safely in Poitiers which was her own capital. She married Henry who arrived soon after and received the homage of her principal vassals. By December 1152, Eleanor was pregnant. She gave birth to Henry's heir, a boy named William, on 17 August 1153. On the same day that William was born King Stephen's son, Eustace, and Henry's rival, died. Whatever the monastic chroniclers and the French may have thought about Eleanor, it appeared that God, for the time being, was smiling upon her new husband. When King Stephen died on 25 October 1154, the Duke of Normandy became King Henry II of England without any contest for the crown. His lands stretched from the Scottish borders to the Pyrenees.

During the first years of their marriage, Eleanor played some part in Henry's administration of his growing territories including taking on the regency in his absences. The court was rarely in one place for long. Henry was like a restless whirlwind moving from one place to the next. Like his grandfather, King Henry II trusted his wife to govern effectively on his behalf. John of Salisbury believed that the queen's authority was equal to Henry's. But after 1163 she almost disappears from the record of charters and legal documents by which women with power can most often be tracked. Her vision of ruling alongside Henry dwindled, in part, because during the first fourteen years of their marriage, she gave her husband eight children. Their first child, William, died in 1156 but Henry, known as the Young King, was born in 1155 and a daughter Matilda was born in June 1156. Seven of her children survived to adulthood including the Young King who died in 1183 from dysentery whilst in rebellion against his father. It was only in her later years that her flair for organisation and statecraft came to the fore. Over time, Eleanor became increasingly concerned about the way in which her husband sought to rule her own duchy of Aquitaine and the power which Henry refused to share with his sons. Tensions erupted into rebellion in 1173.

The Angevin empire was large, the couple were separated for long periods of time and Henry did not remain faithful to his queen. The chroniclers wrote of the king's serial adultery. 'Both in England and in Normandy the king had whoremasters'.[5] He was, incidentally, the monarch who recognised that the growing red-light district at Southwark on land owned by the Bishop of Winchester was a source for additional

Crown income. He issued a set of thirty-nine ordinances to ensure that these brothels were run lawfully and hygienically. One of the stranger rules was that he forbade prostitutes from sleeping with someone for love rather than money. He stipulated that there was to be a quarterly inspection to ensure that none of the women working in Southwark's eighteen brothels or stews had sexually transmitted diseases. The Church and its chroniclers may have condemned sins of the flesh but the girls who worked in Southwark were called the Bishop of Winchester's geese and returned a healthy income for the Crown. Nor did they remain on the south side of the Thames. Walter Map, a clerk in Holy orders and member of Henry's court, wrote about the 'creatures of the night'[6] who could be found lurking on the edges of the royal world.

Amongst them, according to Map, was a Saxon woman called Ykenai or Hikennai described as a 'common wanton'.[7] When he became king, Ykenai presented her son, Geoffrey, to Henry and he accepted the boy as his own. Map questioned whether Geoffrey was Henry's child given the nature of Ykenai's profession but the king seems not to have doubted the matter, raising the boy within his own household alongside his legitimate children before sending him to be educated at Northampton and Tours. Geoffrey had a brother called Peter but he was not Henry's son.[8] It is possible that Map could have exaggerated the low social status of Geoffrey's mother. She may have been a knight's daughter from the Akeny family or even the more noble de Tosny family who owned Acquigny Castle in Normandy as well as lands in England. Henry also fathered a daughter called Matilda on a woman called Joan at about the same time. He arranged for his daughter to become the Prioress of Barking Abbey. She was appointed between 1177 and 1179.[9] In both cases, Henry accepted his illegitimate children, and they grew to serve his interests. However, their mothers remain largely anonymous. He never capitalised on the potential marriages of his mistresses to the same extent as his grandfather but it may also have been that several women he bedded were not of a sufficient social level or standing to use as diplomatic pawns in the medieval marriage game.

During the early years of his reign, Henry granted the manor of Coniscliffe in Durham to Ranulf, Lord Greystoke (the great-nephew of Henry I's mistress Edith Forne Sigulfson) as a wedding gift. The king had granted the lords of Bolam in Northumberland, three vills from his manor of Corbridge in exchange for Coniscliffe. The exchange took place between 1157 when the king recovered territory in Northumberland from King Malcolm IV of Scotland and 1162 when the Greystokes' paid scutage on Coniscliffe. The reason for the gift was that Lord Greystoke married Annabel Balliol, a mistress of the king. The manor was Annabel's dower. It is likely that Henry took Annabel as a mistress very early in his reign during the period when he was campaigning in the north of England to regain control of Cumberland and parts of Northumberland from the Scots. The Balliols had a long association with the north of England. Guy de Balliol possessed lands in Northumberland before his nephew Bernard built Barnard Castle during the reign of William Rufus.

Annabel was widowed before the end of Henry's reign and remarried to Roger FitzHugh taking Coniscliffe with her. Annabel's son William died in 1209 and Annabel's grandson was made the ward of Robert de Vipont, an avaricious favourite of King John. By the autumn of 1214, Annabel was widowed for a second time and paid a fine which included two palfreys to avoid being remarried at the king's behest. She died in 1225 a respectable widow who had once, for a short while, been King Henry II's mistress. For a time before the truth emerged from within the historic record, it was thought that she might have been the mother of William Longspée.

William of Newburgh, erroneously, suggested that Henry only turned to other women once Eleanor who was eleven years older than her husband was beyond childbearing but other chroniclers accused Henry of setting his subjects a bad example much earlier. By 1168 Henry and Eleanor were living almost completely separate lives. Henry's territories were vast and his household was constantly on the move. Besides, Eleanor wished to spend time in her own duchy which had proved difficult for Henry to govern. In December 1168, Eleanor held a Christmas court at Poitiers where she remained with her son Richard who would one day become Aquitaine's duke according to the king's plan for the succession. That same year, in July 1168, Odo de Porhoët, the deposed Count of Brittany accused Henry of seducing his daughter, Alice, whilst she was a hostage in the king's care and presumably part of the queen's household as it would have been inappropriate for a single woman to be part of the king's domestic retinue. Porhoët complained that Henry took his daughter hostage and got her pregnant, 'treacherously, adulterously and incestuously'.[10] Alice's grandmother Maud FitzRoy was King Henry I's illegitimate daughter by an unknown mother. Maud was married by her father to Conan III, Duke of Brittany. Conan III, on his deathbed, repudiated his son as illegitimate and made Bertha, Alice's mother, his heiress. Odo, ruled by right of his wife but when she died in 1155, he refused to relinquish the title to his stepson from Bertha's first marriage. He was deposed by Conan IV in 1156 with the support of King Henry II who wished to extend his lordship into Brittany. Odo was forced to send one of his daughters as a guarantee of peace to Henry's court. John of Salisbury reported Odo's accusations which included the information that Alice had been made pregnant. History does not record what happened to the child but Alice became a nun at Fontevraud in 1188 rising to the position of abbess from 1191. Her rule was noted for being both wise and kind. Queen Eleanor made a donation to Alice, whom she called Alix, in 1199. The letter discussing the rent in Poitevin pounds on the island of Oléron begins 'to our dear alumpna' which means pupil.[11] She died during the Autumn of 1220.

Eleanor, whose grandfather William IX was the notorious troubadour duke of Aquitaine, was unlikely to defy her husband because of his mistresses or illegitimate children. William IX abducted Dangerosa, wife of one of his vassals, and lived with her in his castle at Poitiers. William's wife, Philippa of Toulouse, did not take kindly to her husband turning her home into a love-nest but she was not able to rid herself of her rival and ended her life in Fontevrault Abbey rather than remain in Poitiers. Queens and duchesses, as Eleanor knew, were required to turn a blind eye to their husband's infidelities or withdraw to a convent where they could be conveniently forgotten. And the queen had no intention of going anywhere quietly or without complaint.

Many contemporary sources suggest that problems between Eleanor and her husband arose after the conflict of 1173–1174 when the queen together with her grown-up sons challenged Henry's authority. The king's eldest surviving son, also called Henry, was crowned King of England in 1170, in part to secure the succession – no one wanted another civil war – but he was not permitted to rule. There were also arguments about the allowance granted to the Young King as he was called after his coronation. The Young King and his father's disagreement came to a climax at Limoges during negotiations for the betrothal of Henry and

Eleanor's youngest son, John, to the eldest daughter of Humbert, Count of Marienne, in February 1173. The king had granted his youngest son, John, three castles in Anjou. They were of strategic importance and the king would retain control of them during John's minority. It had the effect of limiting the Young King's control of Anjou which he stood to inherit along with England and Normandy. On 5 March, Young Henry left his father's court at Chinon and fled to Paris into the welcoming arms of his father-in-law, his father's old rival King Louis VII of France. Henry's brothers Richard and Geoffrey soon joined in the rebellion against their father. William of Newburgh and Roger of Howden both agreed that Henry's sons were advised by their mother. The king believed this to be the case. When Eleanor set out to join her sons she was captured and imprisoned, first in Normandy and then in England for the next fourteen years at Winchester and Sarum. Henry pardoned his sons but he decided that his wife's actions were unforgivable. Eleanor remained incarcerated. Her household was disbanded and she was allowed only one woman to serve her, a maid called Amaria. It was only after Henry died that Eleanor would regain her freedom. One of Richard the Lionheart's first acts on becoming king was to send William Marshal to free her.

Periodic rebellions involving his legitimate sons would punctuate the rest of Henry's reign. Of all his children it was Geoffrey, the illegitimate son by Ykenai, who proved the most loyal. After a successful campaign against the Scots and the rebel Roger Mowbray, Henry is said to have said of Geoffrey, 'My other sons are the real bastards. He alone has proved himself legitimate and true'.[12] Like his grandfather, Henry II included his illegitimate offspring in advancing his political interests and assisting with the administration of England. Henry gave Geoffrey several minor clerical offices to provide him with an income and in 1173 he became the Bishop of Lincoln despite the fact that he was not ordained. Geoffrey rose to become Chancellor of England having resigned the bishopric. Once his brother Richard was on the throne, he was forced to become a priest. The Lionheart recognised that ordination effectively neutralised any potential possibility of his throne being usurped in his absence by his illegitimate half-brother.

Eleanor of Aquitaine was sixty-eight years old when she was freed from her captivity upon her husband's death. Now she demonstrated her vigour for statecraft. She even crossed the Pyrenees to fetch Richard's bride, Berengaria of Navarre, before crossing the Alps to meet the king on his way to the Third Crusade. It was a gruelling journey at the best of times. When Leopold of Austria captured Richard on his way home, it was Eleanor who set about raising the ransom and preventing her other remaining son, John, from usurping his brother's throne. She convened councils, demanded oaths of loyalty and wrote sternly worded letters to Pope Celestine III. In 1199, she came out of semi-retirement at Fontevrault to ensure John's succession. The following year she was briefly held captive by Hugh of Lusignan and in 1201 she was besieged at Mirebeau by her grandson Arthur. She returned to Fontevrault where she died in 1204. The black legend of her early years in France perpetuated by chroniclers of the time developed in the eighteenth and nineteenth centuries to depict Eleanor as the villain of the Fair Rosamund love triangle between the queen, her husband and his young lover. She was often depicted as over-sexualised and scheming. In more recent times, in a post-feminist world, Eleanor has been seen in a more positive light, as a capable and intelligent woman. How many medieval queens, not only scandalously lustful ones, choose to depict themselves on their tombs reading a book? What made her different from other medieval mistresses, aside from the fact that she was a queen twice over, was that she recognised that she was a powerful and influential woman. When she attempted to exert that power in a way that was unpleasing to them, the patriarchy around her closed ranks against her and portrayed her as a sinner.

Chapter 11

Rosamund Clifford, Ida de Tosny, Alys of France, Nesta and BelleBelle

In 1165, the year that Eleanor of Aquitaine became pregnant with her youngest child, King Henry II met and fell in love with Jane Clifford, better known as Fair Rosamund, who was about twenty-five years old. Her parents were Walter de Clifford and Margaret de Tosny. Walter was a Marcher lord holding the lordship of Bronillys Castle and the manor of Frampton as well as the barony of Clifford in Herefordshire by right of his wife whose forbears arrived in England in 1066 and who were part of the Conqueror's extended family network. Rosamund, one of six children or more, grew up at Clifford Castle before being sent, according to legend, to Godstow Nunnery where she was educated. If she did spend her formative years in Oxfordshire, there is no written evidence available.

Henry may well have met Rosamund for the first time whilst he was on campaign in Wales, or equally, he might have been hunting close to Clifford's estates. There are stories of the king, by then in his early thirties, meeting Walter's daughter either whilst walking by the river or encountering her at her father's table and being struck by her youthful beauty and good nature. It has been suggested that he was so smitten with Rosamund on first meeting her that he set aside his usual behaviour and remained constantly by her side. From September 1165 until March 1166, Henry remained in Woodstock which was uncharacteristic of the king whose habitual restlessness saw him moving frequently. It is equally possible that the king was unwell or injured rather than making the most of a winter in the arms of a lover. It is only certain that he failed to keep a Christmas court with Eleanor in 1165. It was the first time since their marriage that the couple had celebrated Christmas in different parts of Henry's diverse territories. She was in Angers whilst Henry was at Woodstock. If Henry did seduce Rosamund before Christmas 1165, it was a discrete affair.

The king, always busy with state affairs and projects, began to refurbish his properties at both Clarendon and Woodstock that year. He also ordered a new dwelling to be built at Everswell at the edge of his deer park at Woodstock. The new house included a walled garden or pleasance. He met with his queen at Easter in 1166 when he crossed the Channel to subdue rebellious barons in Maine. It was probably at this time that Eleanor became pregnant with her last child, John, who was born on Christmas Eve 1166. By then she was in Oxfordshire and her husband was with their son Henry at Poitiers. Eleanor was forty-two and she had given birth to ten children.

Following the rebellion of 1173–1174, Eleanor was captured and imprisoned for the rest of Henry's life. By the time she regained her freedom, her youngest child was an adult. A contemporary of the king said that the reason that the queen was locked away was so that the king 'might freely indulge his debaucheries'.[1] If Henry had fallen in love with Rosamund before he had Eleanor locked away it did not prevent him from bedding other women. In 1173, after the Siege of Rouen, Henry is said to have lusted after Rohese Countess of Lincoln, described as 'the most beautiful woman in the realm',[2] the sister of Roger de Clare, Earl of Hertford and the cousin of Richard 'Strongbow' de Clare. Gerald of Wales, the grandson of Nest of Wales, wrote that Henry II 'became an open violator of the marriage bond'.[3] A friend of Becket's, Ralph the Black, denounced the king noting that his subjects hid their wives and daughters from him.

Rumour compounded Henry's insatiable sexual appetites with the information that he took satyrion root as an aphrodisiac. It is unlikely that any medieval monarch would have taken a love potion to render himself irresistibly attractive to the women around him. Very few, if any, females would have found themselves able to reject the advances of a king. Both orchids and ragwort were once known as satyrion. The orchid, coming from the Greek *orchis* meaning testicle because of the shape of its roots, was a signature plant. The ancient doctrine of signatures stated that herbs resembling a specific part of the body should be used to treat the ailments of those body parts. It was accepted that by using the herb that sexual potency would increase and stamina improve. The Greeks believed that when taken with wine satyrion root would enable a man to perform the act of sex up to seventy times in a row. It was also accepted that so much intercourse would lead to exhaustion.[4] When taken in larger doses, satyrion could cause pain, cramp and insomnia. Ragwort is one of the five dangerous weeds covered by a parliamentary act of 1959. If Henry was taking it as an aphrodisiac, he would have to have ingested a vast amount to poison himself. The rumour was not designed to complement Henry on his voracious sexual appetites. Medieval medicine perceived that too much sex was as bad as too little and the Church viewed lustfulness as a variety of mortal sin; not only were Henry's humours unbalanced but he was destined for Hell.

In 1175, Henry's relationship with Rosamund became common knowledge. Gerald of Wales described the young woman who the king kept near his residence at Woodstock as 'the rose of unchastity'[5] but most chroniclers and later writers were kinder than her contemporary who was bitter not to have received preferment from the king. Henry housed Rosamund at Everswell where he had also planted a garden or pleasance. There was a pear orchard or *viridarium* as well as gardens around a spring that fed three pools, which had been created at a cost of £26 9s 4d.[6] The whole construction, enclosed by a wall or a hedge, became known as Rosamund's Bower. Woodstock was also the home to Henry II's menagerie which included lions, camels and a porcupine. It was here that Henry came to escape from court life and from the political difficulties that beset him. Henry's problems at the time included his archbishop Thomas Becket and his subsequent murder, the revolt of 1173–1174 and the threat of French aggression. At Everswell, the lovers could enjoy the changing seasons, inhale the scent of roses and relax, the walls around the garden keeping out unwelcome reality. No wonder Dante Gabriel Rossetti depicted Rosamund in an unoccupied pose. She had nothing to do but to entertain her lover.

The garden at Everswell, with Rosamund at its heart, evoked concepts of courtly love, with its ritualised relationship between a knight and his lady. Chivalry lay at the heart of courtly love and more usually the knight's love was unrequited but in the world of courtly love the ordinary rules of society no longer existed and a secluded garden was the perfect location for a romantic encounter. There was an underlying tension as the garden was symbolic of the Garden of Eden. Dalliances were laced with the sin of sexual temptation, lust and the treachery of women, symbolised by Eve. Stories arose of a secret bower at Woodstock where

Henry kept his lover hidden from his angry and vengeful wife. In time the medieval pleasure garden was remembered as a maze, the centre of which was only accessible with a silken thread. In 1600 Thomas Delaney wrote a popular ballad that described the queen arriving unexpectedly at Woodstock, accessing Rosamund's bower and killing her rival. A fourteenth-century account of the ill-fated love story involved Eleanor poisoning Rosamund. In other interpretations, she stabbed the young woman. The tale was a popular one for Pre-Raphaelite artists of the nineteenth century, resulting in several pictorial versions of the mythical encounter between the queen and her rival. Eleanor is often shown to be angry, pinched and dark while Rosamund is young, fresh and innocent with long flowing hair and billowing robes. Despite the fact that the queen is the woman who has been wronged observers are invited to feel pity for the virginal Rosamund. The king's lover is depicted as the passive damsel in distress whilst Eleanor is shown to be aggressive and unwomanly chiming with the view that medieval chroniclers had of Eleanor as a young woman who wanted to step out from the domestic role of wife and mother in order to rule her duchy. Henry's marriage, despite the drama of Eleanor's escape from Paris into his arms, was a political match whereas his affair with Rosamund had all the romantic elements of thwarted love.

In reality, the queen was kept securely confined until Henry's death in 1189. She had no opportunity for murder. In 1175 or 1176, Rosamund retreated to Godstow Abbey where her mother was buried. It has been hypothesised that she had breast cancer. When she died, she was buried in front of the high altar. Henry is said to have paid for a lavish tomb. It is true that in 1176 Henry sent lathes and roofing shingles from Wallingford to Godstow. He also gave the advowsons of Wycombe and Bloxham to the abbey.[7] Hovedon reported that Rosamund's tomb was covered with silk and rose petals. In 1180, Rosamund's father, Walter, granted the mill at Frampton to the nunnery as well as meadows in Pauntley so that prayers could be said for his wife and daughter. A halo of light created by candles and tapers kept the memory of Rosamund alive until, in 1191, Henry II's friend Bishop Hugh of Lincoln had the tomb removed, describing Rosamund as a harlot. Leland described seeing a stone coffin containing Rosamund's bones being opened and that it released a sweet smell. A stone coffin, since disappeared, was displayed in later times, purporting to have been Rosamund's final resting place but the story was 'no more than the fiction of the vulgar'.[8]

The legend of Fair Rosamund grew during the sixteenth and seventeenth centuries. A member of the Clifford family purchased an estate at Frampton near the River Severn, which had once belonged to the medieval Cliffords. It was at about this time that the village green at Frampton became known as Rosamund's Green and the story spread that she had been born at Fretherne Lodge. Later still part of the Manor Farm came to be associated with Rosamund.[9] There is more myth than reality about the story. Not only did an elaborate murder involving mazes, silk threads and poisoned chalices never happen but history cannot even be sure where Rosamund was born or what she looked like.

Ida de Tosny, a cousin of Rosamund's, was a royal ward and a granddaughter of Isabel de Vermondais. Her parents were probably Ralph de Tosny who died in 1162 and Margaret de Beaumont, a daughter of Robert, 2nd Earl of Leicester. Ida's brother Roger became Lord of Flamstead in her father's place but both children became the wards of the king because of their age. Roger turned to the de Beaumont family for support and patronage, describing himself as 'son of Margaret' even as an adult.[10] Henry could either have arranged marriage for the siblings himself or sold the right to arrange their weddings to a third party. Instead, he first seduced Ida himself. William Longspée was born circa 1176 but it was only the discovery of a charter in 1976 which identified Longespée as Ida's son. Ralph the Black, a supporter of Becket the murdered archbishop, described the king as a 'corrupter of chastity'[11] and it would seem that his accusations were not without foundation. Ida was a gently born virgin not a woman from the lower classes who could be dismissed as a whore or brazen temptress. Medieval monarchs, feudal overlords, set on the throne by God could not truly be guilty of theft because they were the tenant-in-chief. Every baron in the land was a vassal of the monarch. It is perhaps not surprising that many monarchs did not take 'no' for an answer. Sexual assault or *raptus* was not a crime against the victim of the rape. It was a matter to be dealt with between the person committing the assault or abduction and the male members of the victim's family who held legal power over the woman. Any sexual violation against a girl or woman was deemed to financially harm her father, husband or brother, especially if the woman involved was a marriageable heiress. The crime was essential a property crime. The seduction of Ida may not have been rape but Henry stood *in loco parentis* as Ida's guardian. It did not stop the king seeing something he wanted and taking it.

Henry II married his young mistress off to Roger Bigod in 1181. Roger's father, Hugh, was the first Bigod Earl of Norfolk having risen in service to King Stephen. He built a castle at Bungay and by 1166 his was one of the richest families in the country. In 1174, Hugh rebelled against Henry II in support of the Young King along with many of England's magnates. As a consequence, much of his land was confiscated and the earldom taken from his family. Roger began to buy back his father's estates and rebuild the king's trust in his family. During the Christmas festivities of 1181, he married Ida. The king gave the couple estates as a wedding gift that included the manors of Acle, Halvergate and South Walsingham which had been in the Bigod family prior to Hugh's rebellion.[12] In 1189, Roger was permitted to buy back his father's earldom becoming the second earl of Norfolk and Ida his countess. Henry had reverted to his grandfather's stratagem of using his mistresses to bind his barons more closely to him. Having served her purpose Ida was able to return to respectability, and anonymity, until her identity as the mother of Longspée was established in the twentieth century and the jigsaw pieces of history slotted into their rightful places.

William Longspée, having left infancy before Ida's marriage to Roger Bigod, remained in the royal household to be raised as his royal father commanded. His coat of arms proclaimed his heritage for the world to see. The six leoncels on his arms were taken directly from the counts of Anjou. His mother's identity was only established when the cartulary of Bradenstoke Priory in Wiltshire was explored. It contained a charter from William that referred to the 'Countess Ida, my mother'.[13] In addition, a list of prisoners taken at the Battle of Bouvines in 1214 included the earl and his half-brother, Ralph Bigod demonstrating that Ida did not lose all contact with her son and that her Bigod family gained a powerful ally in Longspée. Richard the Lionheart trusted William, creating him the Earl of Salisbury when he provided him with the wealthy heiress Ela of Salisbury as a bride in 1198. He was also close to his half-brother John, who was part of Henry's household when William was a boy. John's accounts reveal that he sent William regular gifts and also divulged that the brothers frequently gambled with one another for various amounts of money each winning on occasion – Longspée was no sycophant.

Another of Henry's illegitimate sons who was close to John was Morgan, named after his uncle who was the last Welsh king of Glamorgan.[14] Morgan was appointed provost of Beverley in 1201 and then became bishop-elect of Durham. A problem arose when Pope Innocent II refused to confirm him as bishop because of his illegitimacy. Innocent tried to compromise by suggesting that if Morgan stated that Ralph, his mother's husband, was his father rather than King Henry II that his claim to the bishopric would be honoured. Morgan refused. Sometime before 1175 his mother Nesta married Ralph Bloet who was part of the de Clare affinity with land in the Lordship of Striguil. Bloet received the manor of Raglan some four years before the marriage making him a significant landowner in the marches between Wales and southwest England. Nesta's father, Iowerth, was the lord of Caerleon and her mother Angharad was the daughter of the Bishop of Llandaff. The match was one that linked neighbouring elite families, tied the troublesome Iowerth who had rebelled in 1172 to Plantagenet rule and promoted a détente along the Welsh March.

In 1175, the same year that Nesta married Ralph, her father did homage to King Henry at Gloucester. It was on this occasion that the king returned Caerleon to her father. It may have been on this instance that Henry first met Nesta. The affair took place sometime between 1175 and 1180. There is very little reference to Ralph Bloet and the date of Morgan's birth is unrecorded. Although she was married, Henry acknowledged his son who was raised alongside Nesta's five legitimate children. Ralph died circa 1200 and following legal disputes with both her brother and brother-in-law, Nesta received a generous dower settlement. This may have come about because Morgan's half-brother, King John, was sympathetic to Nesta. John's marriage in 1189 to Isabelle of Gloucester made John a Marcher lord. Several of Nesta's sons joined King John's household.

In 1177, or thereabouts, Henry took a young woman for his mistress breaking all the rules of traditional morality. He had known Alys of France since she was a child of eight or nine years. In 1159, Henry had arranged for his eldest surviving son, Henry, to be betrothed to Marguerite of France, the two-year-old daughter of Louis VII and his second wife, Constance of Castile. There was a stipulation in the marriage contract that the child would not be reared in the household of Eleanor of Aquitaine who was Louis's first wife. A second marriage was arranged between Marguerite's younger sister, Alys, and Henry II's second surviving son Richard. Both girls were placed in Eleanor's household despite the fact that Louis expressly forbade the arrangement. When Eleanor's household was broken up in 1174, the two princesses travelled to England with the disgraced queen. She was taken to Winchester whilst Alys and Marguerite were sent to Devizes. In time, when Henry's sons came to terms with their father, Marguerite and Alys were made welcome at court. Alys of France was sixteen years old by 1177 and questions were being asked by the French as to why her marriage to Henry's son Richard had not yet taken place. Gerald of Wales stated that not only did Henry take Alys as his mistress but that he intended to marry her himself. Efforts had been made at various times to persuade Eleanor to take the veil. The affair with Alys, and her dower lands, caused an international incident and nearly got Henry excommunicated. Later Richard had to pay Alys's brother ten thousand marks as compensation for not marrying her. Roger of Howden reported that Richard refused to marry the girl because 'my father slept with her and had a son by her'.[15] Howden a chronicler who was at court during the reigns of Henry and Richard tends to be sympathetic to Henry so it is plausible that Richard did say what Howden reported. The *Chronicle of Meaux*, although written later, also claimed that Alys was pregnant by Henry but that the child did not survive infancy. Richard refused to release Alys. Her dowry was the Vexin marching between Normandy and France. It was an important buffer zone that Richard had no wish to relinquish even if he did not wish to marry the bride who went with the land.

Alys, a political pawn between France and the Plantagenets, was not mistress material. She was a princess of France sent as a peace weaver along with her sister. Kings might sleep with as many women as they wished but the daughters of powerful enemies were surely forbidden? It is quite possible that if Henry intended to make Alys his bride, Louis would not have objected. There was talk in 1175 of Henry having his marriage to Eleanor annulled – not only had she rebelled against him breaking her marriage vows but they were also related within the prohibited degrees of affinity. Gerald of Wales stated that Henry intended to rear a new brood of sons to disinherit Eleanor's rebellious offspring. However, if the marriage was annulled Aquitaine would revert to its duchess. She might marry for a third time and make war upon her former husband. It is also possible that the rumours of an affair between Alys and Henry were political posturing and that Henry did not abuse his position *in loco parentis* to the French king's daughter who was placed in Henry's care when she was eight or nine years old. However, there was a pattern of the king asserting his dominance and virility over his enemies by seducing their womenfolk – both Nest Bloet and Alys of France fit the pattern. Odo de Porhoët's claim that Henry seduced his daughter when she was a hostage in his care demonstrates further similarities of behaviour.

After Richard rejected Alys in March 1191, her brother Philip offered her as a bride to Richard's brother John. Eleanor prevented the proposed match. Alys, an innocent in the whole sordid affair, was ruined and had already spent many years in England as a virtual prisoner. She was finally sent back to France in 1195. That summer she married William IV Talvas, Count of Ponthieu. She was eighteen years older than her new husband but the lure of her dowry – the county of Vexin marching between France and Angevin territories was more important than the age of William's new wife. Philip of France may have thought that at thirty-five years old Alys would have no children but, if so, he miscalculated. Alys gave birth to a daughter called Marie circa 1199 who became the *suo jure* Countess of Ponthieu. Alys seems to have given William three children in all, dying when she was forty, in childbed.

Henry had other mistresses though none of them lasted in the way that Rosamund endured in legend if not historical fact. His grandfather created entire families with his mistresses but Henry II's women produced no more than one child with the king and are, as a consequence of their transitory nature, more elusive. Bellebelle appears on the 1184 pipe roll when Henry gave her a gift of cloaks and other clothes at the same time as making a similar purchase for the queen. There were many women called Isabel or Isabella at court so it is impossible to work out who else was dressed like the queen that year. Henry was a notorious womaniser but we know nothing about what the women he shared his bed looked like or even whether they loved the king. Unlike the formidable Eleanor, the rest of Henry's women, whether they were in his bed for sex, companionship or political stratagem, were not so blatant that they incurred the wrath of Henry's chroniclers. Only Fair Rosamund who Charles Dickens called 'the loveliest girl in the world' lingers in popular memory because the King was 'certainly very fond of her'.[16]

Chapter 12

Ela de Warenne, Constance, Clemencia and Agatha de Ferrers and Isabella of Angoulême

K ing John was the youngest of Henry II's legitimate sons to
survive infancy. Like his father and great grandfather, John was a
notorious womaniser both before and after he became king. Many
of the women he bedded slipped quietly into the unknown although like
other medieval monarchs he acknowledged, raised and married off his
illegitimate children when it suited his own ends. His mistresses were said
to include a woman called Hawise, the Countess of Aumale, a woman
called Clementia known as *'regina Clemencie'* by the Tewksbury Annals
and another named Suzanne who was described as a lady-in-waiting as
well as royal mistress. One of his better-known mistresses was his own
first cousin, Ela de Warenne, the daughter of Henry II's illegitimate
brother Hamelin.

In 1164, in the midst of a deteriorating relationship with the Archbishop
of Canterbury, Thomas Becket and the wider Catholic Church, King
Henry II arranged that Hamelin should marry Isabel de Warenne,
suo jure Countess of Surrey. King Stephen made a marriage for Isabel,
when she was eleven years old, to his youngest son, William of Blois but
he died in 1159 whilst on campaign with King Henry near Toulouse.
Henry initially hoped to marry his younger legitimate brother William
to Isabel but the wedding was blocked by Thomas Becket on grounds
of consanguinity. He died a short while afterwards of a broken heart
according to those who disliked the Archbishop of Canterbury. No one
bothered to record Isabel's views on the proposed matches but it is likely
she knew both William and Hamelin Plantagenet. Hamelin's father was
Count Geoffrey of Anjou whose mistress bore a son during the late 1130s
or early 1140s. The marriage between Isabel and Hamelin ensured that
no overpowerful magnate would challenge the king by gaining access to
extensive de Warenne estates. The wedding made Hamelin both wealthy

and powerful with estates on both sides of the Channel, many of them in strategic locations in the North of England and Normandy. The honour of Warenne contained more than 140 knights' fees. The family strongholds included Lewes, Sandal, Conisbrough and Castle Acre in Norfolk. In addition to wealth, Isabel was the niece of Earl Robert of Leicester and Count Waleran of Meulan. Her Beaumont connections linked Hamelin to one of the most powerful factions in the country. Hamelin adopted the name de Warenne which emphasised his status as Earl of Surrey rather than relying on his royal links with Henry II. He was also careful that any charters that he issued emphasised that he was acting on his wife's authority. In time, Isabel provided Hamelin with a family which included three daughters; Ela, Isobel and Matilda, as well as a son named William.

Henry's trust in his half-brother was well rewarded. At the Council of Northampton Hamelin attacked Thomas Becket. He supported Henry in 1173–1174 when his sons rebelled and continued in his loyalty to his legitimate half-brother and his sons throughout his life. Hamelin and his wife were often present at court and their children knew their royal cousins including Henry II's favourite son, John.

Some sources say that Isabel caught John's eyes, others Ela. At this time there is no documented evidence available to identify which of the sisters became pregnant by their cousin. Ela would issue a charter granting land to Roche Abbey but it makes no mention of a son by John. From the contents of the document, it is evident that Ela married firstly to Robert de Newburn about whom nothing is known and for a second time to William FitzWilliam of Sprotborough which was a few miles away from her parents' home at Conisbrough. The status of both her husbands might suggest that as a mother of an illegitimate child, her value on the marriage market had decreased but equally, she was one of several daughters with a living brother to inherit their father's estates. Nor are there any charters that conveniently identify Isabel de Warenne as the mother of John's child. The only piece of circumstantial evidence to support the notion is that when he had children of his own John's son, Richard, named his own daughter Isabel. However, he could have been naming the child after his grandmother or even his mother-in-law. What is certain is that Richard was born at some time during the 1190s. He is identified as FitzRoy, de Warenne and after his marriage as Richard of Dover. His seal incorporated the royal arms and those of the de Warenne family. Following Henry's death in 1189, Hamelin became one of Richard's most influential supporters. He was often in the company of the Lionheart at the beginning of his reign and whist Richard was away in the Holy Land he worked closely with the king's chancellor, William de Longchamp, against the machinations of Prince John. The arrival of an illegitimate child might account for some of the hostility with which de Warenne viewed his nephew. John's antipathy towards de Warenne might also provide circumstantial evidence why Ela was not provided with a better match by the Crown if she were indeed the mother of John's son.

Like her sister, Isabel married a Yorkshire landowner, suggesting that de Warenne was using marital alliances to build a regional affinity rather than relying on his royal or Beaumont connections. Her husband, Robert de Lacy, held the honour of Pontefract but he died in 1193 without children. Within three years Isabel had married for a second time to Gilbert de l'Aigle, Lord of Pevensey. It is possible that Ermengarde de Beaumont, a granddaughter of King Henry I, who married William the Lion of Scotland in 1186, helped arrange the match. After some difficulties in 1204, Gilbert continued to hold land on both sides of the Channel when John lost most of his demesnes. It was impossible for Gilbert to serve both King John and King Philip. His English lands were temporarily seized and granted to Gilbert's father-in-law but as John's need for baronial support grew, Gilbert's lands were returned to his custody. He was in a position where he was welcome in the English, French and Scottish courts.[1] Isabel's first widowhood fits with the timeframe for Richard's birth but it is the flimsiest of evidence for an affair with John who did come to England at that time in contravention of his oath to his brother Richard. After Gilbert's death at the end of 1231, Ela would give a third of the manor of Northease in Sussex, which was part of her dower, to Michelham Priory which she and Gilbert founded in about 1229.[2] Isabel died before 1234 without children raising the question that if she had no children by either of her husbands, how likely was it that she was the mother of John's child?

King John provided for his de Warenne son by marrying him to an heiress, Rose of Dover, in 1214. Her estates included the honour of Chilham in Kent. In 1216, shortly before his death at Newark, John appointed Richard as constable of Wallingford Castle which he would hold until 1227. He served his half-brother as loyally as he once served his father distinguishing himself at the Battle of Sandwich on 24 August 1217. The sea battle was fought to prevent Louis, the Dauphin of France, who had invaded England at the invitation of the rebel barons, from resupplying his men. William Marshal, who served Henry II, his sons and Henry III, would defeat the French at the Battle of Lincoln the following month. Richard joined the Fifth Crusade and began to accrue debts. He dropped from the political scene at both a local and national level. In 1227, King Henry acted on behalf of his sister-in-law, Rose, to prevent Richard from selling or damaging the manor of Northwood which was part of her dower. When Richard died in 1248 his widow paid a fine so that her next husband would be one of her own choosing.

It was rumoured that John broke the laws of consanguinity at a closer level than that of first cousin. Constance, Duchess of Brittany was married to John's elder brother Geoffrey in 1181 but widowed in 1186 when her husband was trampled during a tournament in Paris. In 1196, Richard I named his nephew Arthur as his heir because he did not trust John. By then Constance was unhappily married to Ranulf, Earl of Chester. In 1198, Constance returned to Brittany and sought an annulment from her marriage to Ranulf on grounds of consanguinity. An unverified rumour circulated that the reason behind the annulment was that Constance was having an affair with John. In time it would be suggested that she was the mother of John's illegitimate daughter Joan. She was born whilst John was still in his teens. Taking into account John's location during the 1180s, it is likely that Joan's mother was a Norman. John spent most of the period from 1187 until 1189 in Normandy. After King Henry II died in 1189, Richard and John returned to England on 12 August. John married Isabella of Gloucester at the end of the month. In October, John was required to fulfil his role as a Marcher baron when his brother sent him to subdue the Welsh. The following year, in February, John was back in Normandy where Richard made him swear that he would not return to England for the next three years. John broke his oath almost immediately after Richard departed on the Third Crusade. Joan seems to have spent her early years in Normandy before arriving in England in 1203 according to a pipe roll for that year. Her childhood years, like many other royal children legitimate or not, are poorly recorded.

When John became king, he sent the girl as a bride to the Prince of North Wales, Llewellyn ap Iorweth. When Pope Honorious III legitimated Joan in April 1226, the papal bull stated that at the time of Joan's birth her father was unmarried. She must have been born before 29 August 1189, when John married Isabella of Gloucester. When Joan died in 1237, the *Tewksbury Annals* wrote her obituary. It described her as a daughter of John and Queen Clemencia. It has been suggested that the Old English '*cwen*' meant woman, wife, servant or even hussy as well as the king's wife, which hardly narrows the field.[3]

Clemence or Clemencia is an unusual name but there is more than one woman who could be John's mistress. Clemence de Boteler, for instance, married Nicholas de Verdun of Alton in 1202. In 1228, Henry III gave Joan's daughter Susanna into the care of the de Verduns. If Clemence was Susanna's grandmother it would make sense of where Henry chose to place his niece. Another possibility is Clémence de Fougères, the widow of Alan of Dinan, who became Ranulf of Chester's second wife in the autumn of 1199 after the annulment of his marriage from Constance of Brittany. Her dower included the manor of Twyford. It was granted to Ranulf upon his marriage by John which suggests a familial relationship or a paying off.[4] Ranulf and Clémence were married for thirty years until Ranulf died in 1232. She remained a widow until her own death in 1252. Both Ranulf and Clemencia patronised Savigny Abbey but their existing charters contain no reference to an illegitimate child by John. David Powell writing his *History of Cambria* in 1584 hypothesised that another of John's mistresses, Agatha de Ferrers the daughter of the Earl of Derby was Joan's mother.[5] Dugdale's *Baronage of England* drew on Powell's work. If John's reputation so far is poor, the women who came to be identified with him have suffered undeserved damage to theirs. There is no concrete evidence that Constance, Clémence or Agatha de Ferrers ever slept with John.

'Scurrilous gossip-mongers',[6] did not have far to look for evidence of flaws in John's character so far as women were concerned. He is the only medieval king to have divorced his wife although King Henry II gave thought to annulling his marriage to Eleanor of Aquitaine. John's first wife Isabel of Gloucester was the great-granddaughter of Henry I making them second cousins and related within the prohibited degree of consanguinity. Her maternal grandfather was Robert de Beaumont, 3rd

Earl of Leicester. Isabel's brother died in 1166 making Isabel and her two sisters coheiresses. Henry II sought to provide for his youngest son by a betrothal of marriage for John to Isabella. The king also ensured that Isabel's sisters were excluded from the inheritance and that as a ward of the Crown all of the income from Isabel's lands were available for John to use. John and Isabel were betrothed in 1176 when John was nine years old. The marriage was not finalised by the time of Henry's death because the king continued to look for other opportunities and better matches. The wedding was celebrated on 29 August 1189 at Marlborough Castle when John came to England with his brother Richard. John was twenty-one years old but most historians consider that Isabel was probably closer to thirty. The Archbishop of Canterbury, Baldwin, opposed the marriage because the couple were too closely related, both being great-grandchildren of King Henry I. John promised to seek a dispensation although there is no record of one being obtained. The pair were married for ten years but had no children, living largely separate lives. In 1193, John promised to marry Philip Augustus's sister, Alys of France, who had once been the intended bride of his brother Richard. Nothing came of the proposal thanks to the intervention of John's mother, but it demonstrated that Isabelle's wealth was an insufficient anchor for John. When he became king in 1199, he was crowned without his wife at his side. By 1200, John had formally rejected Isabel and obtained a dispensation on grounds of consanguinity which annulled the marriage.

Isabella was not permitted to manage her own estates. John retained the wealth that remained in John's custody for the next fourteen years and when the king remarried his new bride, Isabella of Angoulême, a child of twelve, she was accommodated with Isabella at Winchester. John also appropriated Isabella of Angoulême's dower, giving her an allowance and presenting her with clothes and jewels. John's new wife and his old one remained in the same household until a few weeks before Isabella gave birth to her first child in October 1207.

John's choice of second wife was viewed as being of dubious morality by some chroniclers including Roger of Wendover. The king chose to abduct and marry a girl who was betrothed to another man. Wendover went so far as to suggest that the king had been bewitched. The chronicler laid the blame for John's military failures in Normandy between 1203 and 1204 at Isabella's feet claiming that the king was so besotted with his queen that he did not act against the French invaders preferring to sleep with her night after night at the expense of the territories which his father had built up. There were rumours that his nights were so filled with lovemaking that he slept until noon.

Isabella was the heiress of Adomar, Count of Angoulême, a territory in south-western France between Poitou and Gascony. She was betrothed to Hugh IX de Lusignan, the Lord of Lusignan and the Count of La Marche, a strategically important territory to the north-east of Angoulême with the support of King Richard who was a friend of Hugh. But if Hugh married Isabella it would have united two factions and created a land barrier between Aquitaine and the rest of John's Angevin territories. The king realised he needed to prevent the wedding. Philip of France, who should not have been trusted, suggested that the best way of doing this was for John to marry Isabella himself. John had already sent envoys to Portugal to negotiate a Portuguese bride but he married Isabella at Bordeaux on 24 August 1200 and they were crowned together in Westminster on 8 October. Chroniclers at the time believed that the king was overcome by lust for his young bride not least because the annulment of his marriage from Isabel of Gloucester was not yet complete. There was also the problem of the bride's age. Chroniclers at the time were uncertain whether or not Isabella had reached the canonical age for marriage which was twelve. Calculations based on her mother Alice de Courtney's marriage to her father Ademar of Angoulême placed Isabella somewhere between eight and fifteen years old at the time of her marriage to John.[7] Most writers conclude that she was no older than twelve. Even worse, the marriage resulted in the Lusignans' revolting against John's overlordship. Hugh had lost his bride, to whom he may have been married by *verba de presenti* lacking only the consummation because of Isabella's tender years, as well as the strategically important county of Agoulême. Lusignan and his brother Ralph of Eu complained to King Philip about the breach of contract. Philip, as he intended all along, declared John's continental lands forfeit when John refused to answer a summons to the French court. In 1202, Isabella became Countess of Angoulême in her own right following the death of her father and John obtained control of the strategically important territory but by the summer of 1204, Normandy, Maine and Anjou had been occupied by the French. John's marriage, made to prevent a united territory of Lusignan, La Marche and

Angoulême imposing upon his own domains, was a disastrous political misjudgement. As time passed Isabella's reputation was blackened. Matthew Paris recorded an account made by Roger of London who went as an ambassador to Morocco in 1211. He said that Isabella, 'has often been found guilty of incest, witchcraft and adultery, so that the King, her husband has ordered those of her lovers who have been apprehended to be strangled with a rope in her own bed'.[8] There is no evidence that Isabella was culpable of any of these crimes rather it spoke of the king's failures as a monarch.

Isabella gave birth to John's first legitimate son, Henry, in October 1207 and went on to have four more children, fulfilling the requirement of every medieval queen to look beautiful and produce healthy heirs to the throne. John continued to be unashamedly unfaithful whilst Isabella's own situation is open to speculation. Although she was crowned queen, she was not permitted to receive the rents from her dower lands or enjoy other revenue. John continued to treat her as a child even after she reached adulthood. She took no part in the administrative process and is largely absent from the historical record contained in charters and grants. She was housed with John's first wife and at Marlborough, she was living with one of John's mistresses. Both she and John possessed fiery tempers and according to the chroniclers, if they were not making love, they were indulging in furious arguments. Gervase of Canterbury described her as being imprisoned in Corfe Castle in 1208 and in Devizes in 1209.[9] It could be that rather than being incarcerated, John, concerned for Isabella's safety whilst the realm was under the interdict following his own excommunication, increased the levels of security surrounding his wife. The high value that John placed on his queen is demonstrated by the fact that he placed her under the protection of one of his most trusted servants, Terric the Teuton. Despite this apparent concern for her safety, she had no political power and little in the way of real financial independence. There were also rumours of a lover and an illegitimate child. During her first pregnancy, Isabella asked John if her half-brother Pierre de Joigny, could visit her in England. An Irish chronicle of the 1230s stated that Isabella had an illegitimate child called Piers the Fair who was killed whilst fighting in the army of Walter de Lacy. There is nothing to substantiate the chronicle, rather it demonstrated the queen's lack of popularity.

In 1215 John rejected the Magna Carta which he signed at Runnymede on 15 June having appealed to the Pope. His barons invited the French dauphin Louis of France to depose the king and civil turmoil erupted. By autumn the king was dead and his son, nine-year-old Henry was proclaimed king. The regency lay in the hands of William Marshal and the bishop of Winchester who was already providing a home and education for John's heir. Isabella was not listed amongst the executors of her husband's will. Even as the dowager queen she had no political power. She made three grants for the salvation of John's soul, demanded her dower rights and left for Angoulême taking her youngest daughter, Joan, with her. In 1220, she made a second controversial marriage when she took Hugh X de Lusignan as her husband. He was her own daughter Joan's betrothed husband and the son of the man she was once supposed to have married. It broke the laws of consanguinity in several ways. She had exchanged, as a child, vows *verba de praesenti* with Hugh IX which made her marriage to his son incestuous. It did not stop her and Hugh from having nine children. Nor had she sought the permission of the king's council in England, as she was required to do. The English stopped her pension and confiscated her lands. Princess Joan remained with her mother but when Isabella threatened to prevent Joan's marriage to King Alexander II of Scotland, King Henry III appealed to the Pope who counter-threatened Isabella and Hugh with excommunication.

Marriage was the only acceptable place for sex in medieval England but Isabella's reputation, 'more Jezabel than Isabel',[10] arose because of the way her husband was viewed at a time when he lost his continental territories. The chroniclers of the period presented a picture of a king distracted by sex. It prevented him from ruling effectively and damaged his relationship with his nobility. The monks who wrote the chronicles had only a limited number of motifs to describe the women they wrote about. Isabella fell into the somewhat formulaic category of temptress. Like Eve who tempted Adam into Original Sin, the monks viewed Isabella as the source of England's ills whilst she was married to John.

Chapter 13

Magna Carta Mistresses

Norman and Plantagenet kings were not models of moral integrity but King John gained a reputation as a sexual predator which had political consequences of a kind that never impacted on his predecessors. John's reputation was blackened by chroniclers like Matthew Paris who wrote of him, 'Foul though it is, Hell itself is defouled by the foulness of John'.[1] Between 1207 and 1215, John's second wife Isabella of Angouleme gave him five children but he also had between eight and twelve acknowledged illegitimate children by different women. All the women who were said to have joined John between the bedsheets were viewed by the Church as temptresses or victims. The former resulted in political damage to the state whilst the latter became a small part of the justification for rebellion against the monarch. One chronicler announced that even John's mercenaries noticed the king's covetousness when beautiful women were involved. The *Chronicle of Meaux* wrote:

> He deflowered the wives and daughters of his nobles, not a woman was spared if he was seized by the desire to defile her in the heat of his lust.[2]

The chronicler continued his account to explain that John's behaviour brought shame to his magnates and it was for this reason he was hated. The king's lecherous designs on the wives and daughters of his magnates became well known. There were many accusations and inferences but less in the way of solid evidence. Many of the stories about John's debasement of nobly born women were written after his barons revolted.

Robert FitzWalter, Lord of Little Dunmow and Constable of Baynard's Castle, claimed that he abandoned John when the king attempted to rape his daughter Matilda. The same account also states that FitzWalter refused to serve an excommunicated king. Matthew Paris, writing from 1236 until his death in 1259, described Matilda as Maud the Fair and

Maid Marion. The tale told by John Stow in his *Chronicles of England* in 1580 was that Matilda turned eighteen and her doting father celebrated with a costly banquet and a tournament which lasted for three days. John, still only the Count of Mortain and plotting against his brother King Richard, attended the festivities and was smitten by the girl. Matilda was not enamoured of John and failed to succumb to his charms. According to tradition, Matilda having spurned John's advances was sent to the Tower where John arranged to have her murdered by means of a poisoned egg. Matilda and the story of her unusual murder are celebrated on the village sign for Diss. On occasion, the egg was substituted with a poisoned bracelet. Stow was retelling an account found in a fragment known as the *Dunmow Chronicle* which had more to do with a chivalric tale than historical reality. By the Victorian period, the story was taken as fact and recorded in Strickland's *Lives of English Queens*. During the seventeenth century, she became associated with the legend of Robin Hood when she appeared as a character in a play by Anthony Munday and concluded her adventures as the Countess of Huntingdon. Sadly, there is no evidence for the story. John had a reputation for imprisoning people. Maud de Braose, the wife of a powerful Marcher baron, was starved to death along with her grandson William at Corfe Castle in 1210. The following year, John, desperate for funds to regain control of his lost French lands, started taking hostages in England and imprisoning them for failure to pay various taxes. It is not beyond the bounds of possibility that Matilda FitzWalter died whilst she was one of John's hostages but there is no written record of it.

John's animosity towards Matilda FitzWalter arose not because she spurned his amorous advances but because of the political activism of her father and husband. She was the first wife of Geoffrey de Mandeville, Earl of Essex. The king accused him of killing a servant and threatened to have him executed. Marian's father is purported to have told John, 'You will see two hundred lanced knights in your land before you hang him'.[3] FitzWalter became a driving force behind the First Barons War but the death of Matilda, whether by egg or bracelet, could be based on fact or it could, just as easily, be propaganda to blacken John's name. There is even some doubt that the effigy in the Priory Church of St Mary the Virgin in Little Dunmow is that of FitzWalter's daughter, although the lady is definitely a part of his family.

To complicate the story still further, the widowed de Mandeville married John's castoff wife, Isabella of Gloucester. Geoffrey paid a fine of 20,000 marks for Isabella's hand in 1214. The *Dunstable Annals* detailed de Mandeville pawning his manors and selling his woods to pay the debt owed to the king.[4] Some historians take the view that de Mandeville asked for Isabella's hand of his own freewill but she was past childbearing age when the marriage was contracted and more than sixteen years older than her new husband. It is a possibility that King John forced his first wife upon de Mandeville making him pay a huge fee that more or less left him bankrupt as a form of punishment. De Mandeville soon defaulted on the payments that he was required to make to pay for his bride. In 1216, he was injured during a jousting tournament and subsequently died but since he was one of the barons who rebelled against the king all of his estates and titles were forfeited to the Crown. John swept up the earldom of Gloucester and its estates leaving his former wife virtually penniless. A year after the death of King John, Isabella's lands were returned to her but she died soon afterwards on 14 October 1217.

According to William of Newburgh, Eustace de Vescy, the lord of Alnwick and most prominent of John's northern barons, was one of FitzWalter's allies who conspired against the king in 1212 because he had no intention that his own wife should be forced into the royal bed. Margaret de Vescy was the illegitimate daughter of William the Lion. King Alexander II of Scotland was her half-brother. Her mother's name was recorded in the *Melrose Chronicle* as 'the daughter of Ada de Hythusum'.[5] The same chronicle reported that William married his daughter Margaret to Eustace de Vescy at Rokeschuch in 1193. She appears to have been a pious woman who gave revenues to Kelso Monastery in 1207 and property to Melrose Abbey. The chronicler tells the tale of the attempted royal seduction, of Eustace substituting another woman in John's bed and of the king congratulating Eustace on the sexual boldness of his wife only to discover that he had been tricked. The story explains Eustace's hatred for John. Whatever the truth of the matter de Vescy fled to Scotland in August 1212 when he was accused of plotting with Robert FitzWalter against John. All of his lands were seized but the king was forced to submit to the Pope the following year. Vescy returned home in May 1213 and his lands were returned although John still conspired to cripple the baron's powers. He refused to fight for John in Poitou, in southwest France, and was forced to pay scutage – money in lieu of military service. So great was de Vescy's dislike of the king that he was warned by the papacy to remain loyal to his sovereign lord. In 1215, he was heavily involved with the northern campaign that led to Magna Carta. In September the same year, he was one of a group of nine barons excommunicated by the Pope for his failure to obey his sovereign lord. De Vescy did seek reconciliation but when John repudiated Magna Carta, de Vescy was one of the men who offered the crown to Prince Louis of France. He travelled with Alexander II of Scotland when the prince invaded. He was with the Scots when they besieged Barnard Castle in August. Hugh de Baliol held the castle for the king but when de Vescy was killed by a crossbow bolt that struck him in the head, the siege was lifted. King Henry III granted Margaret custody of hers and Eustace's son, William, in April 1218.

John pursued the women of his friends and loyal subjects as well as those of his enemies. The fine roll of Christmas 1204 found the wife of Hugh de Neville paying a fee of two hundred chickens to spend one night with her husband. There are innocent explanations. Hugh's wife could have been objecting to the amount of time that her husband was absent from his own hearth on royal service. Alternatively, it could have been that she was a royal mistress who was attempting to remove herself from between the royal sheets. Hugh de Neville, who served John's father and brother, took part in the Third Crusade, before becoming John's Chief Forester. In 1194, he gained the wardship of Joan de Cornhill following the death of her father, Henry de Cornhill, the previous year. Neville married the girl four years later and acquired her family lands in London at the same time. During the same year, he became the custodian of Marlborough Castle and during the next three years, he acquired the sheriffships of Oxfordshire, Essex and Hertfordshire. Isabelle of Angoulême spent long periods of time in Marlborough which was Hugh and Joan's home. Neville also became the chief justice of the royal forests. He was described by Roger of Howden as one of the king's evil councillors. In addition to raising revenue from the royal forests, he was also a witness to many of the king's charters. Their friendship extended to de Neville being John's gambling partner. Despite their friendship, de Neville joined with the barons to revolt against the king in 1216 giving them custody of Marlborough Castle. If John had taken his wife as his mistress, Hugh had reason to be aggrieved. It was only after John's death that de Neville made his peace with the Crown but it was some time before he was reappointed to his forest posts. Joan died before 1234 and Neville married for a second time to Beatrice de Fay. Joan's son John inherited his father's estates and the role of chief forester.

Further circumstantial evidence for many of John's mistresses can be found penned into the accounts. In 1209 an unknown mistress received £30; another received the gift of roses from the justiciar, Geoffrey FitzPeter's, garden. A girl called Susanna described as 'a friend of the king's' was given a tunic and super-tunic in 1213.[6] In 1214, one of the queen's ladies called Alpesia was taken to the king under escort by two guards. A woman called Hawise de Nurdels received a pension of a penny per day. They might all be innocent gifts but John's reputation suggests otherwise. On another occasion, John sent a tun of wine to the wife of Henry Biset, Lord of Kidderminster. There is nothing in the account to suggest an ulterior motive but John's reputation is such that the gift of wine takes on sinister overtones. Biset, as well as being John's steward, was also a household knight who accompanied the king to Ireland in 1204.[7] Biset's wife Isolda Pantolf was widowed in 1208. Biset was her third husband and she was a wealthy woman. She had built up a considerable inheritance including dower lands from three husbands as well as the wardship of Henry's heirs for which she paid the king 1,000 marks.[8]

There is also a tantalising reference in 1210 to Robert de Vaux, Baron of Gilsland, who gave 'five of his best palfreys that the king might hold his tongue about Henry Pinel's wife'.[9] Rather intriguingly Pinel's wife was called Clemence so it is possible that it was Pinel's wife who was the mother of John's daughter Joan. John was an expert when it came to taxing his nobility but the fees were usually in respect of feudal dues rather than juicy scandal. Like many other of the nobility, de Vaux would be required to send members of his family to the king as hostages for his feudal dues in 1212. Although he was made governor of Carlisle Castle in 1215, he took up arms against John when the king repudiated Magna Carta.

Meanwhile, the Bishop of Winchester donated 'one tun of good wine for not putting the king in mind to give a girdle to the countess of Albermarle'.[10] Hawise, was the *suo jure* Countess of Aumale married in 1179 to William de Mandeville, Earl of Essex. The bride was aged somewhere between twelve and fifteen at the time. After de Mandeville's death in 1189, King Richard I arranged for her to marry William de Forz who commanded Richard's crusading fleet. When Hawise resisted the plan Richard seized her belongings. Her objections to the marriage were not recorded but de Forz was a landless knight from Poitou. She acquiesced and was remarried after less than a year as a widow. De Forz died in 1195. Richard arranged a third marriage to Baldwin de Béthune, another of the king's crusading companions, the following year. In 1197, Philip Augustus captured Aumale but Hawise retained the title. Widowed for a third time in 1212, the countess agreed to pay a fine of 5,000 marks to hold her inheritance freely and not be forced to remarry. Richard of Devizes described Hawise as 'a woman who was almost a man, lacking nothing virile except the virile organs'.[11] When the countess died in 1213 her heir, William de Forz, became the third Earl of Aumale. He was the son of her second unwanted husband. Roger of Wendover labelled him a violent and irresponsible troublemaker. John granted him a charter for his mother's lands when he came to England in 1214. His estates were mainly in the northern counties and included the barony of Skipton. The king did not levy the usual fine for de Forz coming into his inheritance although he did insist that de Forz marry Aveline de Montfichet. Taken with the Bishop of Winchester's fine which might have been a joke of some description and the king's later generosity, it has been suggested that although de Forz recognised William as his son, he might have belonged to John, making the Countess of Aumale one of his mistresses.

Earlier kings used their illegitimate children and mistresses more consistently to strengthen their ties to their barony or secure allies. John used only one illegitimate child to create a marital alliance. He offered his illegitimate daughter Joan to Llywelyn ap Iorwerth of Gwynedd. A treaty signed in 1201 was secured by the marriage that followed. It fitted to the pattern of extended kinship established by King Henry I in the previous century and was possible because not only did John recognise Joan as his daughter but so did his contemporaries even if information about who her mother was has been largely lost to posterity.

If John had taken unmarried women from the knightly classes to be his mistresses, no one would have been concerned especially if he had arranged beneficial matches for them afterwards but the accusation of bedding nobly born wives and daughters of his barony, without the usual rewards of land and marriage, helped to blacken his reputation. Nor did it help that John's own marriage destroyed his father's territorial gains rather than growing his own demesne. Hostile monastic chroniclers created a sexual predator who demanded virtuous women from their legal guardians, husbands and fathers for his own pleasures although they did not bother looking too closely for evidence. The chroniclers made no allegations of force nor do they make any reference to the trauma of the women subjected to John's kingly attentions. The stories, true or not, added to the subtext that he was an unfit king and that his barons were right to rebel against him. It appears that John had as similar an appetite for women as his father and grandfather did but not the same aptitude in cultivating relationships with his nobility or developing dynastic networks. It could be argued that one of the consequences of being his father's favourite son was that he was all cock and no crown.

Chapter 14

Piers Gaveston, the Tour de Nesle Affair and the Consequences of Adultery

King Edward II plunged England into civil war because of the influence of his unpopular favourites. His attachment to Piers Gaveston and later Hugh Despenser the Younger ensured that his nobility was polarised and his rule unstable. The antipathy between his wife, Isabella of France, and Despenser helped to destroy Edward's marriage. Isabella, labelled as a She-Wolf during the eighteenth century, described Edward as her 'sweet lord' and 'my very sweetheart',[1] but she deserted him, took a lover and invaded her husband's realm resulting in his forced abdication and subsequent murder.

Edward was betrothed, as Prince of Wales, in 1299 to the daughter of Philip IV of France. It was his fourth betrothal. His father, King Edward I, used his son to further his foreign policy throughout his childhood. At five years old, he was engaged to the queen designate of Scotland, his cousin Margaret the 'Maid of Norway' but she died in 1290 aged only seven having made the journey from her native Norway to Orkney. In 1291, Edward became engaged for a second time to Blanche, a half-sister of King Philip IV of France. The engagement was broken off when King Edward I went to war with the French over the English-held territory of Gascony. The prince then found himself betrothed to Philippa of Flanders in an attempt by the Flemish to maintain their autonomy and by Edward I to foster an anti-French alliance. The agreement was wrecked when the war between the French and the English came to a halt in 1294. Philippa and her father became the prisoners of Philip IV. Guy, Count of Flanders was eventually released but Philippa disappeared into the Louvre Palace, never to be seen again.

A peace agreement between the French and the English brokered by Pope Boniface VIII and completed by the Treaty of Montreuil in June 1299 included a marriage between Philip IV's daughter Isabella and Edward

I's heir. The English king was a reluctant participant in the agreement but a formal betrothal followed in 1303. The treaty also agreed terms for the king's own marriage to Marguerite of France, the sister of Philip IV. Isabella was seven years old and the sixth of Philip and Joan of Navarre's seven children. She became used to being addressed as the Queen of England during her childhood in France. The marriage did not take place until January 1308 and by then there were already rumours about Edward and his handsome favourite Piers Gaveston who he referred to as his 'brother'.[2] Gaveston, a Gascon, was probably a few years older than the prince. Chroniclers speculated about the nature of the relationship that existed between the pair of them. The *Annales Paulini* claimed that Edward loved Gaveston 'beyond measure and reason'.[3] It was not alone:

> When the King's son saw him, he fell so much in love that he entered upon an enduring compact with him, and chose to knit an indissoluble bond of affection with him, before all other mortals.[4]

Gaveston had been appointed to Edward's household along with nine other royal wards by King Edward I as a suitable role model for his son but from 1300 until his death he became increasingly important in Edward's life. The tone is one of condemnation although the criticism is not an overt accusation of homosexuality. The *Lanercost Chronicle* was not so coy when it accused Edward of improper relations with Gaveston but was written with the benefit of hindsight. It also stated that 'the King of England, having married his (Philip IV of France) daughter, loved her indifferently because of the aforesaid Piers'.[5] In France, the *Chronicle of Meaux* recorded that Edward 'particularly delighted in the vice of sodomy'.[6] Current views about Edward's sexuality based on the available sources are divided. Rather than a homosexual relationship, Edward may have tied himself into a knightly brotherhood with Gaveston.

At the same time that some chronicles expressed concern about Edward's sexuality, others criticised him for consorting with harlots.[7] The prince did have an illegitimate son named Adam who was born around the same time as his formal betrothal to Isabella of France. One possibility is that Edward, experimenting with his sexuality, had a liaison with one of his stepmother's ladies. King Edward I had married Marguerite of France in September 1299. The prince was at Dover to welcome the bride and her ladies. He seems to have had a brief sexual encounter, possibly with Alice de la Croix, that resulted in Adam, Edward II's acknowledged son (King Edward I having died in 1307). He was listed as serving in Edward's Scottish campaign of 1322 and provision of arms was made for him. The young man became sick in Newcastle and was dead before the leaves fell that autumn. He was buried in Tynemouth Priory, his coffin shrouded in cloth provided by his father.

King Edward II travelled to France in January 1308 to meet his twelve-year-old bride and to marry her in Boulogne Cathedral before returning to England in February. Isabella, by all accounts a beautiful girl, was on the edge of womanhood and the daughter of a king with a punctilious regard for protocol. She grew up with the stories of Arthurian legend and continued to enjoy them throughout her life. She may have had expectations of her handsome husband which were quickly disappointed. Edward was more concerned with the fact that he had been separated from his favourite. He was met at Dover's dockside by Gaveston who had been appointed regent in the king's absence. Edward greeted Piers as though they had been separated for months. Trokelowe's chronicle reported that the king ran to his favourite kissing and embracing him. The problem lay not in the touching but in Edward's failure to greet his other barons in a similar fashion. It was not long afterwards that several influential members of the nobility demanded that Gaveston should be banished from the realm. Soon after her arrival in England, Isabella discovered Edward's favourite wearing some of the jewellery that formed part of her dowry. During her coronation, the king sat next to his favourite rather than his wife and even worse, rather than displaying her coat of arms during the feasting that followed, it was Gaveston's arms linked with the king's which adorned the walls. Isabella's uncles, Charles of Orleans and Louis of Evreux, were affronted by Edward's lack of respect for his bride. It swiftly became apparent that the king was more interested in his favourite than his wife who was aged only twelve. Matters were not helped when the king presented Gaveston with his stepmother's (Marguerite of France) properties at Hailes and Berkhamstead. Philip IV, offended by the treatment of his daughter and his sister, applied pressure on Edward as well as sending funds to those who sought to dismiss Gaveston from the king's presence. His father-in-law's coercion and his own nobility's demands eventually resulted in

Gaveston's removal. Edward circumvented his favourite's exile by sending him to Ireland as his Lieutenant. He also provided Piers with land in Gascony in compensation for land confiscated at the time of his exile to Ireland.

During the spring of 1309, with Gaveston absent in Ireland, Edward began to treat Isabella with more consideration. He gave her lands in Cheshire and North Wales together with revenue. Her dower lands were still held by her Aunt Marguerite, Edward I's second wife, but in time Isabella would become one of the country's largest landowners. The newfound felicity was not to last although Isabella was now to be found constantly at her husband's side. On 27 June 1309, Gaveston returned to England. By 5 August 1309, he was reinstated to the lands which had been confiscated during his exile. During the parliament held at Stamford the king promised to listen to the barons' grievances but by the following year, several barons were so angry that they refused to attend parliament if the king's favourite was present. Gaveston had learned nothing from his exile, instead he chose to alienate many earls by giving the most powerful of them insulting nicknames. He called the Earl of Warwick the 'Black Dog of Arden' and the Earl of Lincoln 'Burst-Belly' even worse he called his own brother-in-law the Earl of Gloucester 'whoreson' and 'cuckoo bird'[8] which cast aspersions on the morals of Edward's sister Joan of Acre who had been married at the age of twelve to Gilbert de Clare, Earl of Gloucester, who was thirty or so years older than her. The couple had four children before de Clare's death in 1295. The following year Joan secretly married her husband's squire Ralph de Monthermer having persuaded her father to knight him first. The insults made no difference to the king who continued to grant Gaveston land and favours.

When parliament met in February 1310, five earls including Lancaster and Warwick arrived armed and bearing a petition which listed their most recent grievances. Edward was forced to send Gaveston away for his own safety. On 16 March 1310, Edward, under duress, appointed a group of men to reform the royal household. The group of eight earls became known as the Lords Ordainers. When parliament sat in August the following year, the king was presented with the proposed reforms, the demand that Gaveston should be sent once more into exile and that, in future, royal grants should be subject to baronial consent. Edward's favourite left court on 3 November 1311 having been stripped of the earldom of Cornwall and given fifteen days to leave the country. Edward reluctantly agreed to the terms of the ordinances which stripped him of his favourite. Further regulations banning many of Gaveston's adherents from the king's company were passed later in the month. It made no difference, Gaveston was back at court, in York, early in the New Year along with his heavily pregnant wife Margaret. Edward once again revoked Gaveston's exile and returned all lands to him that had been confiscated at the time of his exile. The king was determined not to be ruled by his nobility so rescinded the ordinances. Isabella joined her husband in York and it was here that she conceived her first child.

By the end of March several barons including Edward's own cousin and Isabella's uncle, the Earl of Lancaster, had sworn to kill Gaveston and gathered an army. The king responded by ordering Henry Percy to hand over Scarborough Castle to his favourite. On 5 April, with the Scottish border guarded against Gaveston's escape, the king and his favourite fled north to Newcastle with Isabella. Lancaster's growing force was close behind. Edward, Gaveston and Isabella were trapped between the Scots and a rebel army. Lancaster arrived at Newcastle only to discover that whilst Isabella remained at Tynemouth Priory some six miles away, the king and Gaveston had escaped by sea on 4 May 1312. The king had abandoned most of his household, his pregnant wife and all his baggage in an attempt to save his favourite. The Trokelowe account of Edward's departure describes Isabella begging her husband not to desert her. There is no other corroborating evidence for this episode in the couple's relationship. Lancaster had sent messengers to his niece assuring her of her safety and the royal couple were reunited ten days later at York where Edward was in the process of raising troops.

Gaveston returned to Scarborough where he was besieged by the Earls of Surrey and Pembroke as well as Henry Percy and Lord Clifford. Lancaster's army situated between Scarborough and York prevented the king from going to his favourite's aid. He offered a thousand pounds to ensure Gaveston's continued safety. On 19 May, after a feisty defence, Gaveston surrendered to Aymer de Valence, Earl of Pembroke, who swore that he would be well looked after and given a fair trial. At first, he was placed in honourable captivity in York but by June his captors moved him south towards Wallingford. On 9 June, Pembroke left his prisoner under guard at Deddington Rectory, near Banbury, for the night so that he could spend some time with his own family. Historians are divided as to whether Pembroke purposefully created an opportunity for his captive to be placed in more hostile hands. The Earl of Warwick, the so-called Black Dog of Arden, took Gaveston as his own prisoner in Pembroke's absence early the following morning. A hastily arranged trial with Lancaster and Warwick sitting in judgement followed. On 19 June, Gaveston was executed at Blacklow Hill near Kenilworth by two Welshmen who ran him through before cutting off his head. A contemporary account of the capture, trial and death of Gaveston is contained in the *Vita Edwardi Secundi*. The *Lanercost Chronicle* wrote about the king's anger and his desire for vengeance.

Piers' body was taken to the Dominican Convent in Oxford where it remained unburied for the next two years until Edward was able to get Gaveston's excommunication by the Archbishop of Canterbury reversed. Once this was achieved, the body was moved to the royal manor of King's Langley where it was interred. The king never forgot Gaveston. Throughout his life, Edward paid for prayers to be said for Piers' soul as well as for rich decorations to ornament his tomb. The execution split the Lords Ordainers. Gaveston's judicial murder was an act of extreme violence against a royal favourite that the more moderate Ordainers felt to be excessive. It set in motion an invasion of the North of England by King Robert I and set in train the emergence of Hugh Despenser the Elder as a key supporter of the king. In time Hugh Despenser the Younger became Edward's new favourite. Edward neither forgot nor forgave the murder of Gaveston. It took him ten years before he was able to take his vengeance on the men responsible for the events on Blacklow Hill. Chroniclers recorded that the king turned a smooth face to his enemies but that England now hovered on the periphery of civil war whilst Edward bided his time.

In May 1313, peace restored, Isabella returned to France with her husband. King Edward wished to discuss Gascony with his father-in-law and to secure funds. The reason for Edward's marriage to Isabella lay in the province of Gascony which had come into the possession of the English Crown with Eleanor of Aquitaine. The Treaty of Paris signed in 1259 stated that Gascony remained English with the provision that the king did homage to the French for the lands. The English found it demeaning and the French objected to the amount of territory that the English held. Latent territorial conflict focusing on Gascony erupted into violence on several occasions throughout the period. On 7 June, Edward missed a meeting with Philip IV because he overslept. Godefroy of Paris was unsurprised. He noted that Isabella was the 'fairest of the fair'.[9] He concluded his commentary with a written remark more akin to a nudge and a wink. During the amusements that followed the negotiations, Edward and Isabella were entertained by fifty-four naked dancers. The king gave them a gift of two pounds. On another occasion, Isabella's brothers Louis and Charles gave a puppet show for their guests. Afterwards, Isabella presented her sisters-in-law with embroidered purses.

Previously, in 1305, Louis, dauphin of France and King of Navarre, married Margaret, the daughter of Robert II of Burgundy. In 1308, his youngest brother Charles married Margaret's cousin, Blanche of Burgundy, the younger daughter of Otto IV of Burgundy and Mahaut of Artois. Blanche was eleven years old at the time of the marriage. Philip IV had been unable to resist the dowry that Blanche's mother Mahaut offered to make the match. Louis and Charles' brother Philip had married Blanche's elder sister Joan, the Countess of Burgundy, in 1307. All three marriages were diplomatic unions and part of Philip IV's calculated plan to extend the prestige of the French monarchy by bringing Burgundy under his direct control as well as the county of Artois. Louis, known as the Quarreller, preferred sport to his wife's company. Charles had little time for his wife who was barely out of childhood. The three women formed their own court circle and attempted to make the best of their dynastic marriages in much the same way that Isabella had been expected to make her own marriage to Edward II work.

Isabella returned home to England in July. She and Edward gave a feast at Westminster. They were attended by a group of French knights who accompanied the English court back home. During the course of the evening, Isabella noticed the embroidered purses that she gave to Margaret and Blanche being worn on the belts of brothers Gautier and Philip D'Aunay. Isabella considered why the purses might have changed hands and concluded that the knights were having illicit affairs with her sisters-in-law. It is likely that she found additional evidence to confirm her suspicions as the gift of the purses themselves was not proof of guilt in an era when the etiquette of courtly love required the giving of favours by unattainable women to their chivalrous admirers. For the time being, Isabella remained silent about her suspicions.

In January 1314, news arrived at court that Blanche had given birth to a son named Philip. Given Isabella's doubts, she may have wondered whether her brother was the father of the child. The House of Capet had ruled France since the tenth century and now there was a possibility that one of its heirs was a cuckoo in the nest. It was a disturbing thought for a young woman raised with the idea of sacred royal duty. Her own mother Joan was a role model to which to aspire. The Queen of Navarre in her own right, Joan was raised in France and married Philip in 1284 becoming Queen of France the following year at the age of twelve. The couple enjoyed a close relationship. When Philip IV left his wife as regent of France in October 1294, he wrote of Joan that 'the queen is known for her faith, her tried fidelity, and the zeal of her innate affection'.[10]

The *Speculum Dominarum* or Mirror of Ladies was written as a manual for Joan by her confessor, a Dominican friar named Durand of Champagne. Joan understood from the text that whilst men and women were essentially unworthy, that it was necessary for a queen to acquire wisdom and to use that wisdom to strengthen her family. Isabella's education taught her that a queen must be a role model for her people and her sisters-in-law had behaved in a wholly inappropriate way. In March, Isabella returned to France to present petitions concerning Gascony to her father on behalf of Edward. She arrived in Paris on 19 March, the day after her godfather, Jacques de Molay, the Grand Master of the Knights Templar, was burned to death along with Geoffrey de Charney, the Preceptor for Normandy for the Knights Templar, on the Ile de Cite. The crimes that they, and all the Templars in France, had been convicted of seven years previously were heresy, blasphemy, sodomy and financial corruption but in reality, Isabella's father was behind the unfounded accusations. He was deeply in debt to the Templars and with the support of Pope Clement V took the opportunity to seize the order's wealth for himself. Molay and de Charney confessed under torture but then recanted so were burned alive as lapsed heretics. As smouldering flames licked around him sending him to an agonising death, Molay was said to have cursed the Pope, King Philip and his family.

It must have felt as though the grand master's curse was taking effect when Isabella first shared her suspicions with her father. The moral degeneracy of which he accused the Templars was alive in his own family. He arranged for his daughters-in-law to be watched. By the end of April Isabella was back in Dover. As she arrived, scandal engulfed the French court. Philip IV's agents discovered that Margaret and Blanche had been conducting adulterous affairs with the brothers d'Aulnay at the Tour de Nesle situated on the bank of Seine, opposite the Louvre. The cousins had been entertaining their lovers with evenings of food and wine. Whilst it was acceptable for kings and princes to indulge their passions, royal women were expected to be virtuous. Margaret and Blanche's affairs placed the succession in jeopardy. No one could know whether any children they might have belonged to their husbands or their lovers.

King Philip ordered the arrest of all the suspects; the two adulterous couples and Blanche's sister Joan who was initially accused of being complicit in the affairs but later also accused of adultery. One of the brothers d'Aulnay fled to England but was captured and returned to France where he was tortured. Both brothers confessed to their guilt. They admitted that the affairs were in their third year. Both men were sentenced to death and their property confiscated by the Crown. Margaret and Blanche were also questioned. The Queen of Navarre admitted to leading her cousin astray but it is thought that Blanche never admitted to any wrong-doing. They were tried by the French parliament behind closed doors. In May they were sentenced. Margaret was convicted of adultery. She was stripped of her finery, dressed in sackcloth, her hair was shorn off and then she was sent to the grim fortress, Chateau-Gaillard, for the rest of her life. The same fate befell her cousin Blanche. Both of them were subject to ill-treatment. Margaret was kept at the top of a high tower open to the elements, with no bedding and little food whilst Blanche was incarcerated in an underground cell.

Joan, with the support of her husband, was cleared of adultery but held under house arrest at Dourdan near Paris for several months. She had known of the affairs but not reported them. Nonetheless, she continued to protest her innocence. Her case was helped by the fact that her husband refused to renounce her. Joan's mother, Mahaut, who was her regent in Burgundy also supported her daughter's case. The following year after King Philip IV's death, she was cleared of any crimes by the Paris parliament and allowed to return to court. Joan became Queen of France in 1316 when her husband became King Philip V. Following his death in 1322, she retired to her own domains for the rest of her life.

Before Margaret and Blanche were taken to Chateau-Gaillard in Normandy, the king ordered that they should be taken to Pontoise, to the north of Paris. There, they were made to witness their lovers' deaths. Gautier and Philip were publicly castrated and their private parts thrown to the dogs. Then they were partially flayed alive. Molten lead was poured onto their skin before their tortured bodies were strapped to a wheel and their bones broken with metal bars. At the end of their torment, they were beheaded. Their corpses remained on public display as a warning of what befell men who became amorously entangled with royal wives.

On 29 November 1314, Philip IV died from a stroke whilst hunting. He was forty-six years old. It seemed that God had avenged the deaths of the Templars. Margaret's husband succeeded to the throne as King Louis X. He needed to secure the succession. The legitimacy of his only surviving child, Joan, was suspect because of Margaret's affair. Although Margaret had been found to be adulterous, the pope had not yet granted an annulment to the marriage which meant that Louis was unable to remarry and beget an heir. Perhaps unsurprisingly, soon after Louis became king, Margaret was found dead in her cell. She had been strangled although other sources state that she caught a cold because of her poor treatment and died. Five days later, on 19 August 1315, King Louis married Clemence of Hungary who swiftly became pregnant. Louis did not have long to enjoy his reign or his new wife. He died from pleurisy or pneumonia the following year. At the time, blame was placed on drinking chilled wine after a game of real tennis. His son, John, was born posthumously on 15 November 1316 but lived only five days. Both Louis' brothers wore the crown in their turn and both were dead within the decade without male heirs.

Sources place the birth of Margaret's daughter, Joan, somewhere between 1309 and 1312. Realistically she was a toddler of some two years at the time of her mother's adultery trial. The problem was that no one could say with certainty whether Louis or Margaret's lover was the child's father. As a consequence of the trial, Joan was deemed to be illegitimate but as he lay dying Louis declared that she was his legitimate daughter. Joan later became the Queen of Navarre even though her paternity had been under doubt. However, her uncle Philip was able to secure the French crown for himself after John I's death, bypassing Joan by the use of a law which allowed males to inherit land whilst women could only

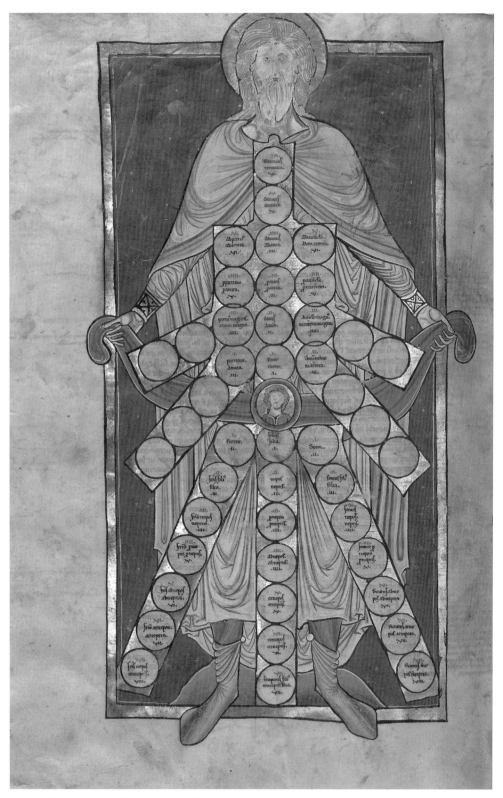

Table of Consanguinity (illumination). (*Getty Center, Public domain, via Wikimedia Commons*)

Is this Edith Swanneck? Bayeux Tapestry – a house is burned by the Normans (wool embroidery on linen). (*Musée de la Tapisserie, Bayeux. Bridgeman Images*)

Falaise Castle. (*Ollamh*)

Peverel Castle. (*The author*)

Robert, Earl of Gloucester, one of King Henry I's illegitimate sons (carved fireplace relief, Cardiff Castle). (*Wolfgang Sauber*)

Osney Abbey, near Oxford, as it appeared in 1640.

Engraved for the Engraving in the Londonensis 1807.

Oseney Abbey founded by Robert D'Oyly the younger on the prompting of Edith Forne Sigulfson.

Eleanor of Aquitaine's effigy at Fontrevault. (Adam Bishop, Public Domain via Wikimedia Commons)

Fair Rosamund, J.W. Waterhouse (oil on canvas, 1917). (*The Pictures Now Image Collection / Mary Evans Picture Library*)

Full-page miniature of lovers walking in a garden, in April, fol 5v. (illumination, circa 1500). (*The New York Public Library, Look and Learn*)

Isabella of Angoulême by W. H. Mote (engraving, nineteenth century) after an illustration by J.W. Wright. (*Public Domain via Wikimedia*)

Matilda FitzWalter, alabaster effigy in the Priory Church at Little Dunmow. (*Hornbeam Arts via Flickr*)

Philip IV and his children (from l. to r. Philip V, Charles IV, Isabella, Louis X and Charles of Valois). (*Alamy*)

Illustration pour la Tour de Nesle: une orgie, Octave Nicholas Francois Tassert, (drawing, nineteenth century). (*Musée Carnavalet, Public domain via Look and Learn*)

King Edward II, alabaster effigy in Gloucester Cathedral. (*Poliphilo, Public Domain via Wikimedia Commons*)

Alice Perrers at the deathbed of King Edward III (illustration, nineteenth century).

Elizabeth Woodville (print, circa 1800). (*Public Domain via Llyfrgell Genedlaethol Cymru – The National Library of Wales*)

The meeting of Elizabeth Woodville and King Edward IV. (Public Domain via British Library and Look and Learn)

F. Bartolozzi R.A. Sculpt.

JANE SHORE,

Give gentle mistress Shore one gentle kiss the more"

King Rich.ᵈ III. Act 3. Sc. I.

London Pubⁱ. as the Act directs Feb². 1.1790. by E. Harding Nº. 132 Fleet Street.

Jane Shore 'Give gentle Mistress Shore one gentle kiss the more' (print, 1790), Francesco Bartolozzi, Harris Brisbane Dick Fund, 1917. (*The Metropolitan Museum of Art*) inherit personal belongings. This fifth-century legal code became known as salic law.

Blanche lingered in her prison cell for the next decade. She remained married to her husband Charles because the Pope refused to grant an annulment. King Philip IV had been careful to gain a papal dispensation from Pope Celestine V on 12 November 1294, which allowed his children to marry any relation in the third or fourth degree. In addition, Philip had acquired a dispensation in 1307 for Charles' marriage to Blanche as they were legally and spiritually related by their siblings' marriage. Blanche eventually gave birth to an illegitimate child in prison thought to be fathered by one of her goalers although the *Chronicle of Guillaume de Nangis* reported that she was made pregnant by her own husband. The arrival of the illegitimate child seems to have prompted the Pope to act. When Philip V died in 1322 and Charles became king, Blanche effectively became Queen of France as the papacy had not yet granted an annulment to her marriage. Witnesses to the marriage were summoned. The evidence demonstrated that Blanche's mother, Mahaut of Artois, drove the marriage negotiations with an offer of a 10,000l dowry, more than twice the value of Marguerite of Burgundy's, which Philip IV found irresistible. The marriage was celebrated at Corbeil in 1308, a week before Isabella married King Edward II. Questions now arose about whether or not Blanche's wedding had been clandestine as no banns had been called prior to the ceremony. Even if the marriage had been completed without all forms of legality being adhered to it would not have invalidated the union as the promise of marriage followed by intercourse would have been sufficient. The marriage was finally dissolved on 19 May 1322 by Pope John XXII on grounds of spiritual consanguinity rather than the embarrassing arrival of an illegitimate child.

Blanche's mother continued to correspond with her daughter throughout her imprisonment and on occasion sent her gifts. Now she demanded the return of Blanche's dowry from the French. Blanche was allowed to become a nun at the Cistercian Abbey of Maubisson, near Pontoise, but her years of ill-treatment had broken her health.

When Charles IV died without a male heir, the Capetian line of kings came to an end as predicted by Maloy. The two contenders for the throne were Philip of Valois, Charles' nephew and Isabella's son, King Edward III of England. The French claimed that Isabella could not inherit the

Crown or pass a claim to a male heir because of the salic law which Isabella's brother Philip V invoked after the death of their brother Louis X in order to succeed to the throne in place of Louis' daughter, Joan. Philip of Valois became King Philip VI. The decision resulted in the Hundred Years War. Edward III invaded France in 1337.

Isabella returned to England as the scandal that came to be known as the Tour de Nesle affair began to unfold and two of her sisters-in-law were condemned. At home, Edward continued to have male favourites including Roger Damory, Hugh Audley and William Montacute. Isabella tolerated them as she had tolerated Piers Gaveston. As a wife, even a royal one, it was her duty to be submissive to her husband's wishes. The *Mirror* stipulated that a queen was the subject of her husband. She was careful not to let any dislike for his favourites become public knowledge. In August, she fulfilled her role as a medieval queen and provided her husband with a second son. Edward gave the messenger who carried the news to him in York £100 and ordered a gown to be made from five pieces of white velvet for his wife. In total, the couple would have four children. As time passed Isabella played a more important part in her husband's life and, until the final years of their marriage, enjoyed a loving relationship. She also gained a reputation as a diplomat and mediator between her husband and his barons. History does not record whether or not she ever considered the fates of the three young women who had once been her sisters-in-law.

Chapter 15

Hugh Despenser, Roger Mortimer, Unhappy Marriages and the Further Consequences of Adultery

Medieval kings married their kinfolk off to extend their power base or to tie their nobility closer to them. Edward continued the pattern he established at the beginning of his reign of marrying his female relations to his male favourites to promote their interests rather than those of the Crown. In 1317, he arranged that Roger Damory and Hugh Audley should marry two of his cousins who became co-heiresses with the death of their brother Gilbert de Clare, Earl of Gloucester. The earl was killed at the Battle of Bannockburn in 1314. His wife, Maud, insisted that she was pregnant so there was the possibility of a posthumous male heir. Almost three years later Edward II put an end to Maud's pretended pregnancy and divided the estates between Margaret, Elizabeth and Eleanor de Clare. Eleanor was already married to Hugh Despenser the Younger but Margaret and Elizabeth were both widows. Damory, a knight, was considerably below Elizabeth in status but the king was determined that they should marry and Elizabeth was forced to agree. Once again Edward's favourites were becoming dominant at court and once again the country teetered on the brink of civil war.

Meanwhile, Isabella's own marital situation was becoming increasingly complex. Eleanor de Clare married Hugh Despenser the Younger in 1306. By 1308 she was one of Isabella's ladies-in-waiting and in 1317 her share of the Gloucester estates made her Lady Glamorgan in her own right. At about the same time Hugh began to rise in the king's affections. He was the son of the only baron who remained loyal to Edward throughout his entire life and he was also part of the extended royal family. Unfortunately for Eleanor's sisters and for Queen Isabella herself, Despenser was a man who had no intention of sharing wealth or power with anyone else. Chroniclers described him as another Gaveston, that he controlled who had access to the king's chamber whilst the *Scalacronica* described him as 'debauched'.[1]

Despenser set about using his power with the king to act above the law and to extend his Welsh lands into the Gower. The Marcher Lords of South Wales were furious when Despenser persuaded the king that John Mowbray had no right to take possession of the Gower which had been in the possession of his own aged father-in-law William Braose. Hugh, a capable administrator, argued that Mowbray required a royal licence to enter into possession of the lands and that consequently, the territory should be forfeit to the king. The Marcher barons took the view that royal writ did not run on the borders. It was a privilege that came from maintaining a safe border against the Welsh. As a consequence of their determination to keep their centuries-old freedoms and to bring Despenser down, the year 1320 saw the beginnings of the so-called Despenser War led by Humphrey de Bohun, Earl of Hereford and Roger Mortimer of Wigmore. Violence erupted on 4 May 1321 and by early summer Edward was considering sending his favourite overseas for his own safety. On 29 July an army from the Welsh marches arrived outside London demanding that the Despensers should be banished from England and that their lands and titles should be declared forfeit. As their anger at the king's prevarication escalated the rebels threatened to depose the king himself but Edward continued to refuse to rid himself of his favourites. Finally, Isabella pleaded, on her knees, that Edward should exile the two men for the greater good of his realm and he agreed because he was afraid of civil war. Hugh Despenser the Younger was exiled in August. The king was also required to pardon the rebels. Later he would protest that he might have agreed outwardly to the banishment of his friends but that he had never inwardly capitulated to the rebels' demands nor did any pardons he made under duress retain their validity once the situation was stabilised.

Edward had no intention of permitting either of the Despensers to languish in exile. By September 1321 the king was plotting the return of his favourites and the downfall of the barons who opposed him. His own popularity continued to wane. He waited until many of the barons were attending a tournament in Witney. Amongst them was Bartholomew Bradlesmere, a half-hearted supporter of the Earl of Lancaster, the king's cousin. Edward began his campaign by seizing Dover Castle and forbidding Bradlesmere from returning to Kent. Bradlesmere ignored this command and ordered that all his castles should be placed on a war footing. Amongst the castles in Kent which now shut their gates was Leeds Castle. This was part of the queen's dower but it was also Bradlesmere's principal residence as he was its governor. Meanwhile, Queen Isabella who did not like Hugh Despencer the Younger, the Earl of Lancaster or challenges to royal authority, made a pilgrimage to Canterbury and returned to London via Leeds Castle where she demanded that Bradlesmere's wife Margaret de Clare should admit her late in the evening of 2 October. Margaret refused to open the gates to the royal party. When Isabella ordered her heavily armed escort to attack, the baroness gave her archers orders to fire on the queen's men – which was an act of treason. The next morning Isabella sent a message to her husband at Porchester where he awaited the return of Hugh Despenser the Younger. By the following week, Edward had raised a royal levy and placed Leeds Castle under siege. Isabella joined her husband who was now at Rochester where she was given control of the Great Seal demonstrating Edward's trust in his wife.

Leeds Castle surrendered and Baroness Bradlesmere found herself imprisoned in Dover Castle before being transferred to the Tower of London where she remained for the next year. The hanging of thirteen of Leeds Castle's garrison was an indication that Edward's patience with his nobility was at an end. Within months the king turned the tables on the rebellious Marcher lords and upon his hated cousin, the Earl of Lancaster. The king commanded his army with a skill that surprised his enemies. At the beginning of 1322, the king's army secured the bridge at Shrewsbury cutting the Mortimers off from the Earl of Lancaster. In February 1322, the king was at Cirencester when the Earl of Hereford, an Ordainer and ally of Lancaster, besieged Tickhill Castle. As the king marched northwards, Lancaster joined with Hereford and the two opposing armies met at Burton-on-Trent. It took the king three days to find a way across the river but when he did his opponents were heavily outnumbered. Lancaster retreated to Pontefract before continuing northwards in the direction of Dunstanburgh where he hoped Scottish assistance would be forthcoming.

The rebels were trapped at the River Ure by Andrew Harclay and an army loyal to the king raised from the levies in Cumberland and

Westmorland. Lancaster either had to turn and face the king's army or force his way across the river and the army led by Harclay. The Earl of Hereford was killed on the bridge as he rushed at his enemy. Lancaster recognised that he was defeated and spent one last night of freedom in Boroughbridge before Harclay's men swept across the bridge the following morning. They found Lancaster inside the church but instead of respecting the sanctuary which the earl claimed, Lancaster was dragged outside, stripped of his finery and sent to York. The Sheriff of Cumberland's victory against the rebel barons on 16 March 1322, at the Battle of Boroughbridge, resulted in the collapse of opposition to the king and his favourites.

Having waited ten years to be revenged against him, Edward ensured that Lancaster was executed for treason 'like any thief or vilest rascal'[2] and all the men who rebelled against him were punished. Mortimer and his uncle submitted to the king and were sent to the Tower. He also ordered the arrest of the wives and children of the rebels. Three of Roger Mortimer's daughters were sent to Sempringham Priory but were eventually released. Joan, the mother of Mortimer's twelve children, was arrested at her home in Ludlow and remained in captivity for the rest of Edward's reign. On 14 July 1322, Mortimer was sentenced to death along with his uncle Roger Mortimer of Chirk. A week later the sentence was commuted to life imprisonment. The reasons behind the king's change of heart are unclear but it is certain that Hugh Despenser the Younger, who hated the Mortimer clan, would not have countenanced the change in sentence. Mortimer of Chirk died in the Tower whilst in custody during 1326. Roger Mortimer escaped from his prison on 1 August 1323, with the aid of accomplices, by drugged wine given to his guards and a rope stretching out across the moat and down to the Thames. He fled to France having discovered that the king intended to have him executed. Sixteenth-century dramatists including Christopher Marlowe speculated that Isabella may have had a hand in Mortimer's getaway but there is no evidence that the pair had any significant encounters prior to the baron's escape and Isabella's own arrival in France. His daring breakout, combined with the death of the Earl of Lancaster, made Mortimer the main focus for opposition to Edward and the Despensers.

Royal rule in England became harsher and more brutal. Despenser, thuggish and land-hungry, treated the widows of the men who rebelled against the king unforgivingly. He was even accused of breaking the limbs of Joan Gynes, widow of Stephen Baret, until she became insane. The torture of Joan was described at the time of his trial in 1326. When Despenser forced his sister-in-law to relinquish valuable lordships the king did nothing to protect her even though she was his niece. Instead, Despenser regained the position of royal chamberlain that had been stripped from him at the time of his exile, received valuable gifts and even had a royal ship, *La Despenser*, named after him. To many, it felt as though Despenser and his father were invulnerable.

Isabella's relationship with her husband deteriorated. She refused to have Despenser or his men anywhere near her. In the autumn of 1322, after the king's disastrous Scottish campaign, nearly resulted in her capture by invading Scots at Tynemouth. It was only the quick thinking of her own household squires that saved her from capture but as the queen and her ladies boarded the ship that would carry them to safety one woman was killed and a second would die later from her injuries. In 1326, it became clear that Isabella held Despenser personally responsible for the situation that her household found itself in during their harrowing escape along the coast. The animosity between Edward's wife and his favourite grew. Isabella who had once been Edward's constant companion found herself living a separate life as Despenser began to move against her. She was the last threat to the Despensers' political dominance over the king. Although she was still a young woman, she and the king had no more children suggesting that they no longer slept together. The queen would later describe Despenser as being an intruder in her marriage and that he had broken the bonds of affection between husband and wife. It might simply be that Despenser poisoned Edward's mind or it could be a thinly veiled reference to a homosexual relationship.

The *Chronographia Regnum Francorum*, not known for its reliability, accused Edward of homosexuality and also of having an affair with his own niece, Eleanor de Clare, the wife of Hugh Despenser. The chronicle's only proof of the incestuous relationship was that Edward gave some of the Earl of Lancaster's land to Eleanor but none to Isabella. The queen benefited from none of the spoils taken after Boroughbridge. By February 1326, Isabella complained that Hugh wished to dishonour her in every possible way. Froissart's *Chronicles* stated that Despenser's evil intent ensured that Edward refused to spend any time in Isabella's company. Of all the king's favourites, Isabella hated Despenser more than any other.

Matters were not helped when Isabella's brother Philip V began building a fort at a site in the English-held village of St-Sardos in Gascony. In October 1323, the French flag was driven into the ground at the location effectively staking a claim to the land. Edward's officers in Gascony responded immediately by burning the flag, killing the man who planted it and destroying the village. Ralph Basset, Edward's steward in Gascony, refused to appear before the French parliament to justify his actions. The conflict and Edward's refusal to do homage for his French lands ensured that Isabella's influence with her husband was reduced still further. When France went to war with England over Gascony in July 1324, Despenser persuaded Edward to treat his wife as an enemy alien and to confiscate her lands in September leaving her, according to the Lanercost chronicler, only 'twenty shillings a day for herself and her whole court'.[3] This happened after she refused to swear an oath of loyalty to Despenser. Shortly afterwards, Isabella's three younger children were removed from her custody on the grounds that she might encourage them to rebel against their father because she was a Frenchwoman. Her two daughters, Eleanor and Joan, were sent to live with Despenser's sister Isabella and her husband Ralph de Monthermer whilst her son John remained in Hugh Despenser's custody. It was normal for royal children to have their own households and governors appointed for their care and education. The men and women chosen by the king to care for his children were part of his own extended family but it did not help that Despenser was involved. The queen was left in even greater isolation when her French servants were sent away and threatened with imprisonment. Eleanor Despenser, Hugh's wife, one of Isabella's ladies was described by the *Lanercost Chronicle* as spying on her and monitoring the queen's correspondence.

The queen hid her increasing dissatisfaction. Unlike her sisters-in-law in France, she had remained loyal to her husband despite the existence of his male favourites throughout their marriage. In December 1324, the last Christmastide that Edward and Isabella might have spent together, the king announced that Isabella would leave court to travel throughout the kingdom on pilgrimage until the following autumn. It is unclear whether Isabella put the miles between the king and herself or whether Edward sent her away. In the same year, Pope John XXII suggested that Isabella go to France on Edward's behalf to negotiate for a cessation in hostilities. The following year, Isabella's brother, Charles IV, also suggested that Isabella negotiate with him on Edward's behalf about the situation in Gascony and that honour could be restored if Edward's eldest son paid homage for Gascony and Ponthieu. Parliament supported the proposal although the king's council protested at the idea of sending the heir to the throne to France. For Edward, the suggestion resolved a problem. He did not wish to go to France as it would leave his favourites in England unprotected from their increasing numbers of enemies.

When she left England on 9 March 1325, Isabella continued to maintain a friendly face to her husband but by the time she was due to return to England that midsummer she had arrived at the conclusion that the time for meekness was over. She would not re-cross the Channel until the Despensers were removed from power. She fulfilled her role as Edward's negotiator and brokered a peace settlement which defused tensions in Gascony even if it did mean that her husband lost his territories of Gascony until he performed the necessary homage due from a vassal. Modern historians are divided as to whether she contrived to have the Prince of Wales sent to her or the extent to which she considered toppling her husband from the throne before the autumn of 1326. She remained in France for her brother's wedding to Jeanne of Evreux. Later rumours would surface that in the queen's absence Edward sought support to annul his marriage. The *Lanercost Chronicle* reported the rumours that Despenser 'was exerting himself at the Pope's court to procure divorce between the King of England and the queen'.[4] Whether the rumours were true or if Isabella knew of them is another matter. However, she now suggested that the Prince of Wales could fulfil the duty of homage to his uncle for Gascony. Isabella and Edward's eldest son left England on 12 September 1325.

As her stay in Paris lengthened, Isabella became a focal point for men who were dissatisfied with Edward II's rule. There were men who fled England after the Battle of Boroughbridge, men with scores to settle against the Despensers and the Earl of Richmond, who was the English envoy in Paris, made himself an opponent of Edward II by supporting the queen. Even the Earl of Kent, the king's half-brother, who was the military governor of Gascony sided with Isabella for a time. In November the king stopped paying his wife's expenses in the hope that it would force her to return to England with their son. As her finances became more constrained, Isabella borrowed money and began to negotiate with Count William of Hainault with a view to one of his daughter's marrying the heir to the English throne.

William of Hainault's wife Jeanne travelled to France. It is likely that the king's enemy Roger Mortimer was in her train. Hainault was in the midst of a trade dispute with England and it is probable that Mortimer approached William for support. The *Monasticon Anglicorum* claimed that Mortimer also had the backing of Charles of Valois, the uncle of Philip V and Isabella. Prior to her arrival in France, Isabella had minimal contact with Mortimer although he needed the queen to back his cause.

King Edward repeatedly demanded that his wife return home but Isabella, wearing widow's weeds, said that someone, meaning Despenser had come between them. There was a third person 'trying to break this bond'[5] of marriage. Safely in France under the protection of her brother, Isabella demanded that Edward should send Despenser away from court, restore her lands and permit her to assume her rightful position as queen. Did Isabella rebel against her husband at this stage? Or was she hoping to force him to rid himself of the hated Despensers? Edward refused to send his favourites away but Isabella's difficulties at home engendered popular sympathy whilst the king and his favourites became increasingly unpopular.

As the king applied more diplomatic pressure on Philip not to provide shelter or financial support for his sister, Isabella drew closer to Mortimer. Isabella needed Mortimer to lead the army which would destroy the Despensers. It was meant to be a political alliance. Both of them hated the king's favourites and shared an interest in Arthurian legend. The pair were attracted to one another and despite the fates of Margaret and Blanche, her own sisters-in-law, Isabella had begun a passionate affair with the rebel baron by December 1325. Whatever the provocation for her actions, Isabella's royal milieu did not lend itself to blatant infidelity. Pope John XXII challenged her behaviour at the time, whilst later writers turned her into a 'she-wolf' because she failed to be a good wife.

Contemporary chronicles initially turned a blind eye to the liaison despite the fact that for a queen to commit adultery was a grievous sin. On 8 February 1326, the king announced that the queen had 'given herself up to the counsel of Mortimer'.[6] He accused her of keeping his company 'in and out of house'[7] which was a euphemism for sexual misconduct. By then the French were prepared to commit finances to an invasion of England. Nonetheless, propriety needed to be maintained. Mortimer was seen once too often at Isabella's side. In May 1326, Charles' new wife, Jeanne of Evreux, was crowned. Isabella and Edward of Windsor were invited but Mortimer was there as well, carrying the prince's train. The king assumed the role of wronged husband in his communications to Charles IV and wrote to Prince Edward berating him for his association with a rebel. He also wrote to Isabella telling her that it was her duty as his wife 'to be in his company and obey his commands'.[8] The queen still refused to return home and wrote to the Archbishop of Canterbury to say that she wished more than anything else to be with her husband but that Hugh Despenser was responsible for the breakdown in the union. Whilst kings could have their lovers and favourites, queens could not be so blatant in their disregard of their marriage vows. Pope John XXII now spoke out against Isabella and French support for the English queen and her lover faded. Charles considered handing Isabella back to her husband. His own adulterous wife, Blanche, had been humiliated and imprisoned by his and Isabella's father in 1314 whilst he and his brothers were mocked for their failure to keep their own wives satisfied. Like Edward, he had been publicly declared a cuckold. Was it possible that Charles regarded his sister's behaviour, whatever the provocation, as hypercritical? Her actions were once again bringing the Capet family into disrepute. Or might his cooling relationship have had more to do with the bribes that arrived from England? In either case, Isabella and Mortimer were forced to go to Hainault where Count William, assured that one of his daughters would marry the heir to the English throne, provided ships for an invasion.

Meanwhile, the Pope wrote to Edward warning him that he should send away any obstacles to a reconciliation with his wife but Edward, when forced to choose between his wife and his favourite, chose Despenser. The summer of 1326 was not a good one for King Edward or Hugh Despenser. In England, there were rumours of treachery and spies. One of their key supporters, Robert Sapy, was horribly murdered. His eyes were put out and his limbs were broken before he was finally killed. Adversaries of the Despencers attacked royal officials and manors. Relations with the Scots deteriorated once more. In Hainault, Isabella was intent upon invasion and in France, Charles IV began the re-occupation of Gascony claiming that he was protecting his nephew's rights. At the end of August, Edward of Windsor was betrothed to Philippa of Hainault without his father's consent. The queen, her eldest son, her lover and a fleet of ships arrived off Orwell in Suffolk on 24 September. By 27 September word arrived in London of her arrival and Edward II ordered that the men of Essex should be arrayed against the invaders. He also offered a £1,000 reward for Mortimer's head. The Essex levies did not assemble, popular sympathy still lay with Isabella. Henry of Lancaster took up his brother's mantle and rallied to the queen as did many other barons with a grudge against the Despensers.

The king and Despenser fled west to Wales at the beginning of October. Part of their reasoning was that the Mortimers were unpopular there and they hoped to garner support. Up until then, the City of London had stood by the king. After his flight, Isabella's appeal for them to bring down the Despensers resulted in the storming of the Tower. The queen proclaimed that she wanted to be rid of Hugh Despenser so that she and the king could be reconciled with one another. Her declaration accused the king's favourite of damaging the realm and the Church as well as the royal marriage. Meanwhile, Isabella was greeted as the nation's saviour. Despenser the Elder was taken captive at Bristol where he was arraigned for treason on 22 October. Isabella pleaded for his life but the Lancastrian component of her army demanded his death. He was executed for treason. Afterwards, his head was sent to be displayed in Winchester while the rest of his body was fed to dogs. Isabella travelled into the Marches where she set up court at Hereford. After a council meeting, it was announced that since Edward II had fled his own kingdom, Prince Edward would be designated *Custos*. Since he was a minor, the new Keeper of the Kingdom needed a regent – Isabella. Meanwhile, rumours flickered like flames across the country. Some people believed that the queen was acting for the welfare of the kingdom, others that she had betrayed her husband. Everyone agreed that Hugh Despenser was the embodiment of an evil counsellor who had done wicked things.

The fear was that if Edward and Despenser reached Ireland they would be able to recruit an army and plunge England back into civil war. However, they were unable to cross the Bristol Channel because of an unfavourable wind. They spent some time at Caerphilly Castle before moving to Margam Abbey, near modern Port Talbot. The king, his favourite and a small band of men loyal to him were finally cornered on 16 November in a wood near Llantrisant. The king was taken to Kenilworth Castle whilst Despenser was taken to Hereford on an old nag with his coat of arms reversed. The abatement imposed by his captors spoke of the stain upon his honour so far as they were concerned. Someone forced a crown of nettles onto his head. Whenever they passed a settlement people emerged from their houses and workplaces to throw things at the fallen favourite. He refused food in an attempt to starve himself to death. The decision was taken to prosecute him in the Marches rather than to move him to London. Despenser went on trial at Hereford on 24 November although he was given no opportunity to defend himself. Just as royal mistresses often suffered moral outrage because of a monarch's lusts, on this occasion Edward's favourite became the scapegoat for the mismanagement of the kingdom, the death of Thomas of Lancaster and the breakdown of Isabella's marriage amongst other charges. The outcome of the trial had never been in doubt.

Once again adorned with a crown of nettles, his coat of arms reversed and exposed to mockery, Despenser's final hours began with verses from the Old Testament tattooed or carved into his torso and arms. Then he was tied to a hurdle and dragged to the town square where he was hanged, drawn and quartered without delay. Isabella was amongst the jeering crowd as Despenser was strung up on the specially built gallows before being cut down and butchered while he was still conscious. His head, parboiled and dipped in pitch, was displayed on London Bridge. Isabella's revenge included having three of the hated favourite's daughters, the youngest aged just four, taken to separate nunneries where they were forcibly veiled. The queen was still in possession of Edward II's Great Seal. Her actions, including the imprisonment of her husband, were entirely legal.

By the end of the year, there were discussions not only about the deposition of the king but also his execution. On 12 January 1327, Isabella told parliament that she could no longer consider a return to her husband. The Articles of Deposition stated that the king was not fit to rule because he was 'led and ruled by others'.[9] The king, now plain Sir Edward of Caernarfon was forced to give his throne to his teenage son who became King Edward III on 1 February 1327. Roger

Mortimer was in the ascendant but the lovers were not free to marry even if Edward were to die. Joan Mortimer, Roger's wife, had remained in Edward II's custody since Roger's imprisonment in the Tower. She had initially been placed under house arrest in Hampshire but was removed from there to Skipton Castle where she was placed in a cell. In July 1326 she was transferred to Pontefract Castle. Imprisoned for five years she now regained her freedom but there was no happy reunion with her husband who was now the most powerful man in the country, in part due to his affair with the queen. The marriage to Joan had made Mortimer wealthy as well as an influential figure in the marches but as Isabella's lover, Mortimer had access to the young king which enabled him to bypass the regency council. Joan returned home without her husband. In 1328, when two of Mortimer's daughters were married Joan found herself in the unenviable position of her husband and his royal mistress staying with her at Ludlow Castle. There was a similar celebration the following year that included a Round Table enactment with Mortimer as a latter-day Arthur.

Isabella, a queen, was expected to live by higher moral standards than the king and his nobility. Isabella had been a much-loved royal consort who was recognised for her political intelligence but now as co-regents, she and Mortimer made the regency council led by Henry, Earl of Lancaster, redundant by their close control of the young king. Isabella's husband was handed into the custody of Thomas, Lord Berkeley and his brother-in-law, Sir John Maltravers. Queens found themselves incarcerated at their husbands' pleasure both before and after the fourteenth century but never before had a reigning monarch been imprisoned by his own wife even if she did send him loving messages and thoughtful gifts.[10] Despite the affection that Isabella still felt for the complicated man who had been her husband for nearly twenty years, the king was murdered on 21 September 1327 at Berkeley Castle. It was announced that he died of natural causes but the first parliament after Isabella and Mortimer's downfall recorded that he had been 'falsely and treacherously murdered'.[11] The *Brut* recorded that he died of sorrow and the *Lanercost Chronicle* hedged its bets by stating that Edward either died of natural causes or was murdered. Holinshed's *Chronicles* written in 1577 reported that Edward was killed by a red-hot poker thrust into his anus providing a moral homily at the same time as recounting the king's death. There is no contemporary suggestion that the king met his death in this manner although as early as 1333 the *Brut* wrote about Mortimer's involvement with his death.

The victors soon fell out amongst themselves. Lancaster's lands were much reduced with estates that he expected to inherit from his brother being given to the queen. Just as Despenser had controlled access to Edward II so Isabella and Mortimer controlled access to his son. Between them, they almost bankrupted the treasury during the four years that she and Mortimer ruled. They also negotiated an unpopular peace treaty with the Scots which included the marriage of Isabella's youngest daughter, Joan of the Tower, to King Robert I's son, David. This caused a breach between Isabella and Edward III who refused to attend his sister's wedding in Berwick. In 1328, Mortimer was created Earl of March and in 1329, when Henry of Lancaster was accused of rebellion Mortimer siphoned off much of the earl's land. Isabella's lover proved as acquisitive as Gaveston or Despenser, in addition to which he came to be regarded as a regicide. Plots and intrigue troubled the kingdom once more. Edmund of Woodstock, Earl of Kent and uncle to Edward III, was arrested on charges of treason when he attempted to free his brother and restore him to the throne, having heard that Edward II was still alive. Kent was given a hasty trial and executed on 19 March 1329. Many people believed that the death of the Earl of Kent was achieved chiefly through the agency of Mortimer, 'who at that time was more than king in the kingdom, forasmuch as the queen-mother and he ruled the realm'.[12] Rather than quelling unrest, the execution of Edmund of Woodstock created more discord than ever. His pleas for mercy had been ignored and his execution was so irregular that he was made to wait an entire day in his shirt before someone could be found who was willing to wield the executioner's blade.

It is possible that Isabella became pregnant by Mortimer in 1329. The only evidence for this is that she appointed Mortimer her heir. She was not known to be ill at the time. However, childbirth was a risky business and she had prepared similar documents prior to the birth of her four children by the king. One theory is that Isabella did carry a child to term but that the scandal and shame of a queen bearing an illegitimate child was so great that Mortimer took the child to Montgomery Castle. However, the fashions of the day did not lend themselves to disguising pregnancy. If she did become pregnant it is more likely that she miscarried. By then her eldest son, Edward III, was a married man with a son of his own. There was no sign that his mother or Mortimer intended that he should assume power when he reached the age of eighteen. Froissart would later report that there were whispers of a pregnancy by Mortimer at the time of parliament sitting in Nottingham in 1330. Edward would have considered that although any child his mother might bear would be illegitimate and had no right to the throne, Mortimer might engineer a situation where any son of his own by Isabella inherited the throne rather than the rightful monarch.

Isabella and Mortimer's blatant adultery resulted in the alienation of the Church. Edward III began corresponding with Pope John XXII at Avignon. It was a considered act. Throughout the four years in which his mother and Mortimer were in power, Edward had quietly created a circle of friends including William Montagu upon whom he could rely. On 15 October 1330, a month before his eighteenth birthday, Edward III and Montagu were accused of plotting against Mortimer before parliament sat at Nottingham. The Earl of Lancaster was also accused and forced to leave the city. Montagu lashed out at Mortimer, accusing him of having the old king murdered. He was then seen to depart the castle, its gates locked and barred against him on his departure. Later, Montagu and a company of men made their way through secret underground passages to the keep of Nottingham Castle. Edward emerged from his chamber and crept downstairs to meet his friends. Then he led them to his mother's apartments where they stormed the queen's bedchamber, killed Mortimer's household knight Hugh Turpilton who died shielding his master and arrested Mortimer in the king's name. Isabella, distraught with worry for Mortimer, was locked in her bedchamber. The next day Edward III took control of his country and arranged for Mortimer to be sent to Leicester in chains.

Mortimer was charged with treason having assumed royal power and kept the king's household within his hands. The charges included ignoring the regency council, abusing royal prerogative, seizing royal treasures, procuring lands and grants for himself, his family and his friends. The last charge was that he plotted to destroy the king's children and turn Edward III into a puppet. Inevitably the charges included the murder of Edward II as well as procuring the death of Edmund of Woodstock, the king's uncle. The indictment rolls made no mention of Mortimer's relationship with Isabella and gave no indication that Isabella played a part in the charges now levelled at her lover. Edward III chose to scapegoat Mortimer for the politics of the previous four years in much the same way that female mistresses were conveniently scapegoated for the personal lusts of the monarchs they bedded and in the same way that Isabella had herself scapegoated the Despensers for their role in the mismanagement of the kingdom under Edward II.

Edward III ignored his mother's personal relationship with Mortimer in a bid to preserve her reputation although there were rumours that she joined the Order of St Clare on the death of her lover. In reality, the Pope had written to the king beseeching him not to 'expose his mother's shame'.[13] She did not have to fear having her hair shorn and being dressed in sackcloth in the way that her French sisters-in-law were humiliated by Philip IV. She would live out her life treated with the honour that was due to the king's mother. It was true that immediately after Edward III seized power, he ordered that his mother should be sent under house arrest to Berkhamstead Castle. Later it would be said that Isabella was mad, a she-wolf, and that her son locked her up in Castle Rising in Norfolk for the rest of her life. In reality, Edward chose to blame Mortimer rather than his mother. Mortimer was executed on 29 November 1330, having been attainted of treason and all his lands confiscated. Amongst the confiscations were Joan Mortimer's dower lands. Once again, she found herself under arrest. It was only in 1336 that Edward III granted her a full pardon and returned her estates. In 1354, Edward III reversed the attainder on Mortimer. Joan reclaimed her husband's body in 1332 and was buried beside him at Wigmore Abbey in 1356.

On 1 December 1330, two days after Mortimer's execution, Isabella surrendered her income and her lands to her son. In return, he allocated an annual income of £3,000 to her whilst his own queen Philippa received the lands as her dower. From Berkhamstead, Isabella was removed to Windsor Castle where she remained for the next two years. It is possible that she lost another baby whilst she was at Berkhamstead and she was grief-stricken by the news of Mortimer's execution. Historians have speculated that Isabella remained out of the public gaze because she suffered a nervous breakdown. Edward III's accounts show many physician's bills for the care of his mother at this time.

In March 1332, Queen Philippa gave birth to a daughter who was named Isabella after her grandmother. Whatever family relationships were like behind closed doors, in public at least Isabella began a process of rehabilitation and a veil was drawn over her affair with Mortimer. That Easter the queen mother joined the royal family at court, Edward settled the bill for the care of his mother with the constable of Windsor Castle. It was only during the eighteenth century that she was described as a 'she-wolf'. Just as medieval chroniclers castigated Eleanor of Aquitaine for challenging her allotted role so too was Isabella vilified at a later time, because she stepped outside the accepted role of wife and mother and took a lover who helped her depose her royal spouse. Perhaps Isabella, a student of Arthurian legend, should have remembered that Guinevere was a beautiful and noble queen whose love for Lancelot rather than Arthur destroyed the fellowship of the Knights of the Round table. The destruction of Camelot was the result of the queen's betrayal of her husband and Guinevere spent the rest of her life regretting her part in the betrayal of Arthur. Isabella died at Hertford Castle on 22 August 1358. She was buried at the Greyfriars Church in London in the dress she wore on her wedding day with her husband's heart next to her own suggesting the depth of her love for the man she deposed from the throne. Edward's loyalty to the Despensers pushed her from loyal wife to scheming adulteress.

Chapter 16

Katherine Mortimer and Margaret Drummond

After the deposition of King Edward II in 1327, Queen Isabella and Roger Mortimer tried to end the war between England and Scotland. King Robert I of Scotland insisted that the English renounce all claims to the sovereignty of Scotland and that his own status as king should be recognised. Even after his defeat at the Battle of Bannockburn in 1314, Edward II had refused the terms that Isabella and Roger now agreed in the Treaty of Edinburgh and which were ratified by the English parliament at Northampton. It was hoped that the marriage of Isabella and Edward's daughter, Joan of the Tower, to the heir of King Robert I of Scotland would guarantee friendship between the two nations. The treaty agreeing the match was signed on 17 March 1328. Since Joan and her husband-to-be, David, were too young to be married it was decided that a wedding would be completed within two months of David reaching the canonical age of fourteen in 1338. If the union did not go ahead then the terms of the treaty would be void and the Scots would be required to pay a fine of £100,000. The pair exchanged their vows at Berwick on 17 July 1328. Isabella travelled north to see her seven-year-old daughter married but neither King Robert nor Joan's brother King Edward III was there to witness it. Edward was said to be so angry about the treaty that he wept tears of fury when he was first informed of its contents. The so-called cradle marriage was unpopular on both sides of the border. In Scotland, Joan acquired the disparaging nickname 'makepeace' and in England Isabella and Mortimer found that the wedding added to their growing unpopularity. Joan accompanied her new husband back to Scotland and became Queen of Scots on 7 June 1329 when King Robert died. Three years later the peace agreement fell apart.

David and Joan were crowned at Scone on 24 November 1331 (without the Stone of Destiny which had been taken to Westminster in 1296).

There were other men with a claim to the Scottish throne who saw an opportunity to displace the five-year-old monarch. Edward Balliol had been a prisoner in England from 1296 as a hostage for his father's (John Balliol), conduct until he was allowed to go to family estates in Picardy during 1315. He returned to Scotland in August 1332 with 2,000 men. He intended to establish himself as king in place of David, subject to Edward III's overlordship whose unofficial support he received before venturing with a fleet into Fife. Balliol's army met with David's at Dupplin Moor near Perth on 12 August and defeated the royal army. On 24 September, he had himself crowned king and suggested that if Joan's marriage with David were to be annulled that he could marry her. Balliol did not have long to enjoy his kingship. David's supporters caused him to flee Scotland in December 1332 but he returned the following year with an army provided by King Edward III. The Scots were defeated on Halidon Hill near Berwick on 22 July 1333. Edward's price for toppling his nine-year-old brother-in-law from his throne was Balliol's vassalage and much of the southern shires of Scotland. David and Joan left Dumbarton Castle for France in 1334 leaving the Guardian of Scotland, Sir Andrew Murray, to act on the young king's behalf. The couple did not return to Scotland until 2 June 1341 when Balliol was finally driven from power by Murray. His situation deteriorated when Edward III turned his attentions from being a bulwark to Balliol's power in Scotland to gaining the French crown by right of his mother, Isabella of France, who was the daughter of Philip the Fair.

When David and Joan returned to Scotland, the king took up the reigns of his kingdom. After the English won the Battle of Crécy against the French in August 1346, the Scots invaded England to support their allies. An army marched south towards Durham led by David but were surprised by a smaller English force led by the Archbishop of York on 17 October 1346. Several Scottish lords including Robert Stewart, David's nephew, abandoned their comrades after seeing the first two divisions of their army being overwhelmed. David was captured at what became known as the Battle of Neville's Cross following a humiliating defeat in which he was wounded in the face by an arrow and fifty or so of his barons were killed. He spent the next eleven years in captivity in England, either in the Tower or at Hertford Castle. Joan remained in Scotland for much of the time, perhaps a hostage for his safety, whilst

David's nephew and heir, Robert Stewart, ruled as Steward of Scotland. Robert did not seize the crown but he made little effort to have his uncle freed. He successfully objected to two treaties that might have secured David's release in 1351 and 1355. He was eight years older than his uncle and unlikely to succeed him but he did have sons who might one day be Scotland's kings if David had no children.

On occasion, safe conducts were issued for Joan to visit her husband and the rest of her family. Despite the opportunity for conjugal visits, she remained childless. Meanwhile, the Scottish king might have been a prisoner but it did not prevent him from meeting with Katherine Mortimer and making her his mistress. There are several theories about who she was including one that made links to a mercantile family in London. She might also have met the king through service as part of Queen Joan's retinue on one of her periodic visits south or even as part of one of the noble retinues that travelled between Scotland and England to negotiate for David's release. Equally, she could have been one of Philippa of Hainault's ladies-in-waiting and met the king whilst David was at Odiham Castle which belonged to the queen. Whatever the case, David had limited freedom so Katherine either met him at Odiham, Hertford Castle or in the Tower of London itself. According to Walter Bower, a fifteenth-century writer, 'the king loved her more than all other women, and on her account his queen was entirely neglected while he embraced his mistress'. [1] Daivd's attitude to Katherine would help to change the role of the medieval mistress from women who met privately with the king and bore illegitimate children barred from the Crown but whose family ties ensured power, wealth and influence at the monarch's discretion, to political players themselves.

In 1357, King David's ransom and release were finally negotiated. The Scots would pay a hundred thousand marks to be paid across ten years during which time there would be no hostilities between the two nations. Scottish hostages were provided as a surety and several Scottish castles were dismantled. Joan asked permission from her husband and her brother to go on pilgrimage to Canterbury to visit the shrine of Thomas Becket which was granted and a safe conduct provided by Edward III. Joan crossed the border into England. She had no intention of returning to Scotland. She was given a pension of £200 a year by her brother, although it did not cover her expenses, and spent much of her time with her mother, Queen Isabella. She remained in contact with her husband and agreed to intercede on his behalf but Joan would not provide David with an heir.

Katherine Mortimer returned to Scotland with her lover in October 1357 because David could not bear to be parted from her. Katherine, a long way down the social hierarchy, had displaced a queen and Joan was complicit in the substitution by permanently removing herself from Scotland. Katherine's story was told in part by Sir Thomas Gray who was captured by the Scots and spent several years in Edinburgh Castle where he wrote the *Scalacronica*. David blamed his nephew Robert the Steward, lieutenant of Scotland, for his lengthy captivity but bided his time. He set about placing his own loyal supporters in control of crucial castles and offices. He also tried to arrange for his ransom to be cancelled in return for recognising one of Edward III's own sons as his heir. Meanwhile, Katherine, living openly with the king, was given a place of honour at the Scottish court. In a short time, she became a focus for discontent when David's nobility realised that they were being excluded by the king from his councils. She became representative of David's unpopular foreign favourites.

In June 1360, when David was in the Borders travelling from Melrose to Soutra with, as always, Katherine by his side, a young man called Richard Holly took the opportunity to talk to Katherine as they rode. Their horses gradually fell back from the main group as the king's mistress chatted. A man named Dewar in the employ of the Earl of Angus, Robert Stewart's cousin, joined with the two riders and together with Dewar stabbed Katherine before escaping. Katherine's body was carried to Newbattle Abbey near Edinburgh where she was buried. According to tradition, David gave the order that she should be buried standing up inside one of the church walls.

Thomas Stewart, 2nd Earl of Angus was imprisoned in Dumbarton Castle because of the suspicion that he was a conspirator in the murder but no one else was implicated. Thomas had been one of the Scottish nobles who negotiated the king's release but he was Robert Stewart's lieutenant in the northeast. Two of Angus's allies, the earls of March and Douglas, opposed David but the king quickly put down the rebellion. Angus died from bubonic plague whilst still imprisoned or was starved to death. David was sufficiently astute to use the death of Katherine for his own political gain and he was quick to find someone else to warm his bed. Margaret Logie, daughter of Sir Malcolm Drummond, became the king's next mistress and like Katherine, she was openly recognised as his 'beloved' much to the interest of the scandalised courts of Europe.[2] Margaret's extended family reaped the benefits of her affair with David. Her husband Sir John Logie profited from the arrangement until his death, as did Margaret's son. Her brother, Malcolm Drummond, was given lands in Perth as well as becoming its coroner. Her uncle John was created Earl of Mentieth. Tension between the Stewarts and the Drummonds began to escalate as David used his mistresses extended kinship network to counterbalance the influence of the Stewarts in Perthshire. His childhood in France and years in captivity had prevented him from fostering alliances within his nobility but now he used the relations of the woman who shared his bed to work his political will. Soon Margaret's brothers, John and Maurice, found themselves involved in a feud with Robert Stewart's family.

By the time Queen Joan died on 7 September 1362, she had been married to David for thirty-four years but because of their estrangement the Scottish king had no legitimate children and he was living openly with Margaret. He decided to marry her. She had already demonstrated her fertility and with John Logie having died or his marriage being annulled at around the same time, there were no obstacles to the union. The marriage of the daughter of an obscure knight to the king of Scotland did not meet with everyone's approval. Robert Stewart was alarmed by the prospect of David having a child of his own to supplant him and his sons as the heirs to Scotland's crown. As the marriage preparations progressed a rebellion arose led by David's potential heirs including Robert Stewart and the Earl of March. David, supported by Archibald Douglas, raised an army and the king's nephew was forced to acquiesce.

The king married Margaret Logie at Inchmurdoch on 20 February 1364. Queen Margaret was the first Scottish-born queen to sit on the throne since the eleventh century but she was far from popular. David gave her extensive lands and customs revenue but she was eager to acquire more, resulting in a dispute with the Bishop of Glasgow. Her son was given Crown lands in Annandale and the Earl of Ross was stripped of his estates. Robert Stewart's eldest surviving son, John found himself married to Queen Margaret's niece, Annabella Drummond. Her popularity plummeted. One chronicler went so far as to suggest that the king had only married her because she pretended to be pregnant. Like Joan, Margaret had provided Scotland with no dowry or territories.

When, by 1369, it was apparent that Margaret was not going to become pregnant, David set about having the marriage annulled in order that he could marry a third time to his current mistress Agnes Dunbar, who was the sister the Earl of Mar and an ally of the king. He gave Margaret a pension of £100. Furious at the loss of her crown, Margaret boarded a ship in secret and made her way to France before travelling to Avignon. She appealed directly to Pope Gregory XI who was sympathetic to Margaret's plight. She submitted an appeal and David was forced to send his representatives to argue the case. She argued that David could not divorce her because of her infertility. She had a son from her marriage to John Logie. If she and David were childless, it was not her fault. The Papal Curia agreed but David died aged forty-seven on 22 February 1371 without any heirs to succeed him before the case was closed. Margaret continued with her lawsuit, the dower rights of a queen were at stake, and demonstrated her piety by taking a pilgrimage to Rome. Before matters could become more complicated and the whole of Scotland found itself excommunicated because of the king's marital difficulties and Margaret's determination to pursue her case, she died on her way back to Avignon. The Pope paid for her burial.

The kings of England's womenfolk had not gained the public notoriety of David's mistresses and no English king had thought it appropriate to marry a woman who had already shared a bed with him. The ideal of courtly love which inspired a lover to acts of chivalry and courage were on the wane, in part, because of the way in which Isabella of France's sisters-in-law, and even Isabella herself, had betrayed their husbands. The elements of sexual attraction and lust were never far from the way medieval kings interacted with their mistresses but it appeared from David's relationships that the women, of the middling rank, were changing from passive possessions to active political players whose voices were no longer silent.

Chapter 17

Alice Perrers

Edward of Windsor, King Edward II's son, was thirteen years old, in 1325, when he was sent to France to perform homage for the Duchy of Aquitaine in his father's stead. Isabella had to flee Paris with Edward when King Edward II's agents arrived to take her son back to England by force if necessary. They stayed for a time with Isabella's cousin who was married to William the Good, Count of Hainault. William had a son and four daughters. As early as 1319, Edward II had made enquiries about the Count of Hainault's daughters. Queen Isabella took the opportunity to negotiate her son's marriage to Philippa in return for military and financial support for her invasion of England.

Isabella and her lover Roger Mortimer landed near Orwell in Suffolk on 24 September 1326 with a fleet and mercenaries funded by William of Hainault. By 1 February the following year, King Edward II was deposed and Edward III crowned. A proxy marriage ceremony was held in Valenciennes in October before Edward's bride travelled to England. By then Edward II was dead and buried in St Peter's Abbey, Gloucester. Philippa celebrated Christmas in London before being escorted north to join King Edward III in York on 23 January 1327. The following day the young couple were married in York Minster. The nave was undergoing reconstruction and unroofed. Snow eddied around the royal couple as they made their vows.

Edward III and Philippa of Hainault had a happy and affectionate marriage. Philippa gave birth to the couple's first child on 15 June 1330. She was a devoted and loving mother who worked discreetly behind the scenes caring for her family and a large number of foster children that she took into her care. In the thirty or so years that they were married the king does not seem to have taken a mistress until Philippa became ill and increasingly bedridden. By then she had given him twelve children, including five sons who survived into adulthood, having accompanied him around his kingdom and abroad on many of his military campaigns.

Two of their children died in infancy whilst a third, Joan, died from the plague on her way to marry Peter of Castile.

Despite this unexpected uxoriousness, there is an ugly tale about Edward dating from a period when Phillipa was pregnant with their eighth child. Edward became enamoured of Catherine Grandison, who was married to William Montagu, first Earl of Salisbury circa 1320. In 1341, Edward, then aged twenty-nine years old, raised a Scottish siege on Catherine's home at Wark Castle. The earl, the man who orchestrated the coup on Edward's behalf to topple Roger Mortimer from power when he was a teenager, was a prisoner in France. It was said that the king, his friend absent, tried to seduce the countess during a game of chess. When she refused him, the king raped her. The story of the rape is told more fully in Le Bel's chronicle. It describes Edward falling in love with the countess when he visited Wark in 1341. In order to see her again, the king held a tournament in London. Salisbury attended with his wife. She remained impervious to Edward's blandishments so he took the opportunity of returning to Wark in 1342 having taken the precaution of sending Salisbury to France where he was captured:

> Come the night, when he had gone to bed in proper state, and he knew that the fine lady was in her bedchamber and that all her ladies were asleep and his gentlemen also, except his personal valets, he got up and told these valets that nothing must interfere with what he was going to do, on pain of death. So it was that he entered the lady's chamber, then shut the doors of the wardrobe so that her maids could not help her, then he took her and gagged her mouth so firmly that she could not cry out more than two or three times, and then he raped her so savagely that never was a woman so badly treated; and he left her lying there all battered about, bleeding from the nose and the mouth and elsewhere, which was for her great damage and great pity. Then he left the next day without saying a word, and returned to London, very disgusted with what he had done.[1]

Le Bel wrote in French rather than Latin. He was a soldier rather than a monk. He served Jean, Count de Beaumont and wrote the 'True Chronicles' at his request. Generally, Le Bel is regarded as reliable as he refused to narrate events unless he or someone he interviewed witnessed them. Although he was French, Le Bel served with the English against the Scots. He called Edward 'valiant', 'gentle' and 'noble'[2] so at first glance it appears not to be a smear against Edward on Le Bel's part. Froissart denounced the tale as untrue, but he did believe that the king was infatuated with Catherine. Whilst Salisbury was the Lord of Wark, is it likely that the king would so far forget himself as to force himself on the wife of his oldest friend? Le Bel's narrative includes Salisbury's confrontation with the king, his renunciation of their friendship and the fact that he left England to die soon after in Spain. It says something about the standards of the time that the chronicler is more concerned that Edward destroyed his relationship with the earl rather than the violence perpetrated by the monarch against the countess. Ormrod's biography of Edward III states that the root of the story lay in French propaganda. Edward III created the Knights of the Garter and was driven by chivalric values including loyalty.[3]

Philippa was thrown from her horse in 1358. She dislocated, or broke, her shoulder and may well have suffered other internal injuries. The queen's deteriorating health coincided with the arrival of Alice Perrers in the royal household. According to financial records, Alice became a member of the queen's household during the 1360s when she was in her mid to late teens. The assumption must be that she was of gentle birth as she was appointed directly to the queen's bedchamber and is described as a *domicella* or damsel in the records. It has been suggested that Edward acquired a mistress to join him between the sheets when Philippa became too infirm to fulfil her part of the marriage debt of coitus that existed between husband and wife. Church law maintained that married couples owed coitus to one another and expressed the view that the duty could only be abrogated by common consent.

Alice's origins have been subject to speculation across the centuries. The written sources were often hostile because of Alice's influence on the king and the wealth she accumulated during that time. At the height of her powers, she controlled fifty-six manors, castles and townhouses across twenty-five counties.

History does not know when she was born or who her parents might have been although in the past, and without any evidence, her year of birth was given as coinciding with the arrival of the Black Death in England in 1348. It was a significant year that wrought chaos on English society thanks to the famine resulting from poor harvests and the deadly disease that killed a third of Europe's population. According to various chroniclers, she was the daughter of a Devon weaver or she was the daughter of a 'thatcher from the town of Henny'.[4] Another version of the same chronicle changes thatcher for weaver. Both of them were skilled workers but a long way down the social ladder and unlikely to have daughters feted by monarchs. It is true that Alice lived during some of the many recurrences of the Black Death. Villages were lost, so it is possible that she grew up in a village that was subsequently deserted but it is unclear to which Devon village the chronicler was referring. Thomas Walsingham, the author of the *St Albans Chronicle*, perpetuated the idea that she came from the lower social orders by making her the daughter of a tiler in Henney in Essex and a domestic servant. There are two villages with the name Henny near Castle Hedingham. In making her father a tiler, Walsingham was suggesting that she came from a family background that turned society on its head. The writer and Jane Perrers lived through Wat Tyler's rebellion during the reign of Richard II. His description of Alice verges upon the vitriolic:

> She was a shameless, impudent harlot, and of low birth, for she was the daughter of a thatcher from the town of Henny, elevated by fortune. She was not attractive or beautiful, but knew how to compensate for these defects with the seductiveness of her voice. Blind fortune elevated this woman.[5]

Walsingham evidently neither liked clever women nor ones who did not know their place. Another theory, dating from the eighteenth century, suggested that Alice was a relative of William of Wykeham, Bishop of Winchester. Much of this supposition is based on where she owned lands. The idea first surfaced in William Bohun's *The English Lawyer*.[6] Bohun claimed that Alice was either Wykeham's niece or sister. He suggested that the bishop found a way of getting Alice into Edward's bed and himself into the management of the kingdom. Bohun went on to claim that Edward's sons, Edward the Black Prince and John of Gaunt, Duke of Lancaster, sought the removal of both the pimping bishop and Alice. Unfortunately, the Black Prince died before this end could be achieved. Undeterred, Bohun claimed that no doubt one of Alice's agents poisoned the prince. The story, obviously a work of fiction masquerading as fact, gained ground. Part of the Bohun's appeal lay in its explanation as to why Alice was able to gain an ascendency over the king when she was not of aristocratic birth and, according to Walsingham, had little to recommend her. By linking her to Wykeham, her pedigree became more appropriate for the mistress of a king and she was reduced to the role of a pawn in the hands of Edward's able friend and administrator rather than being a woman with a mind of her own – which begs the question why would the bishop have needed to reinforce his position with the provision of a sleeping partner for the king? Wykeham did have a niece called Alice who married a man called Perot. She appears to have lived in the West Country and was left £100 by Wykeham in his will.[7] The bishop died in 1404, some four years after Alice Perrers, meaning that Alice Perot and Alice Perrers were two different people and the bishop did not attempt to influence the king through pillow talk.

There is also the small matter of the name Perrers – was Alice unmarried when she became the king's mistress? Historians tended to assume that Perrers was her maiden name. There was a view that she might have been the daughter of John Piers or Perrers of Holt in Norfolk although there was very little evidence for this or of her being married to Sir Thomas de Narford prior to marrying William de Windsor. What these stories did was elevate Alice from the lower classes. By the nineteenth century, one antiquarian went so far as to suggest that Alice was the illegitimate daughter of Earl Warenne by a female member of the Narford family. In 1889, speculation about Alice identity was threaded through *Notes and Queries* based largely on hypothesis and flimsy circumstantial evidence. Another suggestion was that she came from the Hertfordshire family of Perrers. They were landowners near St Albans and in dispute about land with the monastery. Given the hostility that the *St Albans Chronicle* exhibited towards Alice, it became a plausible option. For the Victorians, the case was compounded by the fact that Sir Richard de Perrers led an undistinguished career as a parliamentary representative during the reigns of Edward II and that he was imprisoned in the gaol at Bishop's Stortford in 1349 for 'divers felonies and transgressions'[8] after which he was outlawed. In reality, he was in a protracted dispute with St Albans Abbey. The family continued its legal battles with the church and with the abbey of St Albans. Sir

Richard's son appealed against the sentence of outlawry in 1375 and again in 1377. The case appears in the record books until 1384. This in itself makes it unlikely that Alice was related to Sir Richard because she was at her most influential at the time that Sir Richard's son was pleading his father's case. Surely, she would have interceded if Sir Richard was her own parent? In 1889, it was argued that it must be the case that she was descended from Sir Richard as the arms of William Windsor (Alice's husband in the 1370s) was quartered with the Perrers family of Hertfordshire. Unfortunately, the escutcheon has disappeared and there are question marks over the interpretation of the coat of arms, not to mention when the arms were painted. In the twentieth century, Haldeen Braddy suggested that she was the second wife of William Chaumpaigne of London and therefore the stepmother of the woman who laid a charge of *raptus* against Geoffrey Chaucer.[9]

Analysis of legal documents known as Ancient Petitions held in the National Archives reveals more about Alice's antecedents and the likelihood that she was the daughter of a wealthy gold merchant.[10] John de Kendale of London was owed money by Alice. He petitioned the courts for its return during the reign of Richard II.[11] In 1360, Kendale provided Alice's husband Janyn Perrers with cloth. At that time the couple lived at Gracechurch Street in London. After Alice was widowed, she would have become liable for her husband's debts because she was the executrix of his will. This provides clear evidence that Alice's married name was Perrers, so she cannot have been the daughter of Sir Richard de Perrers or the stepmother of Cecily de Campaigne.

Alice became Edward's mistress soon after she entered Philippa's household, some six years before the queen died. In 1364, Alice gave the king a son called John Southeray. He was followed by two sisters named Joan and Jane. Prior to the birth of John, there is no record of Edward fathering an illegitimate child. Alice's role in Edward's life appears to have been kept quiet. This may have stemmed from respect for Philippa who was widely esteemed or it has been suggested that the secrecy resulted from King David II's scandalous liaisons which included allowing his relatively low-born mistress to flaunt her power within his own household.[12] Edward did not wish to become a figure of mockery like his brother-in-law. Alice departed the queen's household two years after the birth of Southeray to avoid potential embarrassment. The only official gift she was recorded as receiving in that time was two tuns of Gascony wine each year.

Philippa died at Windsor on 15 August 1369. Edward was grief-stricken. She was taken by barge to the Tower from where the body was carried to Westminster Abbey and buried in the Chapel of Edward the Confessor. The queen's household was broken up and the affair became more widely known at court. Alice was about twenty-one years old. Edward's reliance on her made her enemies not least because the king expected everyone to be respectful of her. And Alice had no intention of becoming destitute after Edward tired of her. Although Edward began to give her royal manors, they were gifts that might be forfeit. Alice began to make purchases in her own right swapping the presents she received for property. In London, she purchased a house from Richard Lyons at a lower price than might be expected with the understanding that she would use her influence at court on Lyon's behalf. She acquired the small manor of Pallenswick near Hammersmith and in 1373 she purchased a manor at Gaynes near Upminster. It was conveniently close to Edward's palace at Havering-atte-Bower.

Alice's influence was growing as Edward, without his beloved Philippa to support him, became more dependent upon her. Her role was beginning to be recognised more widely. On 5 January 1371, Pope Gregory XI wrote to the Black Prince, John of Gaunt and to Alice Perrers requesting that they should intercede on behalf of his brother being held captive by the Constable of Aquitaine.[13] The king's bedfellow was being treated like a queen as more and more people realised that she had Edward's ear. The family of Walter, 3rd Baron FitzWalter who had been captured by the French at Vaas Abbey where he sought shelter asked Alice to intercede for help paying his ransom. Alice agreed. She had accrued a sufficient fortune to pay the ransom herself taking the family castle and lordship of Egremont as security for the loan. She was an astute businesswoman who borrowed capital from the Crown for her financial ventures and these were recorded by the Clerk of the Wardrobe. Then Edward gave her Philippa's jewels. It was common for monarchs to take mistresses but it was unthinkable that they should be as inseparable as Edward and Alice were becoming or that the young woman would be gifted with the queen's personal belongings. For many, it was a provocation too far.

In 1374, having already made her wealthy, Edward changed Alice's status. Everyone knew about her existence at court but his relationship was not acknowledged publicly. He decided that there should be a tournament held in Smithfield to mark the end of Lent. It would last for a week and it would be held in honour of Alice. All the knights who took part in the jousting would be required to do honour to the Lady of the Sun as Alice would be styled for the occasion. The king, Alice and his procession travelled from the Tower along Cheapside and Aldersgate to Smithfield which in those times contained pasture for the beasts destined for the shambles, two graveyards for plague victims and farmland for the nearby Charterhouse. The tournament was to be held on a flat grassy area. Alice, dressed as the Lady of the Sun in a cloak of gold tissue lined with red taffeta, was at the heart of the procession and the queen of the lists despite the fact that she was not of aristocratic birth. No one was more important than the king in his own country but he chose to recognise Alice's existence in his life and his love for her and he forced the entire court to show her the same respect when he made her the Lady of the Sun. Edward behaved as though he was a courtly lover humbling himself at his mistress's feet. The tournament was a lavish affair. For seven days there was feasting, jousting and processions.

William Langland was less easily impressed than the majority of London's citizens who watched from a distance. He lived in Cornhill with his wife and daughter. He had already written his allegorical poem, *The Vision of William Concerning Piers the Plowman* but he was revising his work and extending it. Alice became Langland's Lady Meed. The word meant either a reward or a dishonest bribe. Both applied to the king's concubine. She was well rewarded by Edward and took bribes from those who recognised her influence. In Langland's hands, Alice's greed turned her into an allegorical representation of the power of money. Even worse, Alice and her literary self, Lady Meed, were women involved in economic activity. Alice Perrers was not alone in buying land at this time but by stepping out of her allotted place as a wife, mother or daughter, she was destabilising the established hierarchy. Langland did not see Alice as a Jezebel or Eve, he saw her as the original Scarlet Woman – the Great Whore of Babylon to be found in the Book of Revelation.

It might not have been so problematic for Alice or Edward's family had she been content with a domestic role in the king's life. However, she was ambitious and she had stepped out of the shadows where royal mistresses were expected to reside. As Edward retired from public life, access to him was controlled by Alice and by the Lords Latimer and Neville who were Edward's chamberlain and steward. They in their turn benefitted from his patronage. Alice profited from rewards and advantages in exactly the same way as Edward's male courtiers[14] but she was a woman and not of aristocratic birth.

Aware that the king was growing older and frailer and that without her protector she might face an uncertain future, Alice made a secret marriage to Sir William Windsor at some point during the 1370s. De Windsor was part of Lionel of Antwerp's retinue. Lionel was sent as Lord Lieutenant of Ireland in 1361. He returned in 1366. With him was Sir William, the son of Sir Alexander de Windsor, of Greyrigg in Westmorland. He was older than Alice, having seen military service in France. Records put him at the Battle of Poitiers.[15] He returned to Ireland in 1369 having been appointed King's Lieutenant for Ireland. A contemporary account described him as a 'needy knight',[16] although by the time Alice met him, he was a 'knight rich with great wealth which he had acquired by his martial prowess'.[17] Ransoms, loot and Irish bribery made a substantial difference to his fortunes. It is likely that Alice initially provided Windsor with information about the court. In 1371, Windsor was recalled to London following complaints about the methods by which he extorted subsidies from settlers in Ireland. During the enquiry, it became evident that Alice had received the money allocated to de Windsor for his expenses and the payment of his men.

Alice was not alone in her misuse of public money but the time was coming when her notoriety would ensure that she was scapegoated. Edward's involvement in the protracted war against France meant that parliament's voice was heard more clearly. When the king sought to raise taxes to pay his armies the Commons petitioned and bargained to assert their rights before granting subsidies. Matters came to a head when John of Gaunt, the king's third son to have survived to adulthood, led an expedition to Aquitaine in 1373 which was dogged by French ambushes, famine, illness and lack of funds. When John returned home, he found that his elder brother, the Black Prince, was increasingly ill and that his father was growing older and less able to rule. He had to deal with the political backlash of the campaign's failure. It had been three years since parliament last sat when it met in 1376. The king's request for taxation was debated for ten days. The conclusion was that Edward had been poorly advised. He was not the only king to avoid being blamed and for wicked counsellors to bear the brunt of the Commons rage. One of their claims was that parliament 'has the right to influence the selection of the king's servants'.[18] The Good Parliament of 1376, as it came to be called, attacked Lord Latimer, Edward's chamberlain, Neville the steward and Richard Lyons, the Warden of the Mint. Initially, the Commons did not know with what to charge Alice. The problem was that whilst adultery was a mortal sin, kings were expected to enjoy the company of beautiful women. The speaker of the house, Peter de la Mare, accused Alice of defrauding the royal purse of thousands of pounds and that she protected those who were accused and now faced court proceedings.

Initially, John of Gaunt, who was widely regarded as over-ambitious, worked with parliament. The Black Prince, from his sickbed, gave orders to have Alice investigated. Accusations of witchcraft followed. She had withdrawn to her home in Pallenswick. Whilst she was there the speaker's brother, John de la Mare, trapped Alice's physician by pretending to be in search of a doctor. The man, a Dominican, was taken away and before long confessed to preparing portraits of Edward to help draw him closer to Alice. He also alleged that he provided two rings, one to promote the memory and the other to aid forgetfulness. The latter was injurious to the king's health. In addition to the king, he also said that Alice wanted potions to charm the Black Prince and John of Gaunt. His order quietly moved him into a monastery. Eventually, the main charge against Alice was that she sat on the bench beside judges advising them of the verdicts that they should deliver despite the fact that she held no official role. No examples were provided and the problem lay not in corruption of justice but in the fact that Alice was a female. Parliament also complained that she furthered her own interests and those of her friends. Alice was banished from court and stripped of much of her wealth. A royal decree forbidding women from interfering with judicial decisions was obtained.

The king was bereft not only of his mistress but also of the Black Prince who died shortly before parliament concluded its case against Alice. And then Edward's own health suddenly deteriorated. John of Gaunt reversed many of the decisions of the Good Parliament including Alice's banishment. She was able to return to Edward at Eltham from Wendover which had been a royal gift and remain with Edward until his death. Parliament had punished her for a public role, Gaunt permitted her return to his father's side in a domestic capacity, released her associates and returned the fines that had been required. As for Peter de la Mare, the parliamentary speaker, he found himself in a dungeon in Nottingham Castle.

An itemised list of Alice's goods made at this time included Eleanor's jewels, twenty-two manors, advowsons and tenements. In addition, Edward provided for his son John Southeray. Early in 1374, he arranged for him to have £100 a year for his maintenance and in 1375, the king transferred a number of manors to a group of trustees associated with Alice for John.[19] Further grants were made in 1377. In January that year, Edward arranged for Southeray to marry Mary Percy. The girl was Alice's ward and the younger half-sister of the 1st Earl of Northumberland.[20] Mary was the sole heir to the estates belonging to her mother's family. Mary's father, mother and grandmother died shortly after her birth, leaving her a wealthy orphan with property in several counties. Alice purchased the wardship recognising that a marriage to Mary would secure her son's future. The couple were married on 7 January 1377 when John was about fourteen years old. On April 23 1377, Edward was at Windsor where he knighted his grandson Richard of Bordeaux, the heir to his throne. Alongside Richard was his young uncle John.

The king left Windsor and travelled to his palace at Sheen. Alice remained by his side as he grew steadily weaker. His appetite diminished and he was fed broth and bread dipped in goat's milk. He finally took to his bed. He talked to Alice about hunting and hawking, so much so that monastic chroniclers accused her of diverting his attention from the need to confess his sins before he died. Walsingham announced that Edward's other attendants were so horrified that they deserted the king's chamber. Edward died on 21 June 1377 with no one by his side except Alice. According to one story, she stayed only long enough to strip the rings from her lover's fingers before fleeing to her house in Pallenswick. Given the array of charges Alice faced after Edward's death, it seems unlikely that the tale is true because theft from the royal corpse is not amongst them. There is another version of the story that tells of a priest who interrupted Alice and Edward's tete-a-tete to warn the king that he must repent of his sins. Edward, realising that he needed to make his confession, ordered Alice out of his presence.

It wasn't long before Alice found herself facing difficult times. Her house in Pallenswick was stripped of its belongings and her property at Wendover returned to the Crown. The Keeper of the Wardrobe presented a long list of items said to belong to the Crown which needed to be returned. The list ranged from jewels to a length of ribbon. She faced banishment once more, not just from court but from the realm. John of Gaunt, the power behind the throne of his young nephew King Richard II, had acceded to his father's last wishes but wanted to be rid of Alice and her grasping ways.

Mary Percy and her powerful Percy relations took the opportunity to apply to the Pope for an annulment of her marriage to Southeray citing his illegitimacy.[21] The pair separated in 1380. Mary married John Ros, the heir of Lord Ros of Helmsley, in 1382. By then Southeray was with English troops led by his half-brother Edmund of Langley at Vila Vicosa in Portugal. John of Gaunt claimed the throne of Castile by right of his wife Constanza. Fernando I of Portugal was one of Gaunt's allies. Edmund of Langley and his men were sent there by Gaunt to provide military aid to Portugal. It was not a successful campaign. There was widespread discontent with Edmund and to make matters worse the English troops did not receive their pay. The troops mutinied. Froissart recorded that Southeray led a rebellion against Langley accusing him of pocketing the money destined for the soldiers.[22] The English left Portugal soon afterwards. Langley blamed the mutineers for his lack of success. A warrant for the arrest of nineteen of the mutineers was issued but Southeray's name was omitted possibly because he was part of the royal family. After this date, he disappears from the record and it is likely that he died sometime between then and 1400 as he is not mentioned in Alice's will.

After Edward's death, Alice was vilified. Her husband William obtained a grant for much of Alice's property but Wendover was not returned. It had been granted by Richard II to his half-brother Thomas Holland and in 1384, it became part of Anne of Bohemia's dower when she married the young king.[23] William de Windsor died in 1384 leaving many debts. Alice found herself back at court in a series of property disputes against her three sisters-in-law who were William's beneficiaries. Much of William's property was hers, held in her husband's name. Alice even pawned the jewels which Edward gave her to pay for her court cases.

By the mid-1380s, Alice was no longer in the limelight and without influence. History would remember her based on the content of hostile chronicles, legal records and financial accounts. She moved to her home at Gaines in Upminster and returned to the shadows beyond the written record. She left only her will with a bequest for money to be spent maintaining the roads around Upminster and for alms to be given to the poor on the day of her funeral as well as gifts for her servants. She was buried in Upminster Church and despite the instructions she left for a lasting memorial, her grave was lost during the seventeenth century.

Chapter 18

Katherine Swynford

John of Gaunt, one of the most powerful princes of the Middle Ages, made three marriages. His first marriage was to Blanche of Lancaster which provided him with wealth and a title. Blanche died on 12 September 1369, aged twenty-three years. Her death may have been as the result of complications during childbirth or it might have been from plague. In 1371, the duke made a second political marriage to Constanza of Castile, the daughter of Pedro the Cruel, by which he claimed the kingdom of Castile and Leon. His third marriage, made without political or financial gain, was to his long-term mistress. Their story is often regarded as the great love story of the medieval period.

Lancaster's relationship with Kathryn Swynford, who was born in about 1350, caused a public scandal. She and her sister Phillipa were the daughters of Sir Paon Roet, a knight from Hainault who arrived in the retinue of Edward III's queen, Philippa of Hainault. He is not listed in an official role but Froissart, the chronicler, who was himself from Hainault, wrote about Roet. At various times chroniclers pounced upon Katherine's foreignness to vilify her and her paramour. The fact that Roet remained in England after Philippa's marriage to Edward III suggests that he was well thought of by both the king and the queen. But by the early 1350s Roet returned to Hainault where he served Margaret, Countess of Hainault. It has been suggested that Katherine and her sister Philippa were related to Hainault's ruling family. This would explain Roet's presence in Philippa's retinue when she arrived in England and the fact that she cared for his two daughters. Lancaster's own epitaph stated that Roet was a knight but nothing more elevated. He was dead by the mid-1350s and his daughters were in the care of Philippa of Hainault.

Katherine and her sister Philippa served in the queen's household and received their education there. The queen had a brood of twelve children and a large number of foster children including the Roet girls. There is some evidence to suggest that Katherine knew Blanche of Lancaster during her childhood as both of them were part of the queen's household. The sisters would have seen Philippa of Hainault's declining health and the rise of Alice Perrers. Philippa may have been placed in the household of the Countess of Ulster, the wife of the king's son Lionel, in 1357 but the record identifies Philippa Pan and it is unclear whether it is Katherine's sister. The countess died in 1363. Philippa, if it was her listed in the countess's household, returned to the queen and was found a husband by 1366 at the latest when she received a royal annuity of ten marks. Her husband was the poet Geoffrey Chaucer who was patronised by John of Gaunt. Katherine, having received an education, was placed by the queen in the household of Blanche of Lancaster after her marriage to John of Gaunt in 1359.

It was not long though before an appropriate marriage was also arranged for Katherine, now in her teens, from within Gaunt's retinue. She married Sir Hugh Swynford of Kettlethorpe in Lincolnshire before 1365 when she can be found listed in the register of Lincoln Cathedral as Katherine Swynford. He was older than his wife, who was fifteen at the most when she married. Swynford was lord of two impoverished manors, Coleby and Kettlethorpe. Hugh needed his income from being part of the duke's retinue and also from any booty he might take for his part in the Hundred Years War. Katherine and Philippa had a small inheritance in Hainault as well as the favour of the royal family but no dowry. It was an appropriate match. He was a knight and she was the daughter of a knight. Neither of them was wealthy.

The couple had three known children to survive infancy; Thomas, Blanche and Margaret but it is impossible to say whether or not Katherine was happily married. Nor is it possible to imagine how the new Lady of Kettlethorpe made the transition from life at court to running a Lincolnshire manor on behalf of her husband who was often away soldiering in France or Spain. Katherine's eldest daughter, Blanche, named after the duchess was sent to the Lancaster nursery by 1368 but the child still saw her mother who divided her time between service to the duchess, the care of Blanche's children and her own home in Kettlethorpe. Blanche was Lancaster's goddaughter and his accounts show funding of a wardship for her care. In 1375, after he began his affair with Katherine, the duke granted her the wardship of the heir of Sir Robert Deyncourt. As well as providing Katherine with an income from the boy's estate during his minority, it also provided Blanche with an opportunity to marry a landed heir. Margaret was born in about 1364 and Katherine probably became pregnant again the following year. Katherine may have given birth to a third daughter named Dorothy but the evidence is fragmentary.

In 1366, Hugh Swynford was sent to Gascony. Katherine continued in her role in Blanche of Lancaster's nursery. Philippa and Elizabeth had been joined briefly by two boys named after their father but both died during infancy. That Christmas, John's duchess went to Bolingbroke, probably with Katherine in attendance. The duchess gave birth to a son named Henry who was born in April 1367 but Katherine was absent. Once the festivities were over Katherine left the duchess's service as she was heavily pregnant and went to Lincoln. She either rented a house in the cathedral close or became a guest of one of the cathedral's canons. It was there that she gave birth to Hugh's heir, a boy named Thomas. He was baptised on the 25 February 1367 in the Church of St Margaret.

The rumours of the period attached themselves not to Katherine, the model of a virtuous wife, but to her sister, Philippa Chaucer. She also gave birth sometime in 1367 and popular rumour credited the Duke of Lancaster with being the father of the child, Thomas Chaucer, rather than Geoffrey.[1] The theory of Thomas's paternity is based on the heraldic symbolism described on his tomb at Ewelme Church, that Lancaster paid for Thomas's sister Elizabeth to be admitted to Barking Abbey and that the duke's accounts contain generous New Year gifts to Philippa. If Lancaster did have a relationship with Katherine's sister, he did not acknowledge it when he wrote to the Pope asking for a dispensation to marry for a third time. John was known to have mistresses before his marriage to Blanche of Lancaster but there is little or no evidence of him being unfaithful during the years that she was alive. He recognised his daughter by Marie St Hilaire with whom he had an affair before his marriage just as he acknowledged and provided for his Beaufort offspring by Katherine so it is unlikely that either Thomas or Elizabeth Chaucer were his children.

After Blanche's death in 1368, her household would have been disbanded. It would have been inappropriate for Lancaster, as a single man, to maintain a household of women but someone needed to look after his children. In 1369, Blanche's cousin, Alice FitzAlan, Lady Wake, was appointed to the task. The duke's accounts show that Alyne

Gerberge was given a pension for the care she showed to Elizabeth after her mother's death at Tutbury. Alyne went on to serve Lancaster's second wife Constanza of Castile. The evidence also makes it apparent that Blanche Swynford remained in the nursery with her royal companions. Unfortunately, as Lancaster's financial accounts for 1369–1372 do not survive, it is not known what role Katherine played at this time. It is entirely plausible that she returned to Kettlethorpe.

Hugh died in 1372 whilst on campaign with the duke in Aquitaine, making Katherine a widow at the age of only twenty-one or thereabouts. Hugh's estates were now Thomas's but he was still a child. Katherine would receive her dower but the manors of Coleby and Kettlethorpe would be held by the Crown until her son was of an age to hold them himself. Katherine had held the estate in jointure during Swynford's life. In theory, it granted Katherine more financial independence than many women. The family might still have found themselves in financial difficulty which perhaps accounts for a gift of £10 made by Lancaster to Katherine in May 1372. It was a significant sum of money, and worth more than might be expected for an overlord showing consideration to the widow of a loyal retainer. It was the first of many grants and gifts. By the beginning of June, Katherine was in possession of her dower rights with the proviso that she would not remarry without royal permission. Kettlethorpe remained in Katherine's hands, as did one-third of Coleby, thanks to the intercession of someone influential – probably Lancaster.

Lancaster swore that his affair with Katherine did not start before Swynford's death. Besides which, Lancaster was not in England from the middle of 1370 until the end of 1372. He was on campaign in Aquitaine. The love affair began soon after Katherine was widowed as she gave birth to the duke's son, named John Beaufort, the following year. The duke's account books also show thoughtful gifts providing for Katherine's needs including deer that he hunted himself and oak from his estates so that the manor could be kept in good order. She was also called to the service of Lancaster's second wife as was Philippa Chaucer whose role at court came to an end with the death of Philippa of Hainault in 1369. Constanza was at Hertford Castle when the duchess gave birth on 13 March 1373. Katherine, who must have been in London when the news arrived, was sent to tell the king that he had a new granddaughter, named Catherine or Caterina. Her own child by Lancaster had arrived the previous autumn and was a longed-for, but illegitimate, boy. The name Beaufort was taken from the castle of Beaufort in Champagne which had been part of the Lancaster inheritance before the territory was lost to the French.

Few people would have known that Lancaster had taken Katherine to his bed. She divided her time between Constanza and her own home and besides which, the duke was not always faithful to either of the women in his life. In 1381, he confessed to the sin of lechery not only with Katherine but with many other women. Geoffrey Chaucer, who might have had his own grievances, depicted the duke as a man who liked women. However, these other women are unknown to history. Katherine left Constanza's household and became part of the household of Blanche of Lancaster's daughters. She was appointed *magistra* or governess to Philippa and Elizabeth. Henry, aged just six years may still have been part of his sisters' household, certainly he was fond of Katherine when he became an adult. Her appointment may have been made after Lady Wake left Lancaster's employment to raise her own family. Katherine's appointment gave her security as the duke was often on campaign either in France or pursuing his claim to the kingdom of Castile. It also meant that Katherine was able to live separately from Constanza which would have complicated the need for discretion. For Lancaster, there was the security of knowing that his daughters would be educated in the way that Philippa of Hainault would have approved. In other respects, it was not a sensible appointment. Daughters of the nobility were not supposed to be tutored by their father's mistress. Henry of Bolingbroke left Katherine's care in December 1374 when his father appointed a governor and sent him to live in the household of Lady Wake.

Katherine and Lancaster celebrated Christmas together at Eltham with the king and his court where Alice Perrers was in the ascendant. When Katherine travelled home, she was pregnant once again. John, having visited his wife in Hertford, returned to his home in London and ordered a tun of wine to be sent to Kettlethorpe to 'our very dear and well-beloved Dame Katherine de Swynford'.[2] The duke's care for Katherine was that of a man for his wife. He even granted a pension to the woman who nursed her during her early years. His registers often record payments and gifts describing Katherine as 'very dear and beloved'. Katherine grew wealthy but she was never blamed for avarice in the way that Alice Perrers was accused. In 1375, she was fined for not maintaining the Fossdyke at

Kettlethorpe. It was an important waterway joining the River Trent to Lincoln, allowing goods to be moved from the Midlands and Yorkshire. A commission of oyer and terminer appointed in May 1376 heard testimony that Katherine and other landowners along the dyke had allowed the dyke to silt up and were grazing their cattle in the summer on the fertile marsh that was developing.

As Edward III's reign drew to a close, his heir, the Black Prince, sickened and died. Lancaster became the king's chief adviser. He was not only associated with Alice Perrers, but also with a period when England's armies did not achieve their earlier successes and there was a fear after King Edward III's death in 1377 that he might usurp his nephew's throne. Lancaster was too powerful and too arrogant. The duke also offered shelter to John Wycliffe, the theologian who translated the Bible into English and argued that the Pope was not the true head of the church. Unsurprisingly Wycliffe was regarded as a heretic and Lancaster's support for him further blackened the duke's reputation. Thomas Walsingham, the Benedictine chronicler of St Albans, wrote a vitriolic condemnation of Lancaster criticising his leadership during the French wars and castigating him for his general conduct. He even went so far as to repeat a rumour that the duke had arranged for Matilda of Lancaster to be poisoned so that he would inherit the whole of the Lancastrian inheritance by right of his first wife. When the duke reversed the edicts of the so-called Good Parliament of 1376 banishing the king's evil councillors and Alice Perrers from court, the rumour began to circulate that Lancaster was the son of a labourer rather than the legitimate son of Edward III. Walsingham's 'Scandalous Chronicle' became more vituperative with the passage of time. Inevitably Katherine's existence had become public knowledge. The rebukes against Lancaster rebounded on Katherine who was described as an 'unspeakable concubine', 'a whore' and 'a witch'.[3] The monk accused the duke and Katherine of being shameless in the way that they travelled and lived together. The duke's moral turpitude was exemplified by the fact that he had abandoned his wife. Other chroniclers took their cue from the *St Alban's Chronicle* as sympathy for Constanza welled up alongside hatred for Lancaster.

By 1381, Lancaster was the *de facto* ruler of England. His nephew King Richard II was still only fourteen years old. The duke had become increasingly unpopular since the 1370s and was being blamed for the introduction of a hated poll tax. Wat Tyler's rebels camped on Blackheath before ravaging London and destroying Lancaster's home. The Savoy Palace burned for seven days casting a pall of black smoke over a scene of death and destruction. Thirty-two of the rebels, drunk on the duke's wine, had become trapped in the Savoy's cellars as it burned. Across the country, there were a series of attacks on Lancaster's homes, property and servants. Hertford Castle, a residence favoured by Constanza, was ransacked and at Leicester, the castellan removed the duke's belongings to sanctuary in St-Mary-in-the-Newarke Church. Back in London, the murders continued and the Tower breached. Simon of Sudbury, the Archbishop of Canterbury, was dragged out from its sheltering walls and his head hacked off. Lancaster's own physician was found at the same time and suffered the same fate. The following day, 15 June, Richard II met the rebels and the Lord Mayor of London stabbed Tyler to death. Richard's quick thinking and leadership saved the capital from an orgy of killing. He promised that they would all be free – at a stroke, serfdom was abolished or so the rebels thought.

Katherine, the scandalous mistress of the unpopular duke and the daughter of a foreigner, may have travelled north with Lancaster in May stopping with him at Leicester before travelling on to Kettlethorpe. If she was at the manor which had been extended and made more comfortable in the nine years since she became Lancaster's mistress, she was not safe as the Peasants' Revolt gained momentum. As well as the rising in Kent there were also risings in East Anglia. The *Anonimalle Chronicle* stated that she went into hiding. She and her whole family, including her new daughter Joan Beaufort, disappeared from the historical record. It has been suggested that she might have found sanctuary in King's Lynn or an unnamed convent. It is also possible that she was at Pontefract Castle because the castellan refused to open the gate to Lancaster's own wife, Constanza of Castile, who was forced to seek shelter at Knaresborough.

Lancaster met his wife on the road between Northallerton and Knaresborough. She prostrated herself in the road at his feet and he begged her pardon for any harm that he might have caused her. The revolt had been a shock to John. His property had been destroyed, his men killed and his fourteen-year-old son Henry only escaped with his life because he had been smuggled out of the Tower before the rebels stormed it. He publicly repented of his sins. If Katherine and his Beaufort children were to be protected, they had to be distanced from him. The duke renounced his mistress and took the care of his daughters from her charge. At the beginning of September, he raised her annuity to 200 marks a year for life and Katherine took out a lease on a property in Lincoln's Cathedral Close where for the next twelve years she became much respected by the cathedral's canons. On 14 February 1382, Katherine received a legal document known as a 'quit claim' which rendered all accounts between the couple as settled. Neither owed the other anything. All rights that Lancaster had to the gifts he made to Katherine were formally relinquished.

In private, the duke continued to send Katherine and her family gifts and to provide for them. They may still have been in contact, perhaps even conducting their affair more secretly than ever. However, successfully kept secrets are not recorded for posterity and there is no evidence for the suggestion. Thomas Swynford was transferred from the duke's household to the retinue of Henry of Bolingbroke where he remained. Katherine is known to have visited Henry's wife, Mary de Bohun, that year. Mary was only thirteen at the time and in the care of her mother. Katherine busied herself improving her property and extending her landholdings. In 1383, Richard II gave her a licence to enclose a park of three hundred acres of land and woods at Kettlethorpe.

Three years later, Lancaster departed England in the hope of winning his own crown by right of his wife Constanza of Castile. He had put his affairs in England in order before beginning his Spanish campaign. Nine-year-old Joan Beaufort was betrothed to Sir Robert Ferrers of Wem and he went to Lincoln to see his Beaufort children.

Before he departed from Plymouth, Lancaster was required to hush up another scandalous liaison as best he could. His daughter, Elizabeth, who was twenty-three by 1386, was married to John Hastings, Earl of Pembroke, at Kenilworth in 1380. Unfortunately, the groom was half the bride's age. It is perhaps not surprising in the circumstances that she fell in love with John Holland, Duke of Exeter, who was one of Joan of Kent's sons from her marriage to Thomas Holland. Exeter was known for his charm. He had already seduced Constanza of Castile's sister Isabella who was married to Lancaster's brother, Edmund of Langley. He had become besotted with the young countess and now Elizabeth was pregnant by him. Amidst the scandal, John of Gaunt arranged for his daughter's first marriage to be annulled so that she could marry Exeter. The marriage was a happy one although Elizabeth was widowed when her husband was executed by her own brother, King Henry IV, in 1400.

What Katherine thought of Elizabeth's predicament is not recorded. She remained in Lincoln tending to her business and her family. She was probably in the congregation at Lincoln Cathedral when Richard II and his queen, Anne of Bohemia, visited in March 1387. The following month Richard, who was always pleased to see her, made Katherine a Lady of the Garter. She travelled to Windsor in August that year for the ceremony, to wear the splendid new robes that the king paid for and for the feast that followed. Dame Katherine Swynford was respectable once more even if Richard might have hoped that his powerful uncle would have approved.

Lancaster's campaign to win Castile was a failure. The expedition was beset by problems including disease. Philippa Chaucer is thought to have accompanied Constanza as part of the duchess' household. She is likely to have died from dysentery. There is no record of her death other than the discontinuation of her annual pension. Lancaster departed from the Iberian Peninsula for Aquitaine sick in body and heart. He left behind his eldest daughter, Philippa of Lancaster, who was married to King Juan I to seal the Anglo-Portuguese alliance created by the Treaty of Windsor. Her new husband already had a mistress, Inês Pires, and a family. Philippa was well educated and politically astute. Perhaps remembering the influence of Katherine on her father, she insisted that Juan's mistress retire to a convent but the king's illegitimate son and five-year-old daughter, Beatrice, remained at court. Philippa oversaw their education as well as that of her own children. In 1405, Philippa's stepdaughter went to England as the bride of the twelfth Earl of Arundel to further cement the Anglo-Portuguese treaty.

Lancaster, having recognised that he would never be king of Castile, arranged for his daughter Catherine who was sixteen to marry the heir to the throne of Castile. He and Constanza lived separate lives although the duke continued to provide for her. When Constanza finally returned to England, she chose to live mainly at Tutbury. Katherine and her daughter Joan travelled from their home in Lincoln to stay with Henry of Bolingbroke's wife, Mary de Bohun. The timing suggests that her visits often coincided with the birth of Mary's children. Childbed was a dangerous time for a young mother and someone as capable as Katherine would be welcome. It is possible that Henry invited Katherine to please his father but there is evidence that he was warm-hearted to her himself and to his extended family. Some accounts of Katherine's life suggest that she lived with Mary but there is no substantial proof of this. There is evidence that she was often a welcome guest, especially for the Christmas festivities. New year's gifts for Katherine and Joan from Henry and his wife included silk gowns edged with miniver. In 1391, the accounts reveal that Katherine received a diamond set in a gold ring as well as several lengths of expensive white damask. She was an honoured member of the family circle.

When Lancaster arrived back in England on 19 November 1389, there were family matters to attend to including the continuing education of fifteen-year-old Henry who was destined for the church. The Beauforts could often be found with their father. John Beaufort, who was a favourite of Lancaster's, was based in his household. The accounts reveal that Katherine was also stabling twelve horses at the duke's expense.[4] It is likely that Katherine was once again an important part of Lancaster's life although there is no evidence to confirm whether or not they became lovers once more. There was no scandal attached to any of Katherine's visits to the duke's homes and no adverse comment about them being seen together.

Constanza was at Leicester when she died in March 1394. Lancaster was in France negotiating a truce from the intermittent war started by his father King Edward III. The funeral was delayed until the duke was able to attend. At the beginning of July, Henry of Bolingbroke's beloved wife, Mary died as a consequence of childbed fever having given birth to her seventh child. It is entirely possible that Katherine was once again in attendance upon the young woman who had made her a welcome part of the family. Mary was buried the day after Constanza.

Lancaster was fifty-six years old and did something completely unexpected. He sought to marry his mistress within weeks of his return from Aquitaine. The *English Chronicle* explained that the duke had no need to marry a woman with no real status or wealth, let alone a former mistress. Capgrave writing during the fifteenth century stated that the union went ahead contrary to good advice. There was no benefit or gain to be made from the union. The only conclusion that can be drawn is that

Lancaster loved Katherine. The duke wrote to Pope Boniface IX to seek a dispensation to marry. Lancaster was Blanche Swynford's godfather and it created an impediment to a wedding because his relationship to Blanche created a spiritual link. He swore that there had been no carnal relationship prior to Hugh's death and recognised his four Beaufort children by Katherine. A dispensation was duly issued. Having also obtained the king's permission, Lancaster set off for Lincolnshire to claim his prize. Katherine married her duke on 13 January 1396 in Lincoln Cathedral. The widow of Sir Hugh Swynford, a notorious woman, was now a duchess. Her son John Beaufort was already married to the Earl of Kent's daughter, Margaret Holland, who was King Richard II's niece. She had always felt at home within royal circles.

After the wedding, the duke took his new duchess on a trip to some of his northern estates. On their return journey, they stopped at Coventry. It was Easter by the time the couple arrived at court. Froissart stated that their arrival caused astonishment. Richard II had no wife and because Lancaster was the next most important man in the realm, Katherine who had grown up well versed in matters of court etiquette and who counted some of the most important men in the land as her friends automatically became the first lady to whom all others had to give way. Whilst Richard II and her new stepson Henry welcomed Katherine, her female contemporaries did not. Froissart recorded that the Duchess of Gloucester and the Countesses of Derby and Arundel were at best frosty and at worst hostile. Thomas of Woodstock thought that his brother was a 'doting fool'.[5] In September, the Pope validated the marriage and pronounced the Beaufort family to be legitimate. And in October, Katherine was present in France when Richard met Charles VI of France and met his new bride, Isabella of Valois. Katherine travelled with Isabella to England and in due course became one of her chief ladies. She had a reputation for being good with children and the girl who was preparing for her wedding was still only six years old.

On 6 February 1397, Richard II legitimised his four Beaufort cousins by Letters Patent ratified by parliament. Later Henry IV would add a note to the effect that the Beaufort brood were legitimate in all things apart from the right of inheritance to the throne. The changes made Joan Beaufort, recently bereaved by the death of her first husband Sir Robert Ferrers, a much more valuable bride. By the time she and her siblings stood under the canopy of state to be legitimised in law as well as by the Church, she was already married to Ralph Neville, 6th Baron Raby. On 10 February, John Beaufort became the Earl of Somerset and in April, the king made him a Knight of the Garter.

Katherine's presence in the written record is patchy and incomplete. Once she married John of Gaunt and the shock of the social difference faded, she disappeared from the chronicles. Besides, the Plantagenets and the kingdom of England were heading towards civil unrest. John was in favour with his nephew but Henry was in danger. He was one of the Lords Appellants who sought to muzzle the king's favourites in 1388. Richard bided his time until he was in a position to take his revenge against the group of nobles who tried to place restraints on his rule. John retired from the court with Katherine and in his absence the earls of Gloucester, Warwick and Arundel were arrested on the king's orders. There is no record of how John, Katherine or Henry felt when Gloucester was taken to Calais and murdered. As the political tide turned into a tsunami of vengeance, Lancaster's health began to fail. In February 1398, he and Katherine were at Lilleshall Abbey and as soon as they were able travelled to see the king. They were worried that Henry would be the next victim of Richard's vendetta and that the wealth of the Duchy of Lancaster would fall prey to the king's greed. Lancaster's health continued to deteriorate and he was forced to withdraw from public life. He was not present when Richard II insisted that the remaining Lords Appellant, Henry and Thomas Mowbray, the Duke of Norfolk face one another in trial by combat to settle a dispute in which each had accused the other of treason. Lancaster and Katherine were at Gosford Green in Coventry on the morning of 16 September to see Henry fight for his life. Richard stopped the combat at the last minute and banished both participants. Mowbray was exiled for life whilst Lancaster's beloved son was banished for ten years. They were required to leave England by 20 October. At a stroke, and without recourse to law, the king had rid himself of the last two Lords Appellant.

Lancaster was silent in public. Katherine remained by her husband's side. She was with him at Leicester when Richard visited to show that he held no grudge against his uncle. Froissart told the tale of Henry's departure, Lancaster's declining health and his final days. By the fifteenth century, it was claimed that Lancaster 'died of putrefaction of his genitals and body, caused by the frequenting of women, for he was a great fornicator'.[6] The writer, Thomas Gascoigne, continued to describe Gaunt's illness as 'the exercise of carnal intercourse with women'.[7] Whether he was castigating Gaunt for his illicit relationship with Katherine as well as describing the consequences of venereal disease is another matter. What is true, is that the duke's final illness was being used by the Church to demonstrate the consequences of licentiousness. Gascoigne was biased against Gaunt because the duke supported John Wycliffe the reformer who translated the Bible into English.

Lancaster's son, Henry of Bolingbroke, returned to England when his cousin Richard confiscated the duchy of Lancaster and made Henry's exile permanent. Initially Henry said that he only wanted his inheritance but he deposed his cousin Richard II in 1400 and became King Henry IV. The records show that he maintained his links with his stepmother's family, even if he did amend the Beauforts' legitimacy with a handwritten note in the margins of Richard II's patent debarring them from the throne. He referred to Katherine as the 'King's mother', granted her 1,000 marks a year from the Duchy of Lancaster and made her a further gift of four tuns of wine a year. Katherine died on 10 May 1403 having outlived Gaunt by four years. She was buried in Lincoln Cathedral.

Katherine's relationship with Lancaster spanned more than thirty years. She remains famous thanks to Anya Seton's novel which was first published in the 1950s, and which is still in print. History's lens does not offer much evidence about Katherine herself. We do not know how she felt about her royal lover or if she was as strong a character as fiction portrays her. It is unknown whether romance was kindled during Lancaster's visits to his children or elsewhere. Nor can writers be sure about Constanza's relationship with Katherine. The affair between John of Gaunt and Katherine began at about the same time as he married Constanza. The duchess is likely to have felt envy that it was Katherine who provided the duke with sons. The chronicles were as hostile to Katherine only because of her association with Lancaster. Katherine did not set about making herself wealthy or seek to add her voice to the public sphere, she was more successful in manipulating social mores. History has treated her more kindly than Alice Perrers, her contemporary. There is also the small matter that she became the ancestor of the Tudor monarchy, unlike Alice who produced a largely unknown mutineer.

Chapter 19

Elizabeth Wayte

King Edward IV was the second son of Richard Duke of York and Cecily Neville. The duke had a claim to the throne by right of his mother, Anne Mortimer, who was descended from King Edward III's second surviving son Lionel, Duke of Clarence. Richard was also the grandson of Edmund of Langley the fourth son of Edward III. His claim was arguably superior to that of King Henry VI who was descended from John of Gaunt who was Lionel's younger brother. Despite this York served his cousin faithfully in France. By 1452, Richard aspired to being recognised as Henry VI's heir and to destroy his political opponent the Duke of Somerset. He failed in both aims but in August 1453, the English lost their toe-hold in France and King Henry VI had a breakdown. In March 1454, York was appointed protector of the realm. He was hated and feared by Henry's queen Margaret of Anjou who favoured the Duke of Somerset. When the king recovered, she was able to persuade her husband to dismiss York. The duke's response was to take up arms. The opening battle in the war for the Crown between the houses of Lancaster and York took place on 22 May 1455. Hostilities continued intermittently. Richard and his second surviving son, Edmund, Earl of Rutland, were both killed at the Battle of Wakefield on 30 December 1460, their severed heads displayed on Micklegate Bar in York, the duke's head decorated with a paper crown. The fortunes of the House of York were at their lowest ebb but Edward, Earl of March, the eldest surviving son of Richard inherited the dukedom of York and his father's claim to the throne. Thanks to his victories at Mortimer's Cross in February and at Towton that Easter, Edward was crowned on 28 June 1461.

The new king, aged nineteen years, was young and handsome standing at nearly 6ft 4ins tall. The *Croyland Chronicle* described him as a 'tall and elegant of person, of unblemished character, valiant in arms'.[1] It also described him as a man of 'vanities, debaucheries, extravagances and sensual enjoyments'.[2] Sir Thomas More said of him that he was 'of visage lovely, of body mighty, strong and clean made'.[3] He also noted that the king had a 'greedy appetite' for women. Chroniclers described him as generous and a Milanese writer added, 'words fail me to relate how well the commons love and adore him'.[4] It is perhaps not surprising that Edward, who took care to dress well, soon found himself surrounded by women willing to share his bed. Contemporary chroniclers observed that 'he pursued with no discrimination the married and the unmarried, the noble and the lowly'.[5] Edward's lack of chastity is unsurprising given his age and the danger which he endured but a short time before. Commines, who knew Edward, said of him, 'his thoughts were wholly employed upon the ladies'.[6]

Later Edward would jest that he had three mistresses, one was the wiliest, the second the merriest and the third the holiest harlot in the land. The first of the women was Elizabeth Waite. The Victorian historian, James Gairdner, described her as a 'courtesan of obscure birth',[7] suggesting that she went from partner to partner in search of protection and wealth whereas Sir Thomas More was kinder to her and described her as a naïve young girl seduced by Edward's good looks and charm.

A seventeenth-century historian, George Buck, provided Elizabeth with a family name stating that she was the daughter of Thomas Wayte of Hampshire 'a mean gentleman, if he was one'.[8] Edward may have met her in 1461 whilst he was in the south of England. Arthur, Elizabeth's son with the king, according to popular history, was born during the early 1460s. It is not clear whether she was married at the time she became Edward's mistress or was a young widow. In 1472, a royal household account reference to 'my Lord the Bastard' infers that the child was raised in the royal nursery. In 1501, the accounts place 'the Bastard of King Edward's'[9] in the household of his half-sister, Elizabeth of York. He was listed amongst her household at her funeral. He transferred into King Henry VII's household, serving as an esquire of the body and from there he became part of his nephew's household in 1509. He remained close to the king during his early years. His illegitimacy and his mother's obscure birth ensured that his Plantagenet bloodline was not initially a threat to the Tudors. His Tudor nephew made him the keeper of the royal forests at Clarendon and Bere, a Vice-Admiral of England and the Governor of Calais as well as creating him Lord Lisle in 1523 by right of his wife Elizabeth Grey, the widow of Edmund Dudley. Lisle gained a reputation for being charming and easy-going in much the same way that his father was agreeable. Unfortunately, as he aged, Henry VIII became more determined to secure the Tudor succession by eliminating the last remnants of the Plantagenets. As the struggle between protestant reformers and the more conservative members of the nobility intensified, Lisle was implicated as part of the White Rose Faction. He was summoned back to London in 1540 believing that he was to be created an earl. Instead, he found that Thomas Cromwell was to be made an earl and that he was destined for the Tower where his relations, the Poles, had already been executed ostensibly for their religious beliefs but in reality, for their lineage. Lisle was still in the Tower when Cromwell was arrested and executed. On 27 May 1541, Lisle's cousin Lady Margaret Pole, Countess of Salisbury, the daughter of George, Duke of Clarence was executed without trial. Lisle remained incarcerated for the next eighteen months. He was still there when the king's fifth queen, poor foolish Katherine Howard, was executed. It was then that Henry remembered his uncle and issued the warrant for his release. Lisle was so overcome with relief that he died the following day 'through too much rejoicing'.[10]

It is also thought that Elizabeth Wayte was the mother of Elizabeth Plantagenet who married Sir Thomas Lumley in 1477. It is possible that she was also the mother of other unknown children of Edward IV[11] but there is no mention of her after 1467. Elizabeth Plantagenet was less well documented than Arthur. It is possible that she was not Elizabeth Wayte's child at all. The siblings might have been the result of liaisons with two different women. This raises a second possibility about the identity of Edward's wily mistress and an indication as to why Edward should have regarded the young woman he took to his bed as deceitful. A potential clue as to the identity of another woman who Edward may have made his mistress can be found in Polydore Vergil's history of the period. The Italian, who came to England in 1502, was encouraged to write the *Anglia Historia* by King Henry VII. It was first published in 1534 although the manuscript was finished in 1513. He noted that King Edward IV conducted an affair with a relation of the Earl of Warwick whilst visiting his household.

Margaret Lucy was the young widow of Sir William Lucy, a veteran of the Hundred Years War. She was his third wife and had benefited from a marriage settlement which included a life interest in much of his estate. He was killed at the Battle of Northampton in 1460. After Lucy's death, Margaret's dower rights were rejected as the jointure was made without royal licence. It took a further two years before the matter was resolved, leaving Margaret, a childless widow, facing an uncertain future. The *London Chronicle* recorded a further complication;

> And that goode knyght Syr Wylliam Lucy that dwellyd be-syde Northehampton hyrde the gonne schotte, and come unto the fylde to have holpyn ye kynge, but the fylde was done or that he come; an one of the Staffordys was ware of hys comynge, and lovyd that knyght ys wyffe and hatyd hym, and a-non causyd his dethe.[12]

Sir John Stafford, an impecunious Yorkist supporter, took the opportunity to murder his opponent in love, a man who happened to be a Lancastrian, on the battlefield. The *London Chronicle* allowed its readers to think that the men were on the same side because it wanted to emphasise the magnitude of the act. It was inferred Stafford had been having an affair with Margaret and married her within the year of her husband's death. Sir John was killed in his turn at the Battle of Towton.

Margaret, bereaved twice, was fortunate in having powerful relations. She was related to the Montagu family through her mother and her stepfather was the Earl of Exeter. The Earl of Warwick was Margaret's cousin and in 1462, Margaret was part of Warwick's household until her dower rights could be established and a new husband found for her. Given her connections and the prospects of a dower, she was not without suitors. She was courted by Thomas Danvers, an Oxfordshire lawyer, who eventually took her to court for breach of promise to marry. Danvers claimed that he loved Margaret as much as any man could love a woman and had been directed by her half-brother Sir Henry FitzLewis in the matter of attaining her hand. Danvers went on to say that they had exchanged vows *verba de presenti*. The exchange of vows to marry in the present tense constituted a valid marriage. If Margaret and Danvers followed the vow with consummation then an indissoluble marriage took place and even if it was unconsummated, a dispensation from the Pope would still have been required. Money changed hands between FitzLewis and Danvers to seal the agreement. But then Margaret entered a contract to marry Thomas Wake who was one of the Earl of Warwick's retainers.

The matter was sent to the Archbishop of York, who happened to be the Earl of Warwick's brother, for consideration and she remained married to Thomas Wake after she vehemently denied making any agreement with Danvers.

Margaret died on 4 August 1466. It is likely that she died from complications following the birth of her child, John, who was born three months before her death. Her brass, depicting her wearing a butterfly headdress, identifies her husbands through their coats of arms, and can be seen in St Nicholas Church, Ingrave near Brentwood in Essex. The Wake family would rise to prominence during the reign of Richard III and John, Margaret's son, would become one of the king's gentlemen ushers. It is unclear why John was singled out for royal favour.[13] But if Polydore Vergil was correctly informed about Edward IV's illicit affair, the fuzzy story told by Sir Thomas More about Dame Lucy who was seduced by the king might have been a reference to Margaret Lucy rather than Elizabeth.

Chapter 20

Lady Eleanor Talbot Butler and Elizabeth Woodville

Lady Eleanor Butler was Edward IV's holy harlot but she might also have been his wife, and England's unacknowledged queen, if the parliamentary claims laid out in Richard III's *Titulus Regius* were correct. Richard argued that his young nephews, Edward and Richard, were illegitimate because their father had made a secret marriage prior to his subsequent bigamous marriage to Elizabeth Woodville who had also married King Edward IV in a secret ceremony. The act of parliament formally acknowledged that Eleanor was married to Edward but the truth of the matter, for which there is little contemporary evidence, remains the subject of debate.

Commines' account stated that Edward was very much in love and promised to marry Eleanor provided she sleep with him first – which she did. Under canon law, the promise to marry in the future tense followed by consummation was a valid marriage. The Bishop of Bath and Wells was prepared to testify that he had married them when only he and they were present. Commines extended the story by observing that the bishop's fortune during the reign of King Edward IV depended upon the secret being kept. After 1464 he was in receipt of an annual salary and was offered a bishopric. It could have been coincidence or it could have been a reward for his silence.

Eleanor Talbot, the daughter of the 1st Earl of Shrewsbury, was the widow of Thomas Butler, the heir to the lordship of Sudeley. She married him when she was thirteen years old but Butler died before 1461 possibly as the result of injuries sustained at the Battle of Blore Heath. Her dower included two manors; Fenny Compton and Burton Dassett. The Crown seized both the manors because the family was Lancastrian. Eleanor was slightly older than Edward and she was in need of the king's help in gaining what was legally hers. Although her husband and his family were

Lancastrian, Eleanor's father had been one of the principal supporters of Edward's father, the Duke of York. Eleanor's mother was Lady Margaret Beauchamp, her aunt Anne was the Earl of Warwick's wife. The Earl of Warwick also known as The Kingmaker was the man who helped put Edward IV on the throne. Given her family connections, Eleanor may well have thought that Edward would be amenable to helping her gain her dower rights. What she cannot have expected, if the story is correct, is that the king desired Eleanor upon meeting her.

The handsome young victor of Towton had not anticipated that Eleanor, a pious young woman, would refuse his advances and he found it difficult to take no for an answer. In order to get what he wanted; Edward promised that he would marry Eleanor. Under canon law, this exchange of vows to marry was called *verba de futuro* and was a betrothal that could be dissolved unless the promise was followed by sexual intercourse, in which case the couple were regarded as being married. If Edward did go through with a wedding, it is likely that it happened whilst he was making his way south for his coronation in June 1461. Edward may have promised he would marry Eleanor to get her into his bed or he may have gone through a secret ceremony conducted by Robert Stillington who would become the Bishop of Bath and Wells. The king having satisfied his desire left Eleanor behind in the Midlands. Edward never made public acknowledgement of Eleanor and she never demanded the rights of a royal wife. Instead, Eleanor became an oblate at the Carmelite Priory in Norwich. She may have lived at her sister's house at Kenninghall which was within a reasonable distance of the priory.

Since she died in 1468, it was impossible for the parliament of 1483 to find out from her what happened when she encountered Edward. The *Titulus Regulus* is a legal document. It stated that the pre-contract to marry Lady Eleanor Butler was the reason why Edward V was declared illegitimate and his uncle Richard took the throne. The problem for historians is that the very nature of a secret marriage means that there is very little in way of evidence. It is all circumstantial and Edward had a track record for making promises to get into the beds of women he lusted after. He also had a track record with beautiful Lancastrian widows in need of help. Margaret Lucy may have been one, Lady Eleanor Butler the second and Elizabeth Woodville, a third. These private marriages came to be known as irregular or clandestine. Widows whose marriages were private ones sometimes found it difficult to claim their dower rights and children from such unions sometimes found their right to inherit challenged. It was also easier for both the bride and groom to protest that there was no marriage if either of them changed their minds. Where there was secrecy there was more room for deception. Nonetheless, even in the eighteenth century, it was thought that up to one-third of marriages was irregular or clandestine. Edward IV's irregular marriage to Elizabeth Woodville and the claim that he made a secret marriage to Eleanor Talbot are probably the most famous examples of the complications created by medieval nuptial arrangements. Was Eleanor Talbot the unacknowledged Queen of England, making Edward's marriage to Elizabeth Woodville bigamous and his children illegitimate or was Eleanor just another of Edward IV's many mistresses? Without definite proof, the answers are always likely to be controversial.

The Woodville family were no strangers to the difficulties of making secret marriages. Elizabeth's mother Jacquetta was the widow of Henry V's brother, the Duke of Bedford. When he died, without legitimate heirs, Bedford willed her all his lands which would only revert to the Crown when she died. King Henry VI granted Jacquetta the lands that his uncle had left her with the proviso that she should seek permission before remarrying. When she returned to England a knight named Sir Richard Woodville was part of the escort. His family were in Bedford's service. The two became close during the journey home and they either married in secret in 1436 or the following year. The marriage was not a secret for long because Jacquetta fell pregnant with their daughter, Elizabeth. Wavrin's Chronicle recorded the anger of Jacquetta's family in regard to an unequal marriage and suggested that 'she had two children before her marriage'.[1] She and her husband were forced to beg the king's pardon and pay a fine of £1,000.[2] The connection led to Woodville being created Lord Rivers in 1448. The Paston Letters reveal that some of the nobility, Richard Neville in particular, looked down on the Woodville clan because they were 'made by maryage' rather than having an established aristocratic heritage.[3] Despite this, in due course Rivers was able to arrange suitable marriages for three of his children including his eldest daughter.

Elizabeth Woodville married Sir John Grey of Groby who was heir to Lord Ferrers of Groby. Elizabeth's husband was killed at the second Battle of St Albans on 17 February 1461. Whilst Henry VI sat on the throne, he was a loyal knight who served his king faithfully but after Edward's victory at Towton, Grey was posthumously judged to have been a traitor and attainted of treason. His estates became forfeit to the Crown and Elizabeth and her two young sons lost their home at Bradgate Park in Leicestershire. The Woodvilles were also Lancastrians and their estates were escheated to the Crown in May. Elizabeth might have hoped that her in-laws would support her and her children. Her mother-in-law, Elizabeth Ferrers, Baroness Ferrers of Groby, had remarried after John's father died in 1456. The man she married was John Bouchier, one of King Edward's cousins. A disagreement ensued about the income from three manors, totalling 100 marks a year, which Edward Ferrers set aside for his heirs.

At the beginning of June 1461, Edward IV visited Stony Stratford, five miles from Grafton where the Woodvilles lived. The family submitted to the king and begged his pardon. On 12 June Richard Woodville, Lord Rivers was forgiven and the annuity that was Jacquetta's was returned to her.[4] Only a year previously Lord Rivers had been taken to Calais and rated for his low birth by Edward's cousin, the Earl of Warwick. The chronicler Jean de Waurin claimed that Rivers' pardon was due to Edward's love for Elizabeth. Despite the improvement in her parents' circumstances, Elizabeth was still without her dower rights. Weeks turned into months which became years. She wrote to Lord Hastings, who had been given control of the Midlands, on 13 April 1364 and asked for his assistance in gaining her eldest son's rights to his father's estate. Hastings agreed to help Elizabeth but only if she split the rents that accrued from the three contested manors with him. He also stipulated that a marriage should be arranged between Elizabeth's son and any daughter that Hastings might have or, failing that, a suitable female from within his extended family.[5] Had Elizabeth been secure in the king's affections or known she was about to become queen it is unlikely that she would have appealed to the acquisitive Hastings.

Very little is known about Elizabeth Woodville before 1464 but popular history places her under an oak in Whittlebury Forest waiting for the king to petition him for justice. According to the story he fell in love with her and wanted her to be his mistress. Dominic Mancini, writing in 1483 about Richard III's usurpation of his nephew, continued the tale with a story that he was told about the relationship.

The story runs that Edward placed a dagger at her throat to make her submit to his passion, she remained unperturbed and determined to die rather than live unchastely with the king. Whereupon Edward coveted her much the more, and he judged the lady worthy to be a royal spouse who could not be overcome in her constancy even by an infatuated king.[6]

Cornazzano, an Italian poet, wrote that it was Elizabeth who used the knife rather than Edward saying that, as a woman of noble birth, she would prefer to kill herself rather than be dishonoured.[7] His poem depicted the young king as a womaniser. In his poem, Elizabeth is a chaste woman who wins the king's heart. Licence observes that the English chronicles are not so detailed as the foreign accounts of the affair.[8]

Whatever the truth of the story Edward determined to marry Elizabeth Woodville. Fabyan's Chronicle describes Edward pausing at Stony Stratford on 30 April 1464. He was on his way north to join the Earl of Warwick at Bamburgh where King Henry VI was besieged but lingered for a few days. As dawn broke on 1 May, Edward and one or two others went hunting. It was an excuse to explain his absence. Elizabeth and her mother Jacquetta also went out early on May Day to the chapel of St Mary and St Michael near Shaw's Wood. May Day was associated with fertility, couples courting and a time when social rules were flouted which fitted the mood of the king. The chapel belonged to St James' Abbey. Edward awaited them with a priest, Stillington. He exchanged vows with Elizabeth Woodville, consummated their marriage before he returned to Stony Stratford and spent the rest of the day hunting. What history cannot know is whether Edward intended to honour the marriage. It was easily refutable even if it was canonical with consent freely given by both parties followed by consummation. It is entirely possible that he did the same thing to at least one other woman.

Elizabeth was not a suitable candidate for a royal bride. She was older than Edward, a penniless widow and a Lancastrian to boot. Polydore Vergil described the union as the result of infatuation. Unlike other chroniclers he did not linger on the bride's nobility of virtue, instead he looked at the transgression of selecting a woman from a lower social class. Mancini chose to look at the problem through the eyes of Edward's mother, Cecily Neville, who is alleged to have declared her son illegitimate because of his behaviour. A man descended from kings would not have chosen to marry a penniless widow. Later, in 1469, another strand would be added to the story by the addition of the idea that Elizabeth's mother bewitched Edward into marriage.

By the end of May 1464, Edward was in York. He travelled back down through the Midlands in the summer. Parliament opened in Reading in September. Meanwhile, Edward's cousin the Earl of Warwick went to France in order to negotiate a marriage between Edward and a French Princess called Bona, the fourteen-year-old sister of King Louis XI. It was usual for English kings to marry foreign princesses to cement treaties and alliances. Whatever Edward's original intentions he admitted to a marriage at a council meeting. Edward chose to marry from personal preference. The only other monarch or heir to the throne to do this was the Black Prince when he married, in secret, to his cousin, the widowed Joan of Kent – a woman with a scandalous bigamous past. But Joan, a woman of royal blood, never became queen because her husband died before King Edward III and it was her son who became Richard II in 1377.

Rumours flew around the inns of London and from there to France and Italy. The Milanese ambassador wrote to his master that the marriage 'had greatly offended the people of England'.[9] The same report said that Edward had loved Elizabeth for a long time even though she was a widow. Sir Thomas More asserted that Edward's mother, Cecily, accused her son of 'befouling himself with a bigamous marriage'.[10]

Richard's assertion of his brother's bigamy made through the *Titulus Regulus* was believable because Edward IV was a womaniser. Mancini stated that Edward used money and promises where charm and good looks failed. He also noted that Edward soon tired of the women he chased and when he was tired of his mistresses, he passed them to his friends. Vergil suggested that on occasion Edward resorted to violence.

It was only after the Battle of Bosworth in August 1485 and the ascent of the Tudors to the throne that Elizabeth regained her status as Edward IV's wife and her children were re-established as legitimate. All copies of the *Titulus Regius* were ordered to be destroyed. In January 1486, Henry Tudor, the man who was now king by right of his mother Lady Margaret Beaufort, a descendent of John of Gaunt's legitimised children with his mistress Katherine Swynford took Edward IV's daughter, Elizabeth of York, for his wife. Lady Margaret Beaufort was the closest Lancastrian claimant to the Crown but it was a disputed one. Henry IV had accepted the legitimisation of his Beaufort half-siblings in all matters except for the right to wear the crown. Elizabeth Woodville, from her sanctuary in Westminster following Edward IV's death and the disappearance of her sons from the Tower, arrived at an accommodation with Lady Margaret Beaufort that her daughter would marry Margaret's son. Henry swore an oath in December 1483 promising to unite the houses of York and Lancaster with his marriage to Elizabeth. He ruled by right of conquest but Elizabeth added a legitimacy to the Crown and to the house of Tudor that he would otherwise have lacked.

Chapter 21

Jane Shore

Jane Shore started life, born circa 1455, as Elizabeth, the daughter of Amy and her husband John Lambert who was a London mercer and freeman of the City of London. She was part of a large family that included three sons who grew to adulthood. Sir Thomas More told her story and her relationship with Edward IV in his history of King Richard III. According to More, she was the merriest of Edward's mistresses. Like Alice Perrers, she paid the price for being part of the king's life after his death. Her belongings were confiscated, she was imprisoned and she was forced to do public penance through the streets of London. Edward's brother Richard, the Lord Protector, punished Jane Shore to shine a light on his brother's infidelities by the public show of Jane walking bareheaded in her shift through London.

History does not know how many of the women who became royal mistresses went unwillingly to the king's bed but across the centuries very few English royal mistresses might be described as courtesans. Traditionally courtesans plied their trade based on the wealth they could amass from their lovers. Jane Shore is an exception. Unmarried at the time of Edward's death, she transferred her affections to William, Lord Hastings, almost immediately. Jane did not seek the kind of financial independence that Alice Perrers set about accruing for herself from King Edward III nor did she live the lavish life of Agnès Sorel in the court of Charles VII of France although the portrait thought to be a likeness of her at Eton depicts a bare-breasted woman adorned with expensive jewels. Jane sought a new lover after Edward's death because she recognised that without the king to protect her, she was just another vulnerable woman. Or, if the ballads and plays written about her later were correct, she revelled in her sexuality.

John Lambert, Jane's father, was a successful mercer. It is probable that the Lamberts loaned money to King Edward IV so that he could pursue his campaign against Margaret of Anjou and the Lancastrians after he became king in 1461. Jane might have been in the crowds that lined the street when he arrived in London to be crowned king. She would have been about twelve years of age at the time and like many other young women smitten with the golden young man who was the image of heroic chivalry. The Lamberts' wealth and Edward's desire to keep the favour of London's leading merchants ensured that Jane was welcome at court and may even have joined in a royal hunt, of the kind described by ballads dating to the sixteenth century and earlier, in Epping Forest. Edward wished to cultivate London's wealthy merchants as he needed their support. Meanwhile, the Lamberts arranged for their daughter to marry William Shore, a goldsmith and banker of Lombard Street. She was in her teens by then and was turning into a strikingly beautiful young woman who could both read and write. Sir Thomas More, who met her, said:

> She was merry in company, ready and quick to answer; neither mute nor full of babble; somewhat taunting without displeasure and not without disport.[1]

Shore was some fifteen years older than Jane and the marriage was not a success despite the fact that the union secured a comfortable future for the girl.

It is uncertain when Jane became Edward's mistress. It has been suggested that Lord Hastings, Edward's friend and Lord Chamberlain saw her first and was attracted by her beauty. It is easy to imagine the beautiful quicksilver witted girl in Shore's shop becoming a focus for aristocratic lust. Hastings' enemies accused him of pandering for the king although Commines found him to be a man 'of singular wisdom and virtue'.[2] Hastings, if it was he, who saw her first, was rejected. Mancini, who described Edward's court, suggested that the king's friends turned the court into a den of debauchery. It was more difficult to spurn the advances of King Edward IV.

They were changeable times, even for the king. In 1469, the Earl of Warwick, known as the Kingmaker, withdrew his support from his cousin Edward. The king was forced to flee the country and Elizabeth Woodville and her three daughters sought sanctuary in Westminster Abbey. For a brief period, thanks to Warwick, King Henry VI resumed his throne. On 2 November 1470, Elizabeth Woodville gave birth to a son named Edward after his father. He was created Prince of Wales after Edward IV's restoration to the throne following a decisive battle fought in a dense fog at Barnet on 14 April 1471. Warwick's brother was killed during the battle and the Kingmaker died during the rout that followed. Edward's battle for the Crown only ended on 4 May 1471 at the Battle of Tewkesbury with the death of Henry VI's son, Edward of Lancaster. According to some sources, the Lancastrian heir was summarily executed after the battle. Lancastrians who sought sanctuary in the abbey were dragged from within its precincts and put to death. The Yorkist king returned to London in triumph on 21 May. During that night the deposed king, Henry VI, was quietly murdered whilst he was at his prayers probably on King Edward's orders. It was given out that he died of melancholy.

Jane and William's marriage was annulled in March 1476 when Jane was probably already the king's mistress. She had taken her case to the Court of Arches, as the ecclesiastical court was known. She claimed that Shore was impotent and unable to have children. Sir Thomas More described him as frigid. It might have been an invention but in all likelihood, Jane's husband would have been called before a panel of women in a comfortable room. They would have provided him with food and drink, made him comfortable and then exposed themselves to him, touched him and talked to him in a way designed to arouse him; in Shore's case, his wife's case was proved.[3] Sex within marriage without the intention of procreation was deemed as sinful by the Church but Jane's case was an unusual one. The appeal to the ecclesiastical court was not cheap so it is entirely possible that Edward supported Jane's petition.

Jane's relationship with the king continued until his death despite his continued womanising. By then Edward was much changed from the chivalric knight who was first crowned king in 1461. He grew fat, purging himself between courses so that he could continue to feast. She had an apartment at Westminster and came to an accommodation with Edward's wife Elizabeth Woodville who knew that her husband sought sex from other women especially during her pregnancies, a time when the Church frowned upon intercourse. Edward, better known for pursuing women and then having sated his desires moving on, retained an affection for Jane who was known for her kindness. For instance, when Edward decided to abolish the school set up for poor boys by King Henry VI, it was Jane who persuade him otherwise. A picture of Jane Shore still hangs in Eton in recognition of her support for the royal foundation.

After the king died on 9 April 1483, Jane transferred her affections to William, Lord Hastings, who was a member of the Privy Council, chamberlain of England and Edward's friend. She also welcomed Thomas Grey, Marquess of Dorset and Elizabeth Woodville's eldest son from her first marriage into her bed. Dorset and Hastings were rivals and vied to take one another's mistresses for themselves. The political situation in London quickly deteriorated. Edward IV's younger brother Richard of Gloucester, now Lord Protector, took steps to centre power on himself as soon as he gained custody of the young king by having Edward V's uncle Lord Rivers and his half-brother Richard Grey arrested. Elizabeth Woodville hearing that her brother and son had been detained, fled into sanctuary at Westminster Abbey for a second time with her daughters and younger son, Richard Duke of York. Rivers and Grey were subsequently executed on Richard of Gloucester's orders.

The Lord Protector negotiated with Elizabeth Woodville for the release of the Duke of York from sanctuary. He also set about removing men who had been loyal to his brother Edward IV. Richard would allege that Lord Hastings became involved in a plot with the Woodvilles to overthrow him. Richard sent a letter asking for support from his northern supporters on 11 June. Two days later, Hastings went to a council meeting at the Tower of London and was accused of treason. He was dragged out of the chamber and summarily executed. Richard's is the only evidence that there was a plot. Lord Stanley and Bishop Morton were arrested. A proclamation was issued announcing that Hastings had intended to murder the Lord Protector and the Duke of Buckingham. More arrests followed. They included a former secretary to Edward IV and Jane who was accused of carrying messages between Hastings and the queen. It was perhaps thanks to Jane that Hastings and Elizabeth Woodville had formed an alliance after the death of Edward. Prior to the king's death, the two had been part of opposing factions. She and Elizabeth were also accused of sorcery when Richard became unwell and could not sleep. Jane was charged with conspiracy; her belongings were confiscated and she had to do public penance for harlotry at St Paul's Cathedral. She was bareheaded, dressed only in her shift and carried a lit candle in her hand after which she was imprisoned in Ludgate Goal before being released and allowed to go home.

On 16 June, Edward V's younger brother, Richard, was sent from Westminster to live with his brother in the Tower. *The Great Chronicle* recorded the sight of Edward and Richard playing together. It was the last reference of them alive. The following day Edward's coronation, which was scheduled for 22 June, was postponed until November. Nine days after Hastings' execution, Ralph Shaa preached a sermon at St Paul's Cross in London stating Richard's claim to the Crown. Mancini wrote that Edward IV was himself accused of being illegitimate whilst other sources lingered on the allegation that the former king's marriage to Elizabeth Woodville was bigamous because Edward had promised to marry Lady Eleanor Butler simply so that he could have sex with her. The vow followed by intercourse constituted a legally binding marriage. With his brother's children made illegitimate, Richard was next in line for the throne. He was crowned King Richard III on 6 July 1483. What happened next has been the subject of fierce deliberation for more than five hundred years. It is widely believed that the two princes were murdered. At whose hands, is not known for certain.

As rumours and accusations circulated, Jane Shore must have felt increasingly afraid. She might have wondered what her own future would be as it is likely that she was sheltering Elizabeth Woodville's son, the Marquess of Dorset. He left the sanctuary of Westminster in June but did not resurface until the end of the year in Brittany where he joined Henry Tudor. Richard III denounced Grey in his *Proclamation for the Reform of Morals* on 23 October 1483, as a man who took 'sundry maidens… without shame devoured, deflowered and defouled'.[4] The document also announced that Jane was in trouble again. Richard called her a 'shameful and mischievous woman'[5] and she was sent back to Ludgate Goal. Richard used the alleged debaucheries of the anti-Ricardian faction to put down that autumn's rebellion. His concern with vice was just another reminder of King Edward IV's lechery. It was part of a consistent campaign to denounce Edward as a sexual predator and justify Richard's claim to the crown rather than moral outrage. Richard, who kept his own private life well hidden from the public record, had illegitimate children of his own.

But during her time in custody, Jane gained the attention of another admirer, the king's own Solicitor General, a man named Thomas Lynom.

Richard tried to persuade Lynom against the marriage and when that failed, he wrote to the Bishop of Lincoln at the end of 1483 asking for his intervention in the matter.

> By the king. Right reverend father in God, &c. Signifying unto you that it is showed unto us that our servant and solicitor, Thomas Lynom, marvellously blinded and abused with the late [wife] of William Shore, now being in Ludgate by our commandment, hath made contract of matrimony with her, as it is said, and intendeth, to our full great marvel, to proceed to effect the same. We for many causes would be sorry that he should be so disposed. Pray you, therefore, to send for him, and in that ye goodly may, exhort and stir him to the contrary; and if ye find him utterly set for to marry her and none otherwise will be advertised, then, if it may stand with the Law of the Church, we be content.[6]

Jane was released into her father's custody. It is not known whether they stayed in London or went to Plumstead in Kent where Lambert owned property mentioned in his will. John Lambert died in 1487 leaving his daughter a bed of arras and a painted cloth of Mary Magdalen and Martha. Did he choose an image of a repentant prostitute deliberately as a final reminder of the shame that Jane had brought to the family? Jane was married to Lynom by then. John's son-in-law, the King's Solicitor, the man who loved Jane despite her public shame was his executor.

Lynom served Henry VII and his son Arthur becoming a controller of the rolls for the prince's household. He continued to serve the Crown when Henry VIII became king in 1508. Jane faded back into obscurity dying in about 1527 at the age of eighty-two at Hinxworth in Hertfordshire, though it is unlikely that she faced the poverty that Sir Thomas More described. In More's version of her life when Jane lost her protectors and reached an age where she was no longer young and desirable, she was described as living in poverty and dying alone. The scholar needed a moral ending to his tale and the mistress of the king could not end her days in comfort or else it would have appeared that a life of sin was rewarded.

More blackened King Richard III's reputation in his history not only by recounting the disappearance and suspected murder of Edward V and his brother but also by the way Jane was treated. She moved from being a real person into a literary device – 'a tart with a heart' – who cared for widows and orphans. Rather than profiting from her relationship with the king, More claimed that she used her influence to help other people, which also contrasted with Elizabeth Woodville who filled the court with her extended family, granting them titles, power and wealth at the expense of Edward's magnates. Her story inspired plays and ballads. Elizabeth Lynom became Jane Shore in 1599 when Thomas Heywood wrote a play entitled *Edward IV* ensuring that her name, albeit the wrong one, would be remembered.

King Edward IV's son, Edward V, was deposed because of his father's pursuit of women and penchant for promising marriage in exchange for sex. In choosing to marry Elizabeth Woodville, a penniless widow, 'out of love'[7] Edward IV challenged customary English social mores. He forced his realm to accept his choice of bride by making his marriage in secret but he did not take the precaution of repeating his vows under the public auspices of the Church. Even King John, who according to the chroniclers, lusted after Isabella of Angoulême married her out of political necessity. John was the only English medieval king to gain an annulment from a first wife in order to remarry although he was not the first king to consider the idea.

Elizabeth Woodville, a beautiful woman, gained a reputation as a *femme fatale* not least because Sir Thomas More claimed that Elizabeth inflamed Edward's desires before refusing to become his mistress. Earlier medieval kings had no such qualms about bedding women from lower social classes. Royal extra-marital liaisons were to be expected. Edward IV, like his ancestors, had many mistresses but never thought of deserting his queen. But, it was not politically expedient for Tudor writers to lay too much blame at Elizabeth Woodville's feet, she was, after all, the mother of Henry VII's Plantagenet queen. In the next century Edward's grandson, King Henry VIII, would seek the annulment of his first marriage to Katherine of Aragon, his wife of twenty-four years, so that he could marry Anne Boleyn, who refused to become his mistress in the hope that she would beget a male heir. Like Edward IV, and the medieval kings before him, Henry VIII was more used to women saying 'yes'. Anne like Elizabeth Woodville, said 'no'. By recognising the power that they wielded as women and being able to withhold what their pursuers most wanted, both women achieved a crown with far-reaching consequences for themselves, their families and the realm.

Jane Shore, the sexually promiscuous mistress, loved by King Edward IV left an indelible mark on Sir Thomas More who described someone who was beautiful, witty and kind. Nor did she attempt to elevate her position at court. She might have become the personification of lechery thanks to Richard III's proclamation and More's history of the period but she is exactly the kind of woman history expects to find sharing a bed with its medieval kings.

Glossary

Advowson	The right to appoint a member of the clergy as the incumbent of a church.
Affinity	A following which looked to a lord for his influence, aid and support and which repaid the interest shown in his or her affairs with service. A net of political and social connections was created to benefit both the lord and those who served him.
Ætheling	Anglo-Saxon word used to identify male members of the Cerdic royal house of Wessex with a claim to the succession. It was used during the Norman period to identify members of the royal family. William Ætheling or Adelin was the only legitimate son of King Henry I.
Ældorman	A high-status ruling male in Anglo-Saxon England. An ældorman was often of royal birth but their rule of a territory, often a former kingdom, was dependent upon the king's support. The word earl is the nearest modern equivalent.
Annuity	An annual payment or pension.
Bailey	The area around a castle keep enclosed by a ditch and palisade, later by a moat and wall.
Bailiff	In a king or lord's absence, a bailiff was the lord's representative. He was often associated with the collection of rents and managing the domain for which he was appointed bailiff.
Barony	Under the feudal system the king gave land in return for a pledge of loyalty and service. The king's tenant-in-chiefs were known as barons. The landholding was called a barony. The baron, would in his own turn, grant land from within his barony to his own men in return for loyalty and service.
Berewick	An outlying estate belonging to a medieval manor reserved for the lord's own use.
Collegiate church	A community of priests, not monks, who lived under canons (rules) and were celibate. They worshipped together in a collegiate church. Collegiate churches were built most often to sing masses for the souls of a particular family or for the education of boys in preparation for the priesthood.

Concubine	A woman who lived with a man as a wife but without the benefit of marriage. The woman was usually of a lower status than the man.
Consanguinity	The blood relationship of two people descended from a common ancestor.
Courtly love	Cultural ideal that developed alongside knightly chivalric values. Courtly love was based on the idea of falling in love with an unattainable, usually married, lady of high rank. The knight, whose love would be unrequited, owed obedience and devotion to his lady and was required to perform heroic deeds in a bid to win her favour.
Dower	The life interest of a widow in the estates owned by her husband during their marriage. Dower rights typically included one-third of property.
Dowry	Money, goods and estates paid by the bride's family to the groom. Dowries could be reclaimed in the event of a marriage being annulled.
Effigy	A carved monument that became popular in the thirteenth. Effigies were not intended to be exact likenesses.
Feudalism	Hierarchical society based on a pyramid system with the king at the apex of the system, presumed to hold all territory in his realm as his estate. Agricultural labourers formed the bottom tier of a feudal society and were often tied to the land they worked. People at a lower social level received land from those higher to them in rank. In return for land and a place to live, tenants were required to work and fight for their overlords.
Garderobe	A toilet.
Humour	The four bodily humours associated with medieval medicine were organised into the elements; earth, water, air and fire. Physicians identified heat, cold, moisture and dryness to determine bodily ailments and treated them by creating a balance of the humours.
Justiciar	From the Latin *justiciarius* meaning judge. Appointed by the king to dispense justice in his absence a justiciar was the monarch's principal minister of state, second only to the king himself and the guardian of the kingdom in the king's absence.
Knight's fee	The amount of land necessary to support a knight, his family and servants as well as providing an income large enough to equip him and his retinue with horses, armour and weapons. In return, a knight would be required to serve his feudal overlord. The more knights' fees in a lord's possession the more knights he was required to put in the field at time of war.

Letters patent	A legal document issued under the monarch's Great Seal.
Manor	An agricultural estate. The medieval manor system was an essential part of feudalism controlling, tenure, labour and law at a local level.
March	Counties which lay along the border between England and Wales and also England and Scotland.
Marcher	Lords appointed to govern the borders or marches. Marcher lordships are most often associated with the borders between England and Wales. These feudal lords had complete jurisdiction over their tenants without recourse to the monarch. The king had jurisdiction only in cases of treason.
Mark	A mark was worth 13s 4d or two-thirds of a pound. A pound was valued at 20 shillings. Marks were not part of the coinage. It was a value used for accounting and financial transactions.
More Christiano	A marriage blessed by the Church and within the constraints of canon law.
More danico	Marriage 'in the Danish manner' was a customary practice equivalent to handfasting. There is no modern equivalent so is usually interpreted as a common-law marriage.
Pipe roll	Financial records showing payments and debts owed to the Crown as well as the king's expenditure. Although they are the most complete record for the period, they do not record all income or expenditure.
Quitclaim	A waiver to all legal rights on gifts or property.
Scutage	Also known as shield tax. This was the money paid by a vassal to his lord in lieu of military service. It is reflective of the monetisation of society as well as the move away from feudalism towards the so-called bastard feudalism of the later medieval period.
Suo Jure	In her own right.
Tun	252 gallons of wine, oil or honey.
Verba de futuro	Vows between a coupled exchanged in the future tense deemed by the Church to be a betrothal, which could be dissolved, unless the vows were followed by intercourse in which case a marriage was deemed to have taken place
Verba de presenti	Vows exchanged in the present tense for an immediate marriage. Canon law maintained that only the consent of the couple was required in order for a marriage to be valid. No witnesses, banns or priest were required.
Wardship	Feudal land was heritable but in the heir was a minor a guardian was appointed until the heir came of age, and was able to fulfil the duties of vassalage. The estates and the heir were considered to be in wardship to the feudal lord. He

could retain the wardship or else sell or give it to someone else. The guardian drew the profits from the estate during the heir's minority and had the right to arrange the heir's marriage.

Witan   The council of Anglo-Saxon kings in England whose role changed over time. It advised the king and elected rulers based on bloodline, primogeniture and conquest.

Appendices: English Kings, their Mistresses and Children Listed in Chronological Order

Appendix A: Medieval Kings from 978–1066

Monarch & reign	Spouse	Children	Mistress	Children
Æthelred 'The Unraed' 978–1013 1014–1016	Ælfgifu of Northumbria	Athelstan Edmund II Edgar Edred Edric ? Edward? Edwy Egbert Edith Elgiva Wulfhilda Unknown daughter A daughter who became the Abbess of Wherwell		
	Emma of Normandy	Edward Alfred Goda		
Edmund 'Ironside' (23 April 1016–30 November 1016)	Edith widow of Sigeferth	Edward' the Exile Edmund		
Cnut (1016–1035)	Emma of Normandy	Harthacanute Gunhilda	Ælfgifu of Northampton	Sweyn Harold Harefoot
Harold Harefoot (1035–1040)			Elgiva	Elfwine
Harthacnut (1040–1042)				
Edward the Confessor (1042–1066)	Edith of Wessex			
Harold Godwinson (6 January 1066–14 October 1066)	Edith of Mercia	Harold	Edith Swanneck or Swanneshals Also known as 'Edith the Fair' and 'Edith the Rich'	Godwine Edmund Magnus Gunnhild Gytha Ulf

Appendix B: Medieval Kings 1066–1485

Monarch	Wife	Children	Mistress	Children
William I 'the Conqueror' 1066–1087	Matilda of Flanders	Robert Richard Cecilia Adeliza William Constance Adela Henry Agatha Matilda	Putative mistress Maud Peverel	Putative child William Peverel
William II 'Rufus' 1087–1100			unknown	Berstrand? Unreliable source.
Henry I 'Beauclerk' 'The Lion of Justice' 1100–1135	Edith/Matilda of Scotland	Euphemia Adelaide (who adopted the name Matilda) William Richard (?)	Sybilla Corbet	Rainald de Dunstanville William Sybilla of Normandy Gundrada Rohese
			Ansfride	Richard of Lincoln Fulk Juliana
			Nest of Wales	Henry Fitz Henry
			Edith Forne Sigulfson	Robert FitzEdith Adeliza?
			Isabel de Beaumont	Isabel
			Edith	Matilda of Perche

Monarch	Wife	Children	Mistress	Children
			Unknown mistresses	Robert of Caen
				William de Tracy
				Gilbert
				Maud
				Constance
				Eustacia
				Alice
				Matilda
				Elizabeth
				Emma
				Sybilla of Falaise
	Adeliza of Louvain			
Stephen (1135–1154)	Matilda of Boulogne	Baldwin	Dameta	Gervase of Blois
		Eustace		Ralph of Blois
		William		Americ of Blois
		Matilda		
		Mary		
Henry II 'Curtmantle' (1154–1189)	Eleanor of Aquitaine	William	Ykenai	Geoffrey
		Henry	Ida de Tosny	William Longspée
		Matilda		
		Richard	Nesta Bloet	Morgan
		Geoffrey	Joan St Pol?	Fulk?
		Eleanor	Annabel de Baliol	
		Joan	Rosamund Clifford	
		John	Alys of France	
			Unknown	Philip

Monarch	Wife	Children	Mistress	Children
Richard 'the Lionheart' (1189–1199)	Berengaria of Navarre			
John (1199–1216)	Isabella of Gloucester		De Warenne	Richard FitzJohn
			Clemence	Joan
	Isabella of Angoulême	Henry Richard Isabella Eleanor Joan	Hawise Suzanne Hawise, Countess of Aumale	Oliver
			Unknown mistresses	John, a clerk in London Geoffrey Henry Osbert Eudes Bartholomew Maud Isabel Philip
Henry III (1216–1272)	Eleanor of Provence	Edward Margaret Beatrice Edmund Richard John William Katherine Henry		

Monarch	Wife	Children	Mistress	Children
Edward I 'Longshanks' (1272–1307)	Eleanor of Castile	Eleanor Joan John Henry Alice Juliana Joan Alfonso Margaret Berengaria Mary Isabella Elizabeth Edward Beatrice Blanche	Unknown	John Botetourt,
	Marguerite of France	Thomas Edmund Eleanor		
Edward II (1307–1327)	Isabella of France	Edward John Eleanor Joan of the Tower	unknown	Adam
Edward III (1327–1377)	Philippa of Hainault	Edward Isabella Joan William Lionel John Edmund Blanche Mary	Alice Perrers	John de Southeray Joan Jane

Monarch	Wife	Children	Mistress	Children
		Margaret Thomas William Thomas		
Richard II (1377–1399)	Anne of Bohemia			
	Marguerite of France			
Henry IV (1399–1413)	Mary de Bohun	Edward Henry Thomas John Humphrey Blanche Philippa		
	Joan of Navarre			
Henry V (1413–1422)	Katherine of Valois	Henry		
Henry VI (1422–1461 and also 1470–1471)	Margaret of Anjou	Edward		

Monarch	Wife	Children	Mistress	Children
Edward IV (1461–1483)	Elizabeth Woodville	Elizabeth Mary Cecily Edward Margaret Richard Anne George Katherine Bridget	Eleanor Butler Elizabeth Waite Jane Shore Unknown mistress	Edward de Wigmore? Arthur Plantagenet Elizabeth Grace
Edward V (9 April 1483–25 June 1483)				
Richard III (1483–1485)	Anne Neville	Edward		John of Gloucester Richard Katherine

Notes

Introduction
1. Ahonen, p. 449
2. Philips: 2011, p. 97
3. Philips:2006, p. 52
4. Weir:2005, p. 18

Chapter 1
1. Whitelock, p. 241
2. *Anglo Saxon Chronicle* cited in Ingram and Carruthers, eds. p. 170
3. O'Brien, p. 102
4. Jochens, pp. 327–349
5. Bolton, pp. 247–248
6. Ibid, p. 252
7. Ibid, p. 259
8. Stenton, p. 937
9. Adam of Bremen, p. 107
10. Jochens, pp. 327–349
11. Campbell, *Encomium*, III, 1, p. 33
12. O Brien, p. 125
13. Campbell, *Encomium*, III, 1, 40 noted in Bolton p. 253
14. *Anglo Saxon Chronicle*, p. 178
15. Bolton, p. 198
16. Ibid, p. 258

Chapter 2
1. Connolly, p. 153
2. Bridgeford
3. Cited in Given-Wilson & Curteis, p. 189
4. Chibnall, pp. 142–143 cited in Barlow, p. 159
5. Connolly:2018, chapter 3

Chapter 3
1. Tabuteau, pp. 141–169
2. William of Malmesbury, p. 256
3. Ibid
4. Van Houts, pp. 399–405

5. Bates:2016, chapter 1, Robert and Herleva
6. Hallam, pp. 157–158
7. William of Malmesbury, p. 23
8. Borman, p. 23
9. Morris, p. 44
10. William of Malmesbury, p. 260
11. Douglas, p. 382
12. Wilton, pp. 132–133

Chapter 4
1. Planché, p. 275
2. Taylor, p. 223
3. Kemp, p. 55
4. Planché, p. 268
5. Cleveland, p. 1
6. Ibid
7. Weever, p. 395
8. Ibid
9. Ibid
10. Freeman, vol iii, p. 662
11. Carpenter and Sharpe, p. 4
12. Ibid, p. 1
13. Glover, p. 337

Chapter 5
1. Orderic Vitalis, v, p. 299 cited in Cooper p.56
2. The *Anglo Saxon Chronicle* cited in Spencer, p. 71
3. William of Malmesbury, pp. 756–757
4. Henry of Huntingdon, pp. 699–701 cited in Cooper, p. 51
5. Orderic Vitalis, v, p. 295 cited in Cooper p. 56
6. William of Malmesbury, p. 447
7. Given-Wilson & Curteis, p. 61
8. Hoveden and Benedict Abbas cited in Cole, p. 217
9. *Reg. Regum Anglo-Norm.* i, no. 188; *Gesta Stephani,* ed. K. R. Potter, 91 cited in A History of the County of Oxford.
10. Crouch, p. 215
11. Cited in Patterson, p. 3
12. Spencer, p. 93
13. Ibid, p. 119
14. Andreas, p.150
15. Given-Wilson & Curteis, p. 63
16. William of Malmesbury, p. 456

Chapter 6
1. Johns, p. 10
2. William of Malmesbury, cited in Hilton, p. 67
3. *Brut y Tywysogion*, p. 105
4. Ibid
5. Pickering, p. 99
6. *Brut y Tywysogion*, p. 87
7. Gerald of Wales, p. 189

Chapter 7
1. Given-Wilson & Curteis, p. 64
2. Shepperd, p. 95
3. Burton, William of York, ODNB online
4. Norton, p. 16
5. Marshall, p. 57
6. Sincock, pp. 150–151
7. Gorton, p. 82

Chapter 8
1. Dalton, p. 26
2. Kapelle, p. 200
3. Orderic Vitalis, p. 17
4. Green, p. 47
5. Williams, pp. 33–36
6. Sharpe, p. 42
7. Leland, p. 135
8. Ibid
9. Clark, p. 134
10. Drake, p. 9
11. Hollister:2008, p. 229
12. Ibid
13. Power, p. 382
14. Warren, p. 45

Chapter 9
1. Planche, p. 30
2. Crouch, p. 7
3. White, p. 24
4. Given-Wilson & Curteis, p. 62
5. Rüdiger, p. 316
6. Weir: 2008, p. 50
7. For a fuller discussion on gendered silencing and who has the right to speak out see Beard, *The Public Voice of Women*.

Chapter 10
1. John of Salisbury cited in Gold, p. 68
2. Gold, p. 69
3. Evans, pp. 19–45
4. McCracken, p. 249
5. Harper-Bill p. 331
6. Gold, p. 250
7. Ibid
8. Weir:2000, p. 98
9. CCR, V, p. 285
10. Betzig in Smith, p. 62
11. Alvira, pp. 115–116
12. Gerald of Wales, p. 368

Chapter 11
1. Ralph the Black, cited in Gold, p. 251
2. Betzig, p. 62
3. Gerald of Wales cited by Betzig, p. 86
4. Farone, p. 125
5. Burl, p. 16
6. Colvin, p. 18
7. Page, pp. 71–75
8. Hearne, p. 133
9. Morgan and Smith, pp. 139–143
10. Brown, p. 126
11. Ibid, p. 62
12. Morris, p. 2
13. Reed, p. 137
14. Crouch:2016, p. 149
15. Roger de Hoveden, p.211
16. Dickens, p. 88

Chapter 12
1. Pollock, p. 95
2. Clay and Farrer, p. 22
3. Messer, p. 4
4. Ibid, p. 14
5. Ibid, p. 10
6. Warren, p. 4
7. Hilton, p. 169
8. Matthew Paris, *Chronica Majora* cited in Hilton, p. 175
9. McQuinn, p. 126
10. Matthew Paris, *Chronica Majora*, ed. H. R. Luard (Rolls Series, 1872–1883), iv, p. 253

Chapter 13

1. Green, *History of the English People*, p.237 cited in Warren:1961 p. 2
2. Cited in Given-Wilson & Curteis, p. 127
3. *Historie des Ducs de Normandie* cited in Connolly: 2020, p. 143
4. Dunstable Annals, p. 45
5. Chronicle of Melrose, 1191, p. 27
6. Given-Wilson & Curteis, p. 127
7. Church, p. 66
8. Waugh, p.47
9. Strickland, p. 343
10. Ibid
11. Richard of Devizes, p. 10
12. Cazel (ed), pp. 240–243

Chapter 14

1. Cited in Warner, p. 129
2. Ibid, p. 29
3. *Vita Edwardi Secundii*, cited in Weir:2005 p. 19
4. Anonymous chronicle cited in Haines, p. 21
5. *Lancercost Chronicle*, vol 2, p. 196
6. Cited in Weir:2005 p. 20
7. *Vita Edwardi Secundi*, p. 40
8. Lanercost Chronicle, vol 2, p.194
9. Cited in Warner, p. 80
10. Cited in Green, p. 32

Chapter 15

1. *Scalacronica*, p. 10 cited in Warner p. 138
2. *Lancerost Chronicle*, vol 2, p. 234
3. Ibid, p. 249
4. Ibid
5. Cited in Warner, p. 199
6. *Foedera*, II, I, p. 619
7. Doherty, p. 84
8. Cited in Warner, p.203
9. Doherty, p. 23
10. Cited in Warner, p. 235
11. Ibid, p. 242
12. *Lanercost Chronicle*, Vol 2, p. 265
13. Cited in Weir:2005 p. 352

Chapter 16

1. Bower, vol 7, p.321 cited in Webster online edition.
2. Cannon and Crowcroft, p. 598

Chapter 17

1. Jean le Bel:2011, p. 105
2. Jean le Bel, pp. 115–119
3. Ormrod:2011, pp. 302–303
4. Taylor, Childs and Watkiss, eds. And trans., p.43 cited in Ormrod: 2011 p. 220
5. Walsingham. Cited in Ormrod:2006, p. 219
6. Kay, pp. 12–13
7. Ibid, p. 14
8. Ibid, p. 19
9. Brady:1977, pp. 906–11
10. Ormrod:2011 p. 222
11. Ibid, p. 227
12. Ibid, p. 464
13. Kay, p. 91
14. Bothwell, p. 11
15. Kay, p. 65
16. Ibid
17. Ibid
18. Wilkinson, p. 152
19. Given-Wilson & Curteis, p. 138
20. Tompkins, p. 141.
21. Ibid
22. Froissart, Tome X, Livre 2, 253, p. 185.
23. Page:1925, pp. 20–31

Chapter 18

1. Kraus, p. 182 There was no contemporary doubt about Thomas Chaucer's parentage. The question arose in 1872, when F. J. Furnivall raised the possibility in Notes and Queries.
2. Weir:2007, p. 128
3. Ibid, p. 137
4. Ibid, p. 215
5. Ibid, p. 229
6. Thomas Gascoigne, Passages from a book of truths, cited in Weir, Katherine Swynford, p. 246
7. Gascoine, *Loci e libro veritatum* cited in Weir, p. 246

Chapter 19

1. http://www.r3.org/on-line-library-text-essays/crowland-chronicle/part-ii/
2. Ibid
3. http://medieval.ucdavis.edu/YORK.DURHAM/Richard.III.html
4. April 14, Milan: 1461', in *Calendar of State Papers and Manuscripts in the Archives and Collections of Milan 1385–1618*, ed. Allen B Hinds (London, 1912)

5. Cited in Given-Wilson & Curteis, pp. 13–14
6. Cited in Thompson, p. 2
7. Gairdner, p. 92
8. Cited in Ashdown-Hill, p. 490
9. Grummit, ODNB
10. Trevor-Roper, xxiv
11. Given-Wilson & Curteis, pp. 158,161–174.
12. Cited by https://thehistoryofparliament.wordpress.com/2015/07/08/the-battle-of-northampton-and-the-strange-death-of-sir-william-lucy-mp/
13. Penn, p.491

Chapter 20
1. Wavrin, vol 6. p. 455
2. Licence, p. 25
3. Paston Letters, vol 1, letter 88, pp. 160–163
4. Licence, p. 72
5. Ibid, p. 107
6. Mancini, pp. 60–61
7. Licence, p.109
8. Ibid
9. *Calendar of State Papers and Manuscripts in the Archives and Collections of Milan 1385–1618*, vol 1, p. 113
10. Sir Thomas More, cited in Hilton, p. 419

Chapter 21
1. Sir Thomas More cited in Thompson, p. 88
2. Cited in Thompson, p. 40
3. Licence, p. 21
4. Santiuste, p. 137
5. Ibid
6. Orchard, p. 160
7. *Calendar of State Papers and Manuscripts in the Archives and Collections of Milan 1385–1618*, vol 1, p. 111

Bibliography

Printed Primary Sources

Brut y Tywysogion; or, The Chronicle of the Princes, edited by Rev. John Williams ab Ithel, (Longman, Green, Longman, and Roberts, London, 1860)

Calendar of Charter Rolls in the Public Record Office (6 volumes, London, 1916) CCR

Calendar of Papal Registers, Letters, 1342–1362 Volume 3, Bliss, W.H. and Johnson C, eds. (HMSO, London, 1897)

Capellanus, Andreas *On Love*, ed. and trans. Walsh, P.G., (Duckworth, London,1982)

Chroniques de Jean le Bel, ed. Viard, Jules and Dprez Eugene, (Paris 1904)

Dominic Mancini, *The Usurpation of Richard the Third*, trans. and ed. C.A.J. Armstrong (Oxford, 1969)

Encomium Emmae Reginae, ed. A. Campbell (Camden Classic Reprints, Cambridge, 1998)

Gerald of Wales, *The Journey through Wales and, the Description of Wales*, ed. Lewis Thorpe, (Harmondsworth, Penguin, London, 1978)

Le Bel, Jehan, *The True Chronicles of Jean Le Bel, 1290–1360* (Boydell Press, Woodbridge, 2011)

Matthaei Parisiensis, Monachi Sancti Albani, Chronica Majora, ed. H. R. Luard (Rolls Series, 1872–1883)

Richard of Devizes, *Chronicon de rebus gestis Ricardi I regis Angliæ*, ed. J. Stevenson (London, 1838)

Sir Thomas Gray, *Scalacronica; the reigns of Edward I, Edward II and Edward III.* Trans. Sir Herbert Maxwell, (J Maclehose and Sons, Glasgow, 1907)

The Anglo-Saxon Chronicle: Illustrated and Annotated, eds. Ingram, James, and Carruthers, Bob. (Pen & Sword Books Limited, Barnsley, 2013)

The Annals of Roger de Hoveden: Comprising the history of England and of other countries in Europe from A.D. 732 to A.D. 1201, ed. and trans. Riley, Henry T. (H.G. Bohn, London, 1853)

The Chronicle of Lanercost , 1272–1346 ed. and trans. Sir Herbert Maxwell (Llanerch Press, Penbryn Lodge, 2001)

The Gesta Normannorum Ducum of William of Jumieges, Orderic Vitalis and Robert of Torigini, ed. and trans. E.M.C. van Houts, (Oxford University Press, Oxford, 1995)

The Paston Letters, 1422–1509 AD, 2 vols, ed. Gairdner, James (Bloomsbury, London, 1872)

The Plantagenet Chronicles, Hallam, Elizabeth, ed (MacMillan, London, 1995)

Vita Edwardi Secundi, ed. & trans. N. Denkolm-Young (London, 1957)

Wace, *The History of the Norman People: Wace's Roman de Rou*, (Boydell Press, Woodbridge, 2004)

William of Malmesbury, *Gesta Regum Anglorum: The History of the English Kings*, (Clarendon Press, Oxford 1998)

Secondary Sources

Abrams, Lynn, et al. *Gender, Nation and Conquest in the High Middle Ages: Nest of Deheubarth*, (Manchester University Press, Manchester, 2016)

Altschul, Michael, *A Baronial Family in Medieval England: The Clares, 1217– 1314*, (John Hopkins University Press, Baltimore, 2019)

Alvira, Martín, '*Dilecta consanguinea mea*: Ferdinando III's donation to a Nun of Fontevraud' in *The Sword and the Cross: Castile-León in the Era of Fernando III*. Eds. Holt, Edward and Witcombe Teresa (Netherlands, Brill, 2020) pp. 105–135

Ahonen, Mark, 'Galen on Sexual Desire and Sexual Regulation,' *aperion* 2017:50 (4), pp. 449–481

Ashdown-Hill, John, *The Secret Queen: Eleanor Talbot, the woman who Put Richard III on the Throne*, (History Press, Cheltenham, 2016)

Barlow, Frank, *The Godwins: The Rise and Fall of a Noble Dynasty*, (Routledge, London & New York, 2003)

Bartlett, Robert, *Blood Royal: Dynastic Politics in Medieval Europe* (Cambridge University Press, Cambridge, 2020)

Bartlett, W.B. *King Cnut and the Viking Conquest of England*, (Amberley Publishing, Stroud, 2018)

F.D. Blackley, 'Adam, the bastard son of Edward II', *Bulletin of the Institute of Historical Research*, xxxvii (1964), pp. 76–7

Bates, David, *William the Conqueror*, (Yale University Press, New Haven and London, 2016)

Beard, Mary. 'The Public Voice of Women' A London Review of Books Winter Lecture,36 (6) 2014 Retrieved from http://www.lrb.co.uk/v36/n06/mary-beard/the-public-voice-of-women

Beattie, Cordelia., Johns, Susan M, et al, *Gender, Nation and Conquest in the High Middle Ages: Nest of Deheubarth* (Manchester University Press, Manchester, 2016)

Bridgeford, Andrew, *1066: The Hidden History of the Bayeux Tapestry*, (Bloomsbury Press, London, 2004)

Bolton, Timothy 'Ælfgifu of Northampton: Cnut the Great's Other Woman', *Nottingham*

Medieval Studies, 51 (2007), pp. 247–68

Bolton, Timothy, *Cnut the Great*, (Yale University Press, New Haven and London, 2017)

Borman, Tracy, Matilda: Queen of the Conqueror, (Jonathan Cape, London, 2011)

Bothwell, James, *Edward III and the English peerage: royal patronage, social mobility, and political control in fourteenth-century England* (Boydell Press, 2004).

Brady, Haldeen, 'Chaucer, Alice Perrers, and Cecily Champaigne,' *Speculum52* (1977), pp. 906–911

Brown, E. 'Philip the Fair and His Family: His Sons, Their Marriages, and Their Wives.' *Medieval Prosopography*, 32, (2017) pp.125–185

Brown, Reginald Allen, 'Magnates, curiales and the wheel of fortune,' *Proceedings of the Battle Conference on Anglo-Norman Studies: 1979. II* (Boydell Press, Woodbridge, 1980) pp. 97–115

Burl, Aubrey, *Courts of Love, Castles of Hate: Troubadours and Trobairitz in Southern France 1071–1321* (The History Press, Cheltenham, 2011)

Burton, Janet, *William of York (St William of York, Willian fitz Herbert)* 2004, Oxford Dictionary of National Biography online

Brooke, C. *The Medieval Idea of Marriage* (Oxford: Oxford University Press, 1989)

Cannon, John, *The Oxford Companion to British History*, Oxford University Press, Oxford, 2015)

Carpenter David & Sharpe, Richard, *Hatfield Peverel Priory*, https://actswilliam2henry1.files.wordpress.com/2014/10/h1-hatfield-peverel-2016-1.pdf

Cassidy, Richard, 'Rose of Dover (d.1261), Richard of Chilham and an inheritance in Kent' *Archaeologia Cantiana* - Vol. 131 2011, pp305–319

Cazel, Fred A. (ed) *Feudalism and Liberty: Articles and Addresses of Sidney Painter* (The John Hopkins Press, Baltimore, 1961)

Church, Stephen David, and Church, S. D., *The Household Knights of King John. United Kingdom*, (Cambridge University Press, Cambridge,1999)

Church, S.D, ed., *King John: New Interpretations*, (Boydell Press, Woodbridge, 2003)

Clark, Willene B. *A Medieval Book of Beasts: The Second Family Bestiary: Commentary, Art, Text and Translation* (Boydell Press, Woodbridge, 2006)

Cleveland, The Duchess of, *The Battle Abbey Roll with some Account of the Norman Lineages* (3 vols), (John Murray, London, 1889)

Cole, Teresa, *After the Conquest: The Divided Realm 1066–1135*, (Amberley Publishing, Stroud, 2018)

Connolly, Sharon Bennett, *Silk and the Sword: The Women of the Norman Conquest*, (Amberley Publishing, Stroud, 2018)

Connolly, Sharon Bennett, *Ladies of the Magna Carta: Women of Influence in Thirteenth Century England* (Pen and Sword, Barnsley, 2020)

Cooper, Alan "The Feet of those that Bark shall be cut off" timorous historians and the personality of King Henry I,' *Anglo-Norman Studies*, 23, (2002), pp. 47–67

Crouch, David, *William Marshal: Knighthood, War and Chivalry, 1147–1219* (Taylor & Francis, Abingdon, 2014)

Dalton, Paul, 'The Outlaw Hereward 'the Wake': His Companions and Enemies in *Outlaws in Medieval and Early Modern England: Crime, Government and Society, C.1066–c.1600,* (Taylor & Francis, Abingdon, 2016) pp. 7–36

Dickens, Charles, *A Child's History of England,* (Dover Publications, London, 2019)

Doherty, Paul, *Isabella and the Strange Death of Edward II,* (Constable, London, 2004)

Douglas, David Charles. *William the Conqueror: The Norman Impact Upon England,* (University of California Press, Berkeley 1964)

Drake, Henry Holman, *St. Fimbarrus church, Fowey: its founders and their history,* (Lake & Lake, 1876)

Dugdale, William Sir, *The baronage of England, or, An historical account of the lives and most memorable actions of our English nobility in the Saxons time to the Norman conquest, and from thence, of those who had their rise before the end of King Henry the Third's reign deduced from publick records, antient historians, and other authorities*

Dugdale, Sir William and Dodsworth, Roger, *Monasticon Anglicanum,* eds. J. Caley, H. Ellis and B. Bandinel, 6 vols. (London, 1846)

Evans, Michael R., *Inventing Eleanor: The Medieval and Post-Medieval Image of Eleanor of Aquitaine,* (Bloomsbury, London, 2014)

Farrer, William and Clay, Charles, *Early Yorkshire Charters: Volume 8, The Honour of Warenne,* (Cambridge University Press, Cambridge, 2013)

Freeman, E.A., *History of the Norman Conquest* (Oxford, 1870–1879)

James Gairdner, *History of the life and reign of Richard the Third, to which is added the story of Perkin Warbeck: from original documents,* (Cambridge University Press, Cambridge, 1898)

Green, Judith, 'King Henry I and Northern England,' *Transactions of the Royal Historical Society,* vol. 17, (Cambridge University Press, Cambridge, 2007) pp. 35–55

Gillingham, John, *Anglo-Norman Studies XXIII: Proceedings of the Battle Conference 2000,* (Boydell Press, Woodbridge, 2001)

Gillingham, John, *Anglo-Norman Studies XXIV: Proceedings of the Battle Conference 2001,* (Boydell Press, Woodbridge 2002)

Given-Wilson, Chris and Curteis, Alice, *The Royal Bastards of Medieval England,* (Routledge, London, 1984)

Goodman, Anthony, *John of Gaunt: The Exercise of Princely Power in Fourteenth Century Europe,* (Longman, London, 1992)

Gorton, John, *A Topographical Dictionary of Great Britain and Ireland: Compiled from Local Information, and the Most Recent and Official Authorities,* (Chapman and Hall, London, 1833)

Grandsden, Antonia, 'The Alleged Rape by Edward III of the Countess of Salisbury.' *The English Historical Review 87,* no.343, (1972), pp. 333–344

Green, Karen, and Mews, Constant. *Virtue Ethics for Women 1250–1500,* (Springer Netherlands, 2011)

Grummit, David 'Plantagenet, Arthur, Viscount Lisle' Oxford Dictionary of National Biography online, 2008

Haines, Roy Martin, *King Edward II: His Life, His Reign, and Its Aftermath, 1284–1330*, (McGill-Queen's University Press, Montreal, 2003)

Harper-Bill, Christopher, *Proceedings of the Battle Conference 1995*, (Boydell Press, Woodbridge, 1996)

Hilton, Lisa, *Queens Consort: England's Medieval Queens*, (Weidenfeld & Nicolson, 2009)

Hollister, C. Warren. 'King John and the Historians,' *Journal of British Studies 1*, no. 1 (1961) pp. 1–19

Huneycutt, Lois L, *Matilda of Scotland: A Study in Medieval Queenship* (The Boydell Press, Woodbridge, 2003)

Johns, S.M. Gender, *Nation and Conquest in the High Middle Ages: Nest of Deheubarth* (Manchester University Press, Manchester, 2013)

Jones, Michael, *The Black Prince*, (Head of Zeus, London, 2017)

Jones, Timothy, 'Geoffrey of Monmouth, Fouke Le Fitz Waryn, and National Mythology.' *Studies in Philology* 91, no. 3 (1994) pp. 233–49

Kapelle, William E., *The Norman Conquest of the North*, (Croom Helm, London, 1979)

Kempe, Alfred J., *Historical notices of the collegiate church or royal free chapel and sanctuary of St. Martin-le-Grand, London.* (Longman, London,1825)

Krauss, Russell, 'Chaucerian Problems: Especially the Petherton Forestship and the Question of Thomas Chaucer.' In *Three Chaucer Studies*, ed. Carleton Brown. (Oxford University Press, Oxford, 1932)

Licence, Amy, Edward IV and Elizabeth Woodville: A True Romance (Amberley Publishing, Stroud, 2016)

Laslett, Peter, 'Comparing illegitimacy over time and between cultures' in Laslett Peter and Oosterveen, eds., *Bastardy and its Comparative History* (London, 1980)

Lawrence Stone, *The Family, Sex and Marriage in England, 1500–1800* (New York: Harper and Row, 1977)

Leland, John, and Hearne, Thomas. *The Itinerary of John Leland the Antiquary: Published by Mr. Thomas Hearne M. A. To which is Prefix'd Mr. Leland's New-year's Gift: and at the End is Subjoyn'd A Discourse Concerning Some Antiquities Lately Found in York-shire Vol. The first. [- Vol. the ninth, compleating the whole work.],* (Printed at the Theater for James Fletcher, bookseller in the Turk; and Joseph Pote, bookseller at Eaton., 1768)

Lewis, C.S., *The Allegory of Love: A Study of Medieval Tradition* (Oxford University Press, Oxford and New York, 1936)

Matthews, Helen, *The Legitimacy of Bastards: The Place of Illegitimate Children in Later Medieval England* (Pen and Sword, Barnsley, 2019)

Morgan, Kathleen and Smith, Brian S., 'Frampton on Severn: Introduction', in *A History of the County of Gloucester: Volume 10, Westbury and Whitstone Hundreds*, ed. C R Elrington, N M Herbert and R B Pugh (London, 1972), pp. 139–143

Messer, Danna R., *Joan, Lady of Wales: Power and Politics of King John's Daughter*, (Pen & Sword History, Barnsley, 2020)

McQuinn, Kristen, *The Two Isabellas of King John*, (Pen and Sword History, Barnsley, 2021)

Marshall, Susan, *Illegitimacy in Medieval Scotland, 1100–1500*, (Boydell & Brewer, Woodbridge, 2021)

Mason, Emma, *Westminster Abbey and its People 1050–1216*, (Woodbridge,1996)

Mason, Emma, *House of Godwine: The History of a Dynasty*, (Bloomsbury, London, 2003)

Maund, Kari, *Princess Nest of Wales: Seductress of the English*, (The History Press, Cheltenham, 2007)

Meisel, Janet, *Barons of the Welsh Frontier*, (University of Nebraska Press, Lincoln and London, 1980)

Meredith, G., 'Henry I's Concubines', *Essays in Medieval Studies 19* (2002)

Morris, Marc, *The Bigod Earls of Norfolk in the Thirteenth Century* (Boydell Press, Woodbridge, 2015)

Norton, Christopher. St William of York. (York Medieval Press, York, 2006)

O Brien, Harriet, *Queen Emma and the Vikings*, (Bloomsbury, London, 2005)

Orchard, James Halliwell-Phillips, ed. *Letters of the Kings of England: Now First Collected from the Originals in Royal Archives, and from Other Authentic Sources, Private as Well as Public*, (H. Colburn, London, 1846)

Ormrod, W. M. 'Who Was Alice Perrers?' *The Chaucer Review*, vol. 40, no. 3, 2006, pp. 219–229

Ormrod, W.M. *Edward III* (Yale University Press, New Haven, 2011)

Page, William, ed., Houses of Benedictine nuns: The abbey of Godstow' in *A History of the County of Oxford*, Volume 2, (London, 1907) pp. 71–75

Page, William, ed., 'Houses of Augustinian canons: The abbey of Oseney', in A History of the County of Oxford, Volume 2, (London, 1907), pp. 90–93

Page, William, ed. 'The borough of Wendover', in *A History of the County of Buckingham: Volume 3*, ed. (London, 1925), pp. 20–31.

Painter, Sidney, *The Reign of King John*, (Johns Hopkins University Press, Baltimore, 2020)

Patterson, Robert B, *The Earl, the Kings, and the Chronicler: Robert Earl of Gloucester and the Reigns of Henry I and Stephen*, (Oxford University Press, Oxford, 2019)

Payling, S.J. 'Widows and the Wars of the Roses: The Turbulent Marital History of Edward IV's Putative Mistress, Margaret, daughter of Sir Lewis John of West Hornden Essex' in Clark, Linda (ed.) (2015) *The Fifteenth Century: Essays Presented to Michael Hicks*Woodbridge: Boydell & Brewer

Penn, Thomas, *The Brothers York: An English Tragedy*, (Penguin, London, 2019)

Penman, Michael, 'Margaret Logie, Queen of Scotland' in *The Biographical Dictionary of Scottish Women: From the earliest times to 2004*, eds Elizabeth Ewan, Sue Innes, Sian Reynolds and Rose Pipes (Edinburgh University Press, Edinburgh, 2006) pp. 248–249

Philips, Seymour, 'The Place of the Reign of Edward II,' in Dodd, Gwilym and Musson, Antony, eds., *The Reign of Edward II: New Perspectives* (York Medieval Press, Woodbridge, 2006) pp. 220–233

Philips, Seymour, *Edward II* (Yale University Press, Newhaven, 2011)

Planché, James Robinson, *The Conqueror and His Companions*, (Tinsley Brothers, London,1874)

Pollock, M. A., *Scotland, England and France After the Loss of Normandy, 1204–1296: "Auld Amitie"*, (Boydell Press, Woodbridge, 2015)

Powell, W. R., ed., *A History of the County of Essex: Volume 4, Ongar Hundred* (Victoria County History, London, 1956)

Power, L. I. M. H. D., Power, D., *The Norman Frontier in the Twelfth and Early Thirteenth Centuries*, (Cambridge University Press, Cambridge, 2004)

Reed, Paul C. 'Countess Ida, Mother of William Longespée, Illegitimate Sone of Henry II,' *The American Genealogist*, vol. 77, 2002, p. 137

Royle, Trevor, *The Road to Bosworth Field*, (Little Brown, London, 2009)

Rüdiger, Jan, *All the King's Women: Polygyny and Politics in Europe, 900–1250*, (Brill, Leiden, 2020)

Santiuste, David, 'Puttyng Downe and Rebuking of Vices: Richard III and the Proclamation for the Reform of Morals,' in *Medieval Sexuality: A Casebook*. Harper, April and Proctor Caroline, eds. (Taylor & Francis, 2010) pp. 135–153

Sharpe, Richard, 'Norman Rule in Cumbria 1092–1136', *Transactions of the Cumberland and Westmorland Antiquarian and Archaeological Society*, Tract Series vol xxi, 2006

Sincock, William, 'Principal Landowners in Cornwall, AD1165' Royal Institution of Cornwall Journal, (1891) pp. 150–169

Smith Malcolm, ed. Human Biology and History (Society for the Study of Human Biology), (Taylor and Francis, London and New York, 2002)

Spencer, Charles, *The White Ship: Conquest, Anarchy and the Wrecking of Henry I's Dream*, (William Collins, London, 2020)

Strickland, Elisabeth, and Strickland, Agnes. Lives of the Queens of England, from the Norman Conquest. (G Bell and Sons, London, 1882)

Tabuteau, E.Z., 'The role of law in the succession to Normandy and England,' *Haskins Society Journal 3* (1991), pp.141–169

Taylor, Pamela 'Ingelric, Count Eustace and the Foundation of St Martin-Le-Grand' in Gillingham, John (ed) *Anglo-Norman Studies XXIV: Proceedings of the Battle Conference 2001*, (Boydell Press, Woodbridge, 2002) pp. 215–237

Tompkins, Laura 'Mary Percy and John de Southeray: Wardship, Marriage and Divorce in Fourteenth-Century England', *Fourteenth Century England X*, ed. Gwilym Dodd (2018)

Tooke, William, and Weever, John. *Ancient Funeral Monuments, of Great-Britain, Ireland, and the Islands Adjacent: With the Dissolved Monasteries Therein Contained; Their Founders, and what Eminent Persons Have Been Therein Interred. As Also, the Death and Burial of Certain of the Blood-royal, Nobility and Gentry of These Kingdoms, Emtombed in Foreign Nations* (W. Tooke, London, 1767)

Thomson, R. M., *William of Malmesbury*, (Boydell Press, Woodbridge, 2003)

Van Houts, Elizabeth, 'The Origins of Herleva, Mother of William the Conqueror,' *English Historical Review*, 101 (1986), pp. 399–405.

Warner, Kathryn, *Edward II: The Unconventional King* (Amberley Publishing, Stroud, 2015).

Warner, Kathryn, *Philippa of Hainault: Mother of the English Nation*, (Amberley Publishing, Stroud, 2019)

Washington, George, 'King Henry II's mistress Annabel de Greystoke' *Transactions of the Cumberland and Westmorland Antiquarian and Archaeological Society*, Series 2, vol. 64, (1964) pp. 124–129

Waugh, Scott L., *The Lordship of England: Royal Wardships and Marriages in English Society and Politics, 1217–1327*, (Princeton University Press, Princeton, 2014)

Weir, Alison, *Isabella She-Wolf of France, Queen of England* (Jonathan Cape, London, 2005)

Weir, Alison, *Katherine Swynford: The Story of John of Gaunt and his Scandalous Duchess*, (Jonathan Cape, London, 2007)

Weir, Alison, *Britain's Royal Families: The Complete Genealogy*, (Vintage Books, London, 2008)

Wellman, Kathleen, *Queens and Mistresses of Renaissance France*, (Yale University Press, New Haven and London, 2013)

White, Geoffrey H. 'The Career of Waleran, Count of Meulan and Earl of Worcester (1104–66),' *Transactions of the Royal Historical Society*, vol. 17, Cambridge University Press, 1934, pp. 19–48

Whittock, Martyn and Hannah, 1016 & 1066: Why the Vikings Caused the Norman Conquest, (Robert Hale, Ramsbury, 2016)

Wilkinson, Louise, J. 'Joan, wife of Llewelyn the Great' in *Thirteenth Century England X: Proceedings of the Durham Conference 2003* (Boydell & Brewer, Woodbridge, 2005) pp. 81–94

Williams, A., 'Henry I and the English,' in Fleming, D.F, and J.M. Pope, Henry I and the Anglo-Norman World: Studies in memory of C. Warren Hollister, Haskines Society 17, pp. 27–38

Wilson, David M, *The Bayeux Tapestry* (Thames and Hudson, London, 2004)

Wilton, David. *Word Myths: Debunking Linguistic Urban Legends*, (Oxford University Press, Oxford, 2008)

Young, Charles R, 'Hugh de Neville: An Early Thirteenth-Century Problem in Identification,' *Medieval Prosopography2*, no. 2 (1981), pp. 33–40

Acknowledgements

I would like to thank the following people for their kindness and help during my research: the staff of Ashbourne Library, in particular Stefan Bobeszko and James Vaughan. I would also like to thank Karen Deakin of Derbyshire Libraries for her perseverance in locating texts.

Many thanks to Eleri Pipien for her support with the concept of mischievous women and to everyone at Pen and Sword Books for their attention to detail, patience and help. Special thanks to Louise Morgan for her kind assistance sourcing *Hellelil and Hildebrand, the Meeting on the Turret Stairs* by Frederick William Burton. Thanks also to my family and friends who have encouraged me throughout and, as always, to my husband for asking tricky questions and untangling knotted sentences.

Index

Abduction 63, 68, 82, and Nest of Wales 43-46, 48, and Elizabeth de Vermondois 62-63, and Dangerosa 75

Abingdon Abbey, 35, 62

Adam, illegitimate son of King Edward II, 105

Adam of Bremen, 5

Adelaide, Countess of Aumale, sister of Duke William I of Normandy, 20, 23

Adomar, Count of Angoulême, 94

Adultery: xii, 146; accusations 94; Henry I, 72; Isabella of France, 121-123, 128; sisters-in-law of Isabella of France, 109-110, 111, 112, 113

Advowson: 183; Ælfgifu of Northampton, 4-8; Alice Perrers 147; D'Oilly family 57; Henry II 81

Ælfgifu of York or Northumbria, wife of King Æthelred II, 1, 188

Ælfhelm, Ealdorman of Northumbria, 4

Ælfthryth, mother of Æthelred II, 1

Æthelred II, King of England (c.966-1016), 1-3, 25, 188

Alboynus, illegitimate son of Harold Harefoot, 8

Alfred, son of Æthelred II, 3, 7, 10

Alexander I, King of Scots (1107-1124), 52, 53

Alexander II, King of Scots (1214-1249), 95, 98-99

Alnwick, Battle of (1093), 16

Alpesia, mistress of King John?, 100

Alys of France, seduced by King Henry II, 84-86

Amice, daughter of Ralph de Gael, heiress, 3

Anglo-Portuguese marriage alliances, 94, 158

Anglo Saxon Chronicle, 3, 4, 6, 7, 8, 12, 14, 30

Anglo-Scottish marriage alliances, 16, 30, 52, 53, 56, 59, 95, 103, 127, 136

Angharad, mother of Gerald of Wales, 43, 49

Angharad, mother of Nesta mistress of King Henry II, 84

Anglesey, invasion of (1157), 48

Angoulême, 93, 94, 95,

Anjou: castles, 76; coat of arms, 83; counts, 69, 70, 87; French invasion, 93

Anselm, Archbishop of Canterbury, 16-17, 31, 62

Ansfride, mistress of King Henry I: 35-37, 50; her children, 36, 37, 189; mutilation of her grandchildren 37

Ap Bleddyn, Cadwgan, 41, 43, 44, 46

Ap Cadwgan, Owain, 43-48

Ap Rhys, Gruffydd, 41, 46-47, 48

Ap Rhys, Hywel, 41, 46-48

Ap Tewdr, Rhys, 40, 41 46

aphrodisiacs, 78-80

Aquitaine, 71,74, 93, 137, 145, 153, 158

Arthur, Duke of Brittany, 90

Ashingdon, Battle of (1016), 2

Asthall Church, Oxfordshire, 53-54

Audley, Hugh, 1st Earl of Gloucester, 114, 115

Baldwin V, Count of Flanders (1012-1067), 23

Baliol, Hugh, 99

Baliol, Annabel, mistress of King Henry II, 74, 190

Balliol, Edward, 132

Bannockburn, Battle of (1314), 115, 131

Barfleur, Normandy, 37, 38, 59

Barnard Castle, Durham, 74, 99

Barons War (First), xiii, 90, 95, 96, 97, 98, 99, 102

Basset, Ralph, 120

Bayeux Tapestry, 12, 13, 21

Beatrice, illegitimate daughter of King Juan I, 158

Beauchamp, Margaret, Countess of Shrewsbury, 169

Beaufort, Joan, Countess of Westmorland, 156, 157

Beaufort family, 157, 159, 173-174, and origins of the name, 154, and The Peasants Revolt 156-157, and association with John of Gaunt 159, and legitimisation, 160-161, 162, and elevation 161, and Tudor descent from ix, 173, 174

Beaumont, Isabel, mistress of King Henry I, 64-65, 67, 68, 189, and her family 62, 63, 82, 88, 89, 91

Beaumont, Robert de, 2nd Earl of Leicester, 63, 82

Beaumont, Robert de, Count of Meulan and 1st Earl of Leicester, 62-63

Beaumont, Waleran de, Count of Meulan and 1st Earl of Worcester, 63, 64, 65

Becket, Thomas, Archbishop of Canterbury: 53, 59, 80, 87, 88; shrine 133

BelleBelle, mistress of King Henry II, 86

Bellême, Robert de, 3rd Earl of Shrewsbury, 34, 50-51

Berengaria of Navarre, Queen of England, 77, 181

Berkeley Castle, Gloucestershire, 126

Bernard, Abbot of Clairvaux, 70

Beverley, Yorkshire, 84

Bigamy: 10; dukes of Normandy 8, 9; King Edward IV 168, 170, 173, 179; Joan of Kent 173

Bigod, Roger, 2nd Earl of Norfolk, 83

Black Death (1348), xiii, 139-140

Blanche of Burgundy, 109, 110, 111, 112, 113, 123

Biset, Henry, 100

Blanche, Duchess of Lancaster, 150, 151

Blanche-Nef see White Ship

Bloet, Nesta, mistress of King Henry II, 84, 86, 190

Bloet, Ralph, 84

Bloet, Robert, Bishop of London, 36

Bolingbroke, Henry, later King Henry IV of England, 152, 154, 156-157, 158-162

Boniface IX, Pope, 160

Boniface VIII, Pope 103

Bordeaux, Aquitaine, 93, 147

Bosham Church, Sussex, 14

Bosworth, battle of (1485), 173

Bona of Savoy, 173

Boteler, Clemence de, mistress of King John?, 91

Boroughbridge, Battle of (1322), 118, 119, 121

Bourgtheroulde, Battle of (1124), 52

Bower, Walter, 133

Bradlesmere, Bartholmew, 116-117

Braose, Maud de, 97

Bréteuil, Eustace de, 36-37

Bristol: 34, 58; Bristol Channel 15, 124

Brus, Robert de, Lord of Annandale, 57

Butler, Lady Eleanor, mistress and possible wife of King Edward IV, 168-169, 179

Caen, Robert de, 1st Earl of Gloucester, illegitimate son of King Henry I, 33-34, 36, 39

Canterbury, Kent; archbishops, 16, 31, 62, 87, 92, 108, 123, 156; pilgrimage to; 117, 133

canon law, x, 4, 31, 94, 131, 168, 169, 185

Carlisle, Cumberland: 55, 56; castle, 55, 100

Castleton, Derbyshire, 27

Catherine of Valois, 15

Ceredigion, 40, 43, 47, 47

Charles IV, King of France, 109, 113, 121, 123-124

Chaucer, Geoffrey, author, 152, 154

Chaucer, Philippa, 151, 152-153, 158

Chester, 12, 13, 14

Childemaister, Elthelric, 14

Clare, de, family, 65, 79, 84

Clare Margaret de, Lady Bradlesmere, 117

Clare, Basilia de, 65, 67

Clare, Eleanor de Lady of Glamorgan, 115, 120

Clare, Elizabeth de, Lady of Clare, 115, 119

Clare, Gilbert de, 7th Earl of Gloucester, 106

Clare, Gilbert de, 8th Earl of Gloucester and Hertford, 115, 118

Clare, Gilbert de, Earl of Striguil, 65, 66

Clare, Margaret de, Countess of Gloucester and Cornwall, 115

Clare, Maud de, Countess of Gloucester, 115

Clare, Richard de, 'Stongbow', Earl of Striguil, 65, 66

Clemence or Clemencia, mistress of King John, 91, 100

Clifford, Rosamund,'Fair Rosamund', mistress of King Henry II, xii, 52, 78-79, 80-82, 190 and family, 78, 82

Cnoppe, Osgod, 14

Cnut, King of England, Denmark and Norway, 2-3, 4-6, 7, 12, 188

Conan III, Duke of Brittany, 75

Conan IV, Duke of Brittany, 75

concubines and concubinage, x, 5, 6, 7, 11, 14, 16, 22, 25, 44, 49, 144, 155, 184

Coniscliffe, Durham, 73

consanguinity, 10, 62, 90, 91, 95, 113, 184

Constance, illegitimate daughter of King Henry I, 59; and granddaughter, 59

Constance, Duchess of Brittany, possible mistress of King John, 90, 91

Constanza of Castile, Duchess of Lancaster, 148, 150, 154, 155, 156, 159

Convents: education, 15, 31, 78; seclusion, 2, 11,16,17, 31, 75, 113, 125, 169; vows,16, 31

Corbet, Alice, erroneous attribution as mistress of King Henry I, 53-54

Corbet, Gundrada, illegitimate daughter of King Henry I, 50, 51, 189

Corbet, Robert, Lord of Alcester, 50

Corbert, Rogeer, 50-51

Corbet, Rohese, illegitimate daughter of King Henry I, 50, 52, 189

Corbet, Sybilla, mistress of King Henry I, xi, 33, 41, 50-54,

Corbet, William, illegitimate son of King Henry I, 50, 51, 53

Corfe Castle, Dorset, 94, 97

Cornhill, Joan de, possible mistress of King John, 99-100

Council of Oxford (1036), 6

Council of Northampton (1164), 53

Court of the Arches, see ecclesiastical court

courtly love: viii, 80, 109, 136, 144, 184; gardens, 79, 80, 81

Croix, Alice de la, mistress of King Edward II, 105

Croyland Chronicle, 163

Crusade, First (1096-1099), 30, 62

Crusade, Second (1147-1150), 71

Crusade, Third (1189-1192), 77, 101

Crusade, Fifth (1217-1221), 90, 99

Cumberland, 55, 56, 57, 74, 117

D'Aunay brothers, 109, 112

D'Oilly, Alice or Adeliza, illegitimate daughter of King Henry I, 58

D'Oilly, Robert the Elder, 57

D'Oilly, Robert the Younger, 57, 58

Dameta, mistress of King Stephen, 190

Damory, Roger, 114, 116

Danes, 1, 2, 4, 5

Dangerosa, 75

Danvers, Thomas, 166-167

David II, King of Scots (1329-1371), xiv, 127, 131-136

Deheubarth, Wales, 40, 41, 46, 47

Denmark, 4-5, 6, 8, 15

Despenser War (1321-1322), 116

Despenser, Hugh, the Elder, 1st Earl of Winchester, 108, 117, 121

Despenser, Hugh, the Younger, xiii, 103, 108, 115-120, 121, 122, 123, 124, 125

Devon, 15, 24, 53, 57, 59, 140

Dickens, Charles, author, 86

divorce, 4: Eleanor of Aquitaine, 69; Eleanor of Blois, 70; King David II,

136; King Edward II, 12; King John, 91

Domesday Book land holdings, 23, 24, 26, 27, 34, 40, 50, 56

Dover, Kent: Godwin 11; reign of Edward II, 104, 105, 111, 116, 117; William Peverel, 29

dowers and dowries, 2, 15, 23, 35, 59, 85, 86, 92, 94, 95, 100, 105, 106, 109, 113, 117, 129, 136, 148, 151, 153, 166, 168, 169, 170, 171, 184

Drummond, Annabella, 135

Drummond, Margaret, mistress of King David II and Queen of Scotland, 135

Dugdale's Baronage, 25, 29, 91

Dunbar, Agnes, mistress of King David II, 135, 136

Dunstanville, Rainald de, Earl of Cornwall, illegitimate son of King Henry I, 51, 53, 57, 59, 189

Durham: 56, 132; bishop-elect, 84; cathedral 16,

Eadric Streona, Ealdorman of Mercia, 2, 3, 4

Eadric the Wild, 13

Ealdgyth of Mercia, 12-13

Ealdgyth of York, 12, 13

Ecclesiastical court, 177

Edith, mistress of King Henry I, 38

Edith Swanneck, handfasted wife of King Harold II: x, 10-12, 13-15, 188; descendants, 15

Edith of Wessex, wife of Edward the Confessor:11, 15; acceptance of Norman conquest 15; dower rights 14; withdrawal to a convent 11, 16

Edith, widow of Sigeferth, 2, 188

Edmund Ironside, King of England, 2, 16, 188

Edmund of Langley, 1st Duke of York, 148, 157, 163

Edmund of Woodstock, 1st Earl of Kent, 127, 128

Edward I, King of England (1272-1307), 192, and love for Eleanor of Castile xv; marriage alliance xv, 103, and Piers Gaveston 104

Edward II, King of England (1307-1327): 110, 114-126, 131, 192; alleged murder 126, 127; deposition 124-126; Gascony 108, 110, 120, 121; Hugh Despenser the Younger, 115, 116; illegitimate child, 104; Lords Ordainers 106,107, 118; male favourites xiii, 114, 115, 116, 119, 126; Piers Gaveston 104-107, 108; relationship with Isabella of France 103, 105, 107, 109, 114, 115, 117, 120, 121, 122, 123, 130,

Edward III, King of England (1327-1377), 127-131, 132, 137, 138-155, 192-193

Edward IV, King of England (1461-1483): 163, 164, 168, 169, 170, 171, 172, 173, 174, 176, 177, 178, 179, 194; illegitimate children, 165, 194

Edward of Woodstock, the Black Prince, xv, 140, 143, 145, 146, 155, 173

Edward 'the Confessor', King of England 7, 8, 10, 11, 12, 26, 27, 188

Edwin, Earl of Mercia,12, 13, 28

Ela of Salisbury, *suo jure* Countess of Salisbury, heiress 83

Eleanor of Aquitaine, Queen of England: 69-72, 74-79, 81, 85, 86, 91, 108, 130, 190; 'black legend' xii, 71; 'Fair Rosamund', 77, 81; divorce, 69

Eleanor of Blois, 70

Eleanor of Castile, Queen of England, xv, 192

Eleanor crosses, xv

Elizabeth of Lancaster, Duchess of Exeter, and scandalous marriage 154, 157-158

Elizabeth of York, Queen of England, 3, 164, 176, 179, 194

Emma of Normandy, Queen England, 1, 3, 5, 6, 7, 8, 188

Emma of Paris, 8-9

Enconium Emmae Reginae, 5, 7, 8

Enguerrand, Count of Ponthieu, 23

Essex: 25, 26, 27, 99, 124, 140, 167; earls of; 37, 97, 100

Eustace, son of King Stephen, 72, 190

Eustace of Bréteuil, 36-37

Eustace, Count of Boulogne, 11

Everswell, Woodstock, England, 79, 80

excommunication, 6, 23, 70, 94-95, 96, 99, 108, 136
Exeter: 1, 15, dukes of, 157-158; earls of, 166

Falaise, 18, 19, 20
Fergus of Galloway, marriage to illegitimate daughter of King Henry I, 32, 56
Ferrers, Agatha de, possible mistress of King John, 91
Ferrers of Groby, Elizabeth, 6th Baroness, 171
Ferrers of Wem, Robert, Sir, 157, 160
fines, 46, 74, 90, 98, 99, 100, 101, 131, 147, 154, 170
FitzAlan, Alice, Lady Wake, 152, 154
FitzEarl, Otuel, 35, 38
FitzEdith, Robert, illegitimate son of King Henry I, 56, 57, 189
FizGerald, David, Bishop of St David's, 48
FitzGerald, Maurice, 48
FitzGerald, William, 48
FitzGilbert, Richard see Richard of Tonbridge
FitzHamon, Mabel, suo jure Countess of Gloucester, heiress, 33, 35
FitzHenry, Henry, illegitimate son of King Henry I, 43, 48
Fitz Herbert, Herbert, Chamberlain of England, 51, 52
FitzLewis, Henry, Sir, 166
FitzOsbern, William, 14
FitzRichard, Mabel, heiress, 53
FitzRoy, Maud, illegitimate daughter of King Henry 1, 75
FitzStephen, Robert, 48, 49
FitzStephen, Thomas, mariner, 38, 39
FitzWalter, Matilda, xv, 96-97
FitzWalter, Robert, Lord of Little Dunmow, 96, 98
FitzWilliam, Raymond, 'le-Gros', 66, 67
Flanders, 11, 61
Fontevrault Abbey, Anjou, 75, 77
Forne, Lord of Greystoke, 56, 57
Forz, Willaim de, 3rd Earl of Aumale, 101

Fougères, Clemence de, mistress of King John?, 91
Froissart's Chronicles, 119, 128, 139, 148, 150, 160, 161
Fulbert, the Tanner, 19, 20
Fulk, illegitimate son of King Henry I, 35

Gael, Ralph de, 15
Gaimar, Geoffrey, 3
Gascony, xv, 93, 103, 106, 108, 110, 120-121, 124, 152
Gaveston, Piers, xiii, 103, 104, 105-108, 114
Gay or Gayt family, 34
Geoffrey, Count of Anjou, 70, 87
Gerald of Wales, chronicler, 49, 66, 70, 79, 80, 85
Gerald of Windsor, 42-43, 44, 45, 46, 47, 48, 51
Gervase of Canterbury, chronicler, 94
Gifts: to monastic foundations and churches, 29, 34, 57, 81, 98; to mistresses and favourites, 52, 73-74, 83, 86, 100, 109, 119, 143, 147, 148, 152, 153, 154, 157, 159, 162
Gilbert, Count of Brionne, 22, 23
Guy, Count of Brionne, 23
Gisla, daughter of Charles the Simple, 8
Glaber, Ralph, 22
Gloucester: 16, 84; duchess of, 160; earls of, xiv, 53, 57, 98, 106, 115, 161; St Peter's Abbey, 137
Gloucestershire, 51
Godstow Abbey, Oxfordshire, 78, 81
Godwin, Earl of Wessex, 6, 7, 10, 11
Godwinson, Harold later King Harold II of England, x, 10, 11, 12, 13, 14, 188
Good Parliament (1376), xiv, 155
Grandison, Catherine, alleged rape by King Edward III, 138
Gregory XI, Pope, 136, 143
Grey of Groby, John, Sir, 170
Grey, Thomas, Marquess of Dorset, xv, 178, 179
Greystoke, Barony of, 56, 57
Greystoke, Ivo, 56
Greystoke, Walter

Gunnhild, sister of Sweyn Forkbeard, 1
Gunnhild of Wessex, daughter of King
    Harold II, 11, 15-16
Gytha of Wessex, daughter of King
    Harold II, 15
Gunnor, mother of Emma of Normandy,
    1, 8-9, 22, 61, 62
Guy, Count of Flanders, 103
Gwynedd, Wales, 46, 47, 101
Gynes, Joan, victim of Hugh Despenser
    the Younger, 119

Hait the Fleming, 48
Harclay, Andrew, 1st Earl of Carlisle,
    117-118
harlot, xiv, 24, 81, 104, 140, 164, 168,
    178
Harold 'Harefoot' later King Harold I of
    England, 6, 7, 8, 188
Harthacnut, King of England, 6, 7, 8,
    188
Haroldson, Godwin, 11, 15
Haroldson, Magnus, 15
Haroldson, Edmund, 15
Hastings, Battle of (1066), 10, 13-14, 21,
    26, 50, 57, 62, 65
Hastings, John, 3rd Earl of Pembroke,
    157
Hastings, William, 1st Baron Hastings,
    171, 175, 176, 178, 179
Hatfield Peverel Priory, Essex, England,
    28-29
Hawise, Countess of Aumale, possible
    mistress of King John, 87, 100, 101,
    191
Helen of Wales see Nest of Wales
Hellelil and Hildebrand, viii
Henry, 3rd Earl of Lancaster, 124, 126,
    127, 128
Henry of Huntingdon, chronicler, 3, 32,
    63
Henry I, King of England (1100-
    1136): xi, 16, 29, 30-39, 40-53, 189;
    illegitimate children, xi, 32-33, 35, 36,
    43, 48, 52, 55, 56, 57, 58, 59,61-62, 64,
    75 189-190
Henry VI, King of England (1421-1471),
    170, 193

Henry VIII, King of England
    (1509-1547), xv, 165, 180, 181
illegitimate children of King Henry II,
    69, 73, 76, 82, 84, 85, 190
Henry, The Young King, 72, 75, 76
Herleva of Falaise, x, 18-24, and
    extended family, 20, 21, 22, 24
Herluin, Vicomte de Conteville, 21, 23,
    24
Hiémois, Normandy, 18, 19
Holland, John, 2nd Duke of Exeter,
    157
homosexuality, xiii, 104, 105, 110, 119
Honour of: Conisbrough, 61; Peverel,
    27, 29; Pontefract, 89; Warenne, 88
hostage-taking as surety, 2, 11, 33, 37,
    42, 74, 86, 97, 100, 132, 133
Hugh, Bishop of Lincoln, 19, 81
Hundred Years War (1337-1453), xiv,
    114, 151, 165
Hythusum, Ada de, mistress of William
    the Lion, 98

illegitimacy, xi, 3, 7-8, 9, 10, 21, 25, 27,
    39, 53, 70, 84, 88, 101, 127, 133, 148,
    158, 168, 169, 179
influence of mistresses, xiv, 103, 133,
    139, 141, 143, 144, 146, 181
Ingelric, 25, 26, 28
Ireland, 11, 15, 41, 42, 46, 48, 49, 66, 67,
    100, 106, 124, 145
Isabella of Angoulême, queen of
    England: xii, xiv, 92, 96, 191; age
    at marriage, 93; reputation, 94, 95;
    second marriage 95
Isabella of Castile, 157
Isabella of France, Queen of England:
    xiii, 15, 103, 104, 106, 107, 108-109,
    110, 111, 113, 114, 115, 116, 117, 118,
    119-123 127-128; Arthurian Legend
    viii, 105, 122, 126, 130
Isabella of Gloucester, uncrowned queen
    of England, 90, 92, 94, 98
Ivry Castle, Normandy, 36

Jeanne of Evreux, Queen of France, 123
Jeanne of Valois, Countess of Hainault,
    122

Joan, mother of Matilda the illegitimate daughter of King Henry II, 74

Joan, Lady of Wales, illegitimate daughter of King John, 90, 91, 101, 191

Joan Grenville wife of Roger Mortimer 1st Earl of March, 118, 126, 129

Joan of Acre, 106

Joan of Burgundy, 109, 111

Joan of Kent, 157, 173

Joan of the Tower, Queen of Scots, xiv, 131, 132, 133-134, 135, 136

Joan, Queen of Navarre, xii, 110, 104, 110

Joan, Queen of Scots, legitimate daughter of King John, 95

Joan II, Queen of Navarre, 112

John, Duke of Bedford, 170

John, King of England (1199-1216): xiii, 74, 77, 79, 83, 84, 86, 87-89, 90-102, 19; Alys of France, 86; the role of wives and mistresses in the Barons War, xiii, 95, 96, 97, 98, 99, 100; betrothals 75-76, 84, 92, 93; illegitimate children, 87, 88, 89, 90, 91, 96, 100, 191; Isabella of Angouleme, 93-94, 96; Matilda FitzWalter, 96-97

John I, King of France (1316), 112

John of Gaunt, Duke of Lancaster: xiv, xv 143,145, 146; claim to throne of Castile by right of his wife 148, 150, 151, 153, 154, 155, 157, 158; illegitimate children 140, 150, 152, 153, 154-160, 161-162, Peasants Revolt 156, 159, 160, 161; unlikelihood of children by Phillipa Chaucer 152

John of Salisbury, chronicler, 70, 71, 72, 75

John of Worcester, chronicler, 6, 7, 11, 34

John XXII, Pope, 113, 121, 122,123, 128

Joigny, Pierre de, supposed lover of Isabella of Angouleme, 94

Juan I, King of Portugal (1385-1433), 158

Judith of Lens, 28

Juliana of Fontevrault, illegitimate daughter of King Henry I, 36-37

Kettlethorpe, Lincolnshire, 151, 155

King's Langley, Hertfordshire, 108

Lacy, Walter de, 94

Lambert II, Count of Lens, 23

Lambert, John, 175, 180

Lambert, Jane see Shore, Jane

Lambert, John, 175, 176, 180

Lanercost Chronicle,104, 108, 120, 121, 125

Lanfranc, Archbishop of Canterbury, 31

Langland, William, author, 14, 144

Leeds Castle, Kent, 117

legitimation: of Joan Lady of Wales 91; of the Beaufort family, 160, 162

Leicester, earls of see Beaumont

Leinster, Ireland, 49, 66

Leo IX, Pope, 23

Leopold V, Duke of Austria (1177-1194), 77

Liber Vitae, 5

Life of Harold,14

Lincoln: battle, 90; bishops, 19, 36, 76, 81, 180; cathedral, 151, 158, 160, 162; earls, 106; Katherine Swynford, 153, 157, 158

Lincolnshire, 55, 61, 155

Little Dunmow church, 97

Logie, John, Sir, 135

Logie, Margaret, see Drummond Margaret

London: xiv, 2, 3,11, 12, 25, 99, 116, 117, 124, 125, 133, 137, 138, 143, 144, 145, 153, 154, 156, 165, 173, 175, 176, 177, 178, 179, 180; bishops, 44; Greyfriars' Church, 130,

Longspée, William, 3rd Earl of Salisbury, illegitimate son of King Henry II, 69, 74, 82, 83, 84, 190

Longsword, William, Duke of Normandy (c.900-942), 8

Lords Appellant, 161

Lords Ordainers, 106, 108, 117

Louis VII, King of France (1137-1180), 69, 70, 71, 76, 84, 85

Louis X, King of France (1314-1316), 109, 112, 114

Louis XI, King of France (1461-1483), 173

Lucy, Margaret, mistress of King
    Edward IV 165-166, 167, 169

Lumley, Thomas, Sir, 165

Lucy, William, Sir, 165-166

Lusignan, 93, 94

Lusignan, Hugh IX, Seigneur de
    Lusignan, and Count of La Marche,
    77, 93, 94

Lusignan, Hugh X, Seigneur de
    Lusignan, count of La Marche and
    Count of Angoulême, 95

Lynom, Thomas, 179-180

Lyons, Richard, 143, 146

Mac Murchada, Dairmait, King of
    Leinster, 66

Magna Carta, 95, 99, 100

Magnus the Good, 6

Mahaut of Artois, 109, 111, 113

Maid Marian, *see* FitzWalter Matilda

Maine, 24, 59, 69,79, 93

Malcolm III, 'Canmore', King of Scots
    (1058-1093), 16, 52, 61

Malmesbury Abbey, Wiltshire, 2

Maltravers, John, Sir, 126

Mancini, Dominic, chronicler, 171, 172,
    173, 176, 179

Mandeville, Geoffrey de, Earl of Essex,
    97, 98

Mandeville, William de, Earl of Essex,
    100

Map, Walter, chronicler, 73

Mare, Peter de la, 146, 147

Mare, John de la, 146

Margaret 'Maid of Norway', Queen of
    Scots, 103

Margaret of Anjou, Queen of England,
    163, 175, 193

Margaret of Burgundy, wife of Louis X
    of France, 109, 112

Margaret, sister of Edgar the Ætheling,
    later Queen of Scots and saint, 16, 52,
    61

Marguerite of France, wife of Henry the
    Young King, 84, 85

Marguerite of France, queen consort of
    King Edward I, 104, 105, 106, 192

marriage: annulment, 23, 62, 70, 71, 85,
    90, 91, 92, 112-113, 132, 135, 136,
    148, 158,177, 181, 184; banns 113, 185;
    Christian, ix-x, 3, 6, 8, 9, 1, 39, 62,
    139, 169, 185; clandestine, 168, 169,
    179, 185; Danish, ix-x, 3, 4-5, 8, 9, 10,
    14, 18, 185

Marshal, William, 67, 76, 90, 95

Matilda, Abbess of Barking Abbey,
    illegitimate daughter of King Henry
    II, 73

Matilda of Flanders, 23, 25, 26, 27, 31,
    189

Matilda, Countess of Perche, illegitimate
    daughter of King Henry I, 38, 59

Matilda, Empress, daughter of King
    Henry I born Adelaide, 31, 33, 53, 58,
    69

Matilda of Scotland (also known as
    Edith), Queen of England, 16, 30-31,
    42, 43, 50, 61

Meaux Chronicle, xiii, 85, 96, 104

Medieval medical theories and sex, xi,
    36, 80, 184; doctrine of signatures,
    78

Mercia: 2, 4, 55; earls of, 6, 12, 28, 55

Meschin, Ranulf le, Earl of Chester, 55,
    56

Molay, Jacques de, Grandmaster of the
    Knights Templar, 110, 113

Montagu, William, 1st Earl of Salisbury,
    128, 138

Montgomery, Arnulf de, 41, 42, 43, 51

Montmorency, Hervey de, 66, 67

Monthermer, Ralph de, 106, 120

Montreuil, Treaty of (1299) 103

Morcar, Earl of Northumbria, 12, 13

More, Sir Thomas, 163, 164, 167, 173,
    175, 176, 177, 180, 181, 182

Morgan, Bishop-elect of Durham,
    illegitimate son of King Henry II, 84

Mortimer, Katherine, mistress of King
    David II, xiv, xv, 133-134

Mortimer, Roger, 1st Earl of March:
    Despenser War, 116, 117, 118; and
    Isabella of France 122-123, 124,
    126-130, 131; and possible illegitimate
    child, 127; and family 118, 126, 163

murder: xiv, xv, 1, 2, 3, 4, 7, 14, 22, 46, 59, 65, 80, 81, 82, 97, 103, 108, 123, 126, 127, 134, 156, 161, 166, 177, 178, 179, 180

Nest of Wales, mistress of King Henry I: xi, 33, 40-49, 50, 54, 66, 67; Carew Castle, 43, 48; Cilgeraran Castle 43; children 43; FitzGerald descendants, 49, 67
Nesta *see* Bloet, Nesta
Neville, Cecily, Duchess of York, 163, 172
Neville, Hugh de, 99-100
Neville, Hugh de, wife of, possible mistress of King John 99
Neville, Richard, 16th Earl of Warwick, 'The Kingmaker', 170, 176
Neville, Ralph, 6th Baron Raby, 161
Neville's Cross, Battle of (1346), 132
Niger, Alan (also known as 'the Black'), 17
Normandy, dukes of, 11,18, 22, 23, 26, 30, 69, 72
Normandy, 1,2, 3, 7, 8, 12, 20, 30, 33-34, 37, 47, 51, 61, 63-64, 76, 85, 90, 92, 93-94, 112,
Northampton: 73, 88, 131; Battle of (1460), 166
Northamptonshire, 27
Nottingham: 27, 29, 128; castle, 26, 128, 147
Nottinghamshire, 27
Northumbria: 2, 4, earls of; 4, 12, 13
Norway, 5, 6,13,104
Nurdels, Hawise de, mistress of King John?, 100

Odo, Bishop of Bayeux, 21, 24
Odo, Count of Champagne, 23
Osbern, 21
Oseney Abbey, Oxford, vii, 57, 58, 57
Oxford, England, 1, 6, 7, 58, 108
Oxfordshire, 27, 53, 58, 78, 79, 99 cluster of mistresses of Henry I; 34, 35

Pantolf, Isolda, mistress of King John?, 100

papal dispensations, 62, 71, 92, 113, 152, 160, 166-167
Paris: 71, 76, 81, 90, 110, 112, 121, 137; Treaty of (1259), 108
Paris, Matthew, chronicler, 40, 69, 94, 96
Parliament, 106, 111, 120, 121, 125, 126, 128, 131, 145, 146, 147, 155, 160, 168, 169, 173,
Paston Letters, 170
Peasants Revolt (1381), 140, 155-156
Pembroke: castle, 41- 43, 46, 48, 51, 65; earls, 107, 108, 157, lordship, 65
penance, xiv
Percy, Henry, 107
Percy, Mary, heiress, 147, 148
Perrers, Alice, mistress of King Edward III, xiii, xiv, 139,140-145, 147, 148, 149
Perrers, Janyn, 142
Petronella of Aquitaine, 69-70
Peverel family, 26, 29
Peverel, Maud, alleged mistress of William the Conqueror, x, 25-29
Peverel, Ranulph, 26, 27, 28
Peverel, William, 27, 28, 29
Philip Augustus, Philip II, King of France (1190-1223), 92, 101
Philip IV, 'the Fair', King of France (1285-1314), xii, 103, 104, 105, 109, 110, 111, 112, 113
Philip Le Bel, chronicler, 138, 139
Philip of Valois later Philip V, King of France, 110, 114, 120, 122
Philippa of Flanders, 103
Philippa of Hainault, Queen of England: 124, 129, 137, 139, 142, 143; and Roet family 150-151, 192
Philippa of Lancaster, Queen of Portugal, 154, 158
Philippa of Toulouse, 75
Piers the Fair, alleged illegitimate son of Isabella of Angoulême, 94
Pinel, Clemence, mistress of King John?, 100
Pinel, Henry, 100
Planché, J. R., 25, 26, 28
Plantagenet, Arthur, Lord Lisle, illegitimate son of King Edward IV, 164-165, 194

Plantagenet, Geoffrey, Archbishop of York, illegitimate son of King Henry II, 69, 73, 76

Plantagenet, Elizabeth, illegitimate daughter of King Edward IV, 165, 194

Plantagenet, Hamelin see Warenne, Hamelin de

Pole family, 165

Poppa, 8

Porhoët, Alice de, mistress of King Henry II, 74, 75

Porhoët, Odo de, Count of Brittany, 74

Powys, 40, 41, 43, 44, 46, 47

Raoul I, Count of Vermandois, 69-70

raptus laws, 45, 63, 82, 142

Raymond of Antioch, 71

Richard I, Duke of Normandy (932-996), 1

Richard I 'the Lionheart', King of England (1189-1199): 74, 76, 77, 89, 90, 93, 190, 191; Alys of France, xiii, 83, 85, 86; marriages made to heiresses 67, 76, 83, 101; fines paid by widows, 90

Richard II, Duke of Normandy (996-1026), 1, 3, 18

Richard II, King of England (1377-1399), 147, 148, 155, 156, 157, 158, 160, 161, 162

Richard III, Duke of Normandy (1026-1027), 18

Richard Duke of Gloucester later Richard III, King of England (1483-1485), 177, 179, 194

Richard, Duke of York, younger son of King Edward IV, 178

Richard of Lincoln, illegitimate son of King Henry I, 36, 37, 38, 39

Richard of Tonbridge: 22, 24; de Clare family, 65

Robert I, King of Scots (1306-1329), 131

Robert I 'the Devil', Duke of Normandy (1037-1035), x, 18, 19, 20

Robert Curthose, Duke of Normandy (1087-1106), 30, 33, 42, 50, 61, 62, 64

Robert of Caen, Earl of Gloucester, 33, 35, 36, 39, 53, 57 potential mothers, 34, 42, 50

Richard of Dover, illegitimate son of King John, 88

Roger of Howden, chronicler, 76, 85, 99

Rouen: 20,34, 52, 64; bishops of, 20, 21; siege of (1173), 79

Roet, Katherine, *see* Swynford, Katherine

Roet, Paon, 160

Roet, Philippa *see* Chaucer, Philippa

Rohese, Countess of Lincoln, 79

Roger of Howden, chronicler,76, 85, 99

Roger of Wendover, chronicler, 92, 101

Rollo, Duke of Normandy, 8

romance, viii, xii, 45, 63, 80, 81

Rose of Dover, heiress, 89, 90

Rufus, Alan (also known as 'the Red'), 15, 16

Sainte-Foi, 8

salic law, 113, 114

Seacourt, Ansfride de, mistress of King Henry I, 35-37

Seacourt, Anskil de, 35

Scarborough Castle, 107

Sex: attitudes towards, x, xi, xiii, 5, 32, 35, 36, 63, 71, 73, 79-80, 82, 86, 95, 96, 98, 123, 139, 177; sin, x, xi, 29, 32, 73, 80, 95, 154-155, 177; prostitution, xiv, 24, 72, 73, 98; venereal disease, 73, 161-162

Shaa, Ralph, 179

Shore, Jane *also known as* Elizabeth, xiv-xv, 175-182

Shore, William, 180

Shrewsbury: 13, 44, 117; abbey, 50; earls of 41, 42, 50, 51, 168

Sigeferth, 2

Sigulf, 56

Sigulfson, Edith Forne, mistress of King Henry I, 55-59, 73, 189

Simon of Sudbury, Archbishop of Canterbury, 156

Somerset Herald, 25, 27

Southeray, John, illegitimate son of King Edward III, 142, 147, 148

Southwark brothels, 73

Speculum Dominarum, xii, 110

Spot, Wulfric, 4

St Brice's Day Massacre (1002) 1

St Hilaire, Marie, mistress of John of
  Gaunt, 152
St-Martin-le-Grand, London, 25-26, 28
St Olaf, 5
Stafford, John, Sir, 166
Stamford Bridge, Battle of (1066), 13
Stewart, John, 135
Stewart, Robert, Steward of Scotland,
  132, 133, 134, 135
Stewart, Thomas, 2nd Earl of Angus,
  134
Stillington, Robert, Bishop of Bath and
  Wells, 169, 172
Stephen, Constable of Cardigan Castle,
  48
Stephen, Count of Blois, afterwards
  Stephen, King of England
  (1135-1154), 38, 39, 58, 65, 69, 70, 72,
  87, 190
Suzanna, friend of King John, 100
Suzanne, mistress of King John, 87
Susanna, daughter of Joan, Lady of
  Wales, 91
Sussex, 13, 14, 52, 61, 89
Sweyn Estrithson, King of Denmark, 16
Sweyn Forkbeard, King of Denmark
  (d.1014), 1-2, 4
Swynford, Blanche, 160
Swynford of Kettlethorpe, Hugh, Sir,
  151, 152
Swynford, Katherine, xiv, xv, 150-162
  and Anya Seton viii, and Bohun, Mary
  de, 157, 158 and Swynford children,
  151-153
Swynford, Thomas, 157
Sybilla of Normandy, illegitimate
  daughter of King Henry I, 52, 56

Talbot, Eleanor, Lady, see Butler,
  Eleanor, Lady
Taillebois, Ivo, 55
Talvas, William IV, Count of Ponthieu,
  86
Terric the Teuton, 94
Tewkesbury Annals, 87
The Anarchy (1138-1153), 29, 34, 54, 65
The Tower of London, 97, 117, 118,
  132-133, 143, 144, 156, 165, 178, 179

Thomas, 2nd Earl of Lancaster, 106, 107,
  116, 118
Thomas of Walsingham, 140, 141, 156
Thorkelsdottir, Gytha, 10, 11, 13, 14, 15
Tintern Abbey, 66
Titulus Regius 168, 173
Tracy, family of, 59
Tracey, William de, illegitimate son of
  King Henry I, 59, 190
tomb: Alice Perrers, 149: Eleanor of
  Aquitaine, 77; Edith Forne Sigulfson,
  58; Katherine Mortimer, 134; Matilda
  FitzWalter, 29; Piers Gavetston, 108,
  Rosamund Clifford, 81-82
Tosny family, 73
Tosny, Ida de, Countess of Norfolk,
  mistress of King Henry II, 82-83, 190,
  and Tosny family 73, 78, 82
Tour de Nesle, 111
Towton, Battle of (1461), 163, 166
Trokelowe's Chronicle, 105, 107
Tudor, Henry, later King Henry VII
  (1485-1509), ix, 3, 179, 180
Tudor, Owain, 15
Turold, 21, 22

Uhtred, son of Fergus Lord of Galloway,
  33

Valence, Aymer de, 2nd Earl of
  Pembroke, 107
Val-ès-Dunes, Battle of (1047), 23
Vaux, Robert de, Baron of Gilsland, 100
Verdun, Nicholas de, 91
Vergil, Polydore, 165, 167, 172, 173
Vermandois, Elizabeth, 61-65
Vermandois, Hugh de, Count of
  Vermondois, 62
Vescy, Eustace de, 98, 99
Vescy, Margaret de, illegitimate daughter
  of William the Lion, 98
Vexin, The, Normandy, 34, 64, 85, 86
Victorian viewpoint, 45, 97, 141, 164
Virty-sur-Marne, burning of (1143), 70
Vitalis, Orderic, chronicler, 19, 21, 22,
  30, 31, 32, 34, 37, 42, 53, 56, 62, 64

Wake family, 167

Wake, Thomas, 166-167
Wake, John, 166
Wakefield, Battle of (1460), 163
Wales: 12, 13, 40, 42, 43, 46, 47, 65, 78, 9, 106, 124, ; Marches of, 41, 51, 54, 84, 116, 185
Wallingford Castle, 57, 58, 64, 89
Waltham Abbey, Essex, 14
Walter, brother of Herleva, 22
wards, 42, 74, 82, 92, 99, 147, 151, 185
Warenne, Ela de, mistress of King John?, 87-89
Warenne, Hamelin de, Earl of Surrey, illegitimate son of Geoffrey of Anjou, 87, 88, 89
Warenne, Isabel de, *suo jure* Countess of Surrey, 87
Warenne, Isabel de, mistress of King John?, 88,89
Warrenne, William de, 2nd Earl of Surrey, 61, 62, 63, 64, 65, 68
Wars of the Roses (1455-1487), 163, 165, 166, 168, 169, 171, 172, 173
Wayte, Elizabeth, mistress of King Edward IV, 164, 165, 167
Wendover, Buckinghamshire, 146, 147
Westminster: xv, 109, 177, 179; abbey, 7, 16, 30, 93, 131, 143; sanctuary, 174, 176, 178
Wessex: 1,4 earls of, 6,7, 10,11; royal house, 16, 23, 28, 30, 31, 52, 61, 183
White Ship, 38-39, 55, 59
William I, Count of Hainault (1304-1337), 122, 123, 137
William I, Duke of Normandy and King of England (1066-1087), 20, 21-24, 25, 26, 30, 189
William II, 'Rufus', King of England (1087-1100), 30, 31, 35, 40-41, 42, 55, 61, 65, 189
William IX, Duke of Aquitaine, 75
William Ætheling, only legitimate son of King Henry I, 33, 35, 37, 38, 39, 183, 189
William Clito, 64
William of Jumièges, chronicler, ix, 9, 14, 21

William of Malmesbury, chronicler, 18, 19, 20, 21, 22, 31, 32, 33, 37, 38, 43, 52, 55
William of Newburgh, chronicler, 69, 71, 74, 76, 88
William of Poitiers, chronicler, 13, 14
William the Lion, King of Scots (1165-1214), 59, 89, 98
Wilton Abbey, Wiltshire, 15, 16, 17, 31
Winchester, Hampshire; 5, 6, 7, 8, 15, 30, 76, 85, 92, 124; bishops, 72, 95, 100, 101, 140; Siege and rout of (1141), 53, 57
Windsor, Berkshire: 42, 129, 130, 143, 147, 158; Treaty (1386), 158
Windsor, Alexander, de, Sir, 145
Windsor, Gerald de, 42, 44, 51
Windsor, William, Sir, 141, 142, 145, 148
witchcraft, 92, 94, 146, 155, 173
Woodstock, Oxfordshire, 34,78-79, 81
Woodville, Elizabeth: xiv, 169, 170, 171-173, 174, 178, 181, 194; possible bigamy, 179 ; birth of Edward V in sanctuary, 176, 177; children, 194; clandestine marriage 168, 172 178
Woodville, Jacquetta, Countess Rivers, 170
Woodville, Richard, 1st Earl Rivers, 170
women: attitudes towards xii, xiii, 36, 45, 60, 95; biblical stereotypes, ix, xi, xiv, 95, 96,144; law, 6, 41, 43, 45, 73, 95, 112-113, 139, 146, 166, 168, 169, 185; social rank, 36, 59-60
widows, 12, 31, 36, 142, 169-170
Wulfstan, Archbishop of York, 5, 6
Wulfstan, Bishop of Winchester, 16
Wycliffe, John, theologian, 155, 162
Wykeham, William, Bishop of Winchester, 140-141Ykenai, mistress of King Henry II 73, 190

York: 12, 13, 56, 107, 114, 118; archbishops, 5, 51, 132, 167, minster; 137, 173
York Gospels, 5
Yorkshire, 51, 56, 61, 89, 155